Understanding the Gospel of Luke:
A Study of the Jewish Roots Using the Hebrew Heritage Bible Translation

by Dr. Nancy Cook

Understanding the Gospel of Luke: A Study of the Jewish Roots Using the Hebrew Heritage Bible Translation

© 2020 by Nancy Cook

Published by Timothy Publishing Services
3409 W. Gary St.
Broken Arrow, OK 74012
918-924-6246

All rights reserved. No part of this book may be reproduced or transmitted in any form or by any means, electronic or mechanical, including photocopying and recording, or by an information storage and retrieval system, without permission in writing by the author.

Unless otherwise identified, Scripture references are taken from the Hebrew Heritage Bible New Testament, Copyright © 2019 by Brad H. Young. The Hebrew Heritage Bible Society, P.O. Box 703101, Tulsa, Oklahoma 74170. E-mail: bradyoung@bradyoung.org. Used by permission. All rights reserved.

Scripture quotations marked (NIV) are taken from the New International Version®. Copyright © 1973, 1978, 1984, 2011 by Biblica, Inc. ™ Used by permission. All rights reserved worldwide.

Scripture quotations marked (ESV) are taken from The Holy Bible, English Standard Version®. Copyright © 2001 by Crossway, a publishing ministry of Good News Publishers. Used by permission. All rights reserved. ESV Text Edition: 2016.

Scripture quotations marked (NRSV) are taken from the New Revised Standard Version®. Copyright © 1989 by the Division of Christian Education of the National Council of the Churches of Christ in the United States of America. Used by permission. All rights reserved.

ISBN-13: 978-1-940931-22-7

Library of Congress Control Number: 2020915226

Printed in the United States of America

Illustrations by Debbie Willey – debbiesuewilley@gmail.com

Cover Design and content layout by Amy Smith – amysmith@cressidadesigns.com

Cover Photo: The synagogue at Capernaum compliments of David Anderson

All rights reserved.

Endorsements

"Dr. Cook has developed an excellent educational tool for use in many settings including high school, college, seminary, and church education. A critical need exists today for this type of educational material regarding the Jewish context as related to Christianity. Dispersed throughout the book are quotes from Dr. Cook's high school students about their own personal experiences studying the Jewish background of New Testament. The design of this work is most impressive. The format is easy-to-read, educational in its content, and the information is rich in research. Students will be immersed in a learning experience as they engage in each lesson."
— *Dr. James Barber, Director of the Doctor of Ministry Program, Assistant Professor of Practical Theology and Director of Field Education Oral Roberts University Graduate School of Theology and Ministry*

"Dr. Nancy Cook's carefully-crafted running commentary on the Hebrew Heritage Bible Translation of the Gospel of Luke targets high school Bible classes, but it is also appropriate for adult Bible classes or small group studies. This accessibly-organized work contains insightful, relevant questions, activities, and illustrations that not only promote learning but also assist users in discovering and appreciating the Jewish roots of Christianity. Based on scholarly sources, Dr. Cook's book clearly supports her theory that 'Only when we see our Jewish roots can we understand our Christian faith.' It is a wonderful resource for Christian teen and adult Bible studies."
— *Nancy Pettus, Director of Holocaust Education, Jewish Federation of Tulsa and The Sherwin Miller Museum of Jewish Art*

"Dr. Nancy Cook has done an admirable job of making the Gospel of Luke accessible and attractive. It works both for young audiences, who might not want to make the investment in time and energy to understand it, and older readers, who might be put off by a wealth of obscure terms. Her erudition and turn of phrase employed in illuminating little known cultural and historical phenomena makes reading the work a pleasure. Furthermore, Nancy's exemplary nonjudgmental character clearly comes across in the way she explains small nuances in different religions."
— *L. Alexander Wolfe, Jerusalem, Israel*

About the Author

Dr. Nancy Cook currently teaches Middle Eastern Archaeology, Anthropology, and Bible to high school students for dual university credits. Her teaching activities also include adult education and lectures at various institutions and venues. She received a master's from the University of Oklahoma, and a Master of Arts in Practical Theology and Doctor of Ministry from Oral Roberts University. Helping students understand the Jewish roots of the Christian faith has been her passion for the last twenty years. For more information or questions, contact Nancy at drnancycooktulsa@gmail.com.

For additional teaching materials and resources including videos visit:
Dr. Nancy Cook Understanding the Bible: Jewish Roots Learning Resources
Link: https://sites.google.com/view/drnancycookunderstandthebible/

I am blessed by an amazing group of people who helped me make this book a reality. Thank you for sharing your talents. I am very grateful to Dr. Brad Young for his incredible dedication to the work of the Lord and brilliant insight into the lives of first century Jews and the teachings of Yeshua. Thank you, Dr. Young, for sharing your knowledge with me and the countless other students you have blessed over the decades. Thank you to my students; never stop asking questions.

"...remember that it is not you that gives life to the root, but rather it is the root that nourishes you." (Romans 11:18b, HHB)

"Dr. Nancy Cook is an uncommon person, teacher, and researcher. My visit to her classroom was a unique experience. The way she illustrated the ancient environment of the Holy Land with its mythological sites to her students left me speechless."
— *Dr. Ron Avni, Ben-Gurion University of the Negev, Beersheba, Israel*

Table of Contents

Introduction to the Gospel of Luke	7
History of the Jews: Lesson 2	17
The Gospel of Luke Chapter One: Lesson 3	47
The Gospel of Luke Chapter Two: Lesson 4	61
The Gospel of Luke Chapter Three: Lesson 5	73
The Gospel of Luke Chapter Four: Lesson 6	87
The Gospel of Luke Chapter Five: Lesson 7	105
The Gospel of Luke Chapter Six: Lesson 8	119
The Gospel of Luke Chapter Seven: Lesson 9	133
The Gospel of Luke Chapter Eight: Lesson 10	147
The Gospel of Luke Chapter Nine: Lesson 11	161
The Gospel of Luke Chapter Ten: Lesson 12	175
The Gospel of Luke Chapter Eleven: Lesson 13	187
The Gospel of Luke Chapter Twelve: Lesson 14	201
The Gospel of Luke Chapter Thirteen: Lesson 15	211
The Gospel of Luke Chapter Fourteen: Lesson 16	221
The Gospel of Luke Chapter Fifteen: Lesson 17	231
The Gospel of Luke Chapter Sixteen: Lesson 18	241
The Gospel of Luke Chapter Seventeen: Lesson 19	253
The Gospel of Luke Chapter Eighteen: Lesson 20	267
The Gospel of Luke Chapter Nineteen: Lesson 21	277
The Gospel of Luke Chapter Twenty: Lesson 22	293
The Gospel of Luke Chapter Twenty-One: Lesson 23	307
The Gospel of Luke Chapter Twenty-Two: Lesson 24	321
The Gospel of Luke Chapter Twenty-Three: Lesson 25	337
The Gospel of Luke Chapter Twenty-Four: Lesson 26	349
Resource Map for Teachers	362
Additional Notes	363
References	366

INTRODUCTION TO THE GOSPEL OF LUKE

Lesson 1

Who wrote the Gospel of Luke?

The author of the Gospel of Luke is never named in the Gospel, but very early church tradition and most scholars agree that Luke wrote the Gospel that bears his name. The "we" sections of Acts and the letters of Paul in Colossians 4:14, "Luke, the beloved physician, sends you his greetings of shalom…" and in Philemon 1:24, "…and Luke, my colleague…" point to Luke as the author of the Gospel.[i]

Who was Luke?

The biblical text says that Luke was a physician (Colossians 4:14) and sometimes traveled with the Apostle Paul as his colleague.[ii]

Biblical scholars say that Luke was either a:

A. Hellenistic Jew:[iii] Hellenistic Jews were Jewish in matters of faith, but they had adopted the Greek language and customs. Most of these Jews had roots in the Greco-Roman world of the Diaspora. The Diaspora is the scattered Jewish community who are living outside of the land of Israel. This was a result of persecution of the Jews.[iv]

- Hellenistic Jews were Jewish in matters of faith, but they had adopted the Greek language and customs.
- The term "Diaspora" means the scattered Jewish community who are living outside of the land of Israel. This was a result of persecution of the Jews.

B. Greek convert to Judaism.[v]

or

C. God-fearing Gentile.[vi] God-fearers were Gentiles who were associated with the synagogue, prayed the Jewish prayers, gave to the poor, and showed deep interest in Judaism. They had not fully converted to Judaism because they were neither circumcised nor baptized.[vii]

> God-fearers were Gentiles who were associated with the synagogue, prayed the Jewish prayers, gave to the poor, and showed deep interest in Judaism. They had not fully converted to Judaism because they were neither circumcised nor baptized.

More and more scholars today believe that Luke was a Hellenistic Jew.

Luke was from Syrian Antioch. He was well educated in Greek culture[viii] and had a thorough understanding of the Hebrew Scriptures (Old Testament) (TANAK).[ix]

> "By studying the Bible, I have been able to understand the Jewish contexts of the New Testament, and I have grown more confident in my faith. The word of God is the strongest force I've ever experienced, and it is the most living literary work ever written."
> Wade Gerhardt – Class of 2020

Fun Fact

Letters were written on papyrus scrolls – like thick paper. Papyrus was a plant.

- **What is a synagogue?** A synagogue is a building where a Jewish congregation meets to study the Hebrew Scriptures, worship, and pray. The word "synagogue" is of Greek origin and means "place of assembly." Ancient synagogues also had guest rooms for travelers.
- **Who are the Jewish people?** God's plan in history was to establish his covenant through a man called Abraham. All Jews trace their ancestry to Abraham as father of the Hebrew nation. The religious teaching of the Jews is rooted in the Hebrew Scriptures (Old Testament) (TANAK).

(*Our Father Abraham: Jewish Roots of the Christian Faith*, 1989, pp. 3, 4, 32, & 189)

Did Luke write anything else?

Luke also wrote the book of Acts. Both the Gospel of Luke and Acts are addressed to Theophilus, and the writing styles are the same.[x] Luke wrote Acts after he wrote the Gospel. They were a single work in two volumes, and the two should be read together.[xi] Together, the Gospel of Luke and the Book of Acts comprise over 25 percent of the New Testament.[xii]

Fun Fact

At the time of Luke, the Hebrew Bible was written on parchment scrolls. This parchment must be made from the skin of a kosher animal – an animal that chews its cud and has a cloven (split) hoof like a cow, goat, or sheep. Today the Hebrew Bibles used in Jewish synagogue services are still written on parchment scrolls.

(*The Bible in the Shrine of the Book*, 2006, Jerusalem: Israel)

What was the Gospel of Luke originally?

The Gospel of Luke was written as a personal letter to Theophilus. It is the longest book in the New Testament.[xiii] Most letters like this would eventually be copied and shared with the public. Likewise, this letter written by Luke was copied and shared.

> Gospel means "Good News" – one of the first four books of the New Testament.

To whom was the Gospel of Luke written?

Luke wrote this letter to Theophilus. Theophilus was a common name and means "dear to God." Theophilus was a real person who was probably pretty important because Luke calls him "most noble." Many scholars have believed that Theophilus was an important Roman official.[xiv] However, there is archaeological evidence from an ancient inscription found in Jerusalem that there was a high priest named Theophilus from AD 37-41.[xv] So, it is possible that Theophilus was Jewish. The Greek name "Theophilus" is "Yedidyah" in Hebrew.[xvi] Ancient writers often dedicated works to a person of prominence which helped them to promote the book or letter.[xvii]

> "Most students that hear they're going to study a book of the Bible will think it's going to be boring. They'd be surprised how interesting it actually is. It will help you understand your religion and help you grow in your faith. It will make you ask questions and open your mind. So, I'd say it's actually worth it."
> Jack Wells – Class of 2020

Theophilus means "dear to God."

When was it written?

Luke probably wrote this Gospel in AD 61-62.[xviii] It was most likely not written later than AD 65.[xix]

Where was it written?

Luke probably wrote this Gospel from Rome while the Apostle Paul was in prison.[xx]

What was the purpose of the Gospel of Luke?

Luke wrote to reassure Theophilus, a socially significant person, of the things he had learned.[xxi]

- **What is the Hebrew Bible?** The Hebrew Bible is called the "Old Testament" by many Christians. It is the Scriptures of the Jewish community.
- **What is the TANAK?** The Jewish tradition arranges the Hebrew Bible into three units called the Torah (Law), Nevi'im (Prophets), and Ketuvim (Writings). TNK or TANAK is an acronym for these three sections. The Hebrew Bible, TANAK, and "Old Testament" are all referring to the same thing.

Fun Fact

A "codex" was written on sheets of papyrus or parchment that were folded, sewn, and bound together as a book. One of the oldest "codices" [plural of codex] of the Christian Bible was written in the 4th Century AD (around AD 330-360). Christians adopted the technology of making books from the Roman method of joining wooden slats coated with wax. Both sides of the paper could be written on, making it cheaper and easier to read and copy.

(*The Bible in the Shrine of the Book*, 2006, Jerusalem: Israel)

How was the Gospel of Luke written?

Luke wrote like a historian. Historians in the ancient Mediterranean world where Luke was from would normally consult eyewitnesses whenever possible and were very careful in their investigation of the facts. This investigation included interviewing witnesses and traveling to the sites where events occurred. Oral transmissions (people telling stories) were usually very accurate, especially where Luke lived. People who lived in these ancient cultures had memories that were carefully trained, both among the educated and uneducated.[xxii] It is also quite likely that Luke had access to a written record about the Hebrew life of Jesus that he used when he wrote his letter to Theophilus.[xxiii]

Hebrew Names

Yedidyah – "Friend of the LORD"

Fun Fact

Luke's Gospel has 19,482 words - the maximum size that a 35-foot papyrus scroll could contain. That's a long letter!

(*The ESV Archaeology Study Bible*, 2017)

- **What is the New Testament?** The New Testament is also called the "Christian Bible." It was written by different people who were all believers in Jesus. It contains four types of writings: the Gospels, the history of the church (the book of Acts), the letters, and the Apocalyptic writing of Revelation. It covers the time between the birth of Jesus and the spread of the Christian church – less than 100 years. (Hoffmeier, 1989)

Not-So-Fun Fact

In AD 138, a wealthy man named Marcion from northern Turkey went to Rome to argue that the Hebrew Bible was not important for Christians. Marcion was an early church leader who said that the "cruel god" of the "Old Testament" was inferior to the "Good God" of the New Testament. He wanted the "Old Testament" to be removed from the Christian Bible. Marcion said "that the church was wrong in attempting to combine the gospel with Judaism. Indeed, Marcion's principal goal was to rid Christianity of every trace of Judaism." In AD 144, the church officially stated that Marcion's teachings were false, and he was excommunicated (put out of the church community). His teachings, even though they were officially rejected by the church, contributed to many years of rejection and persecution of the Jews.

(*Our Father Abraham: Jewish Roots of the Christian Faith*, 1989, pp. 108-109)

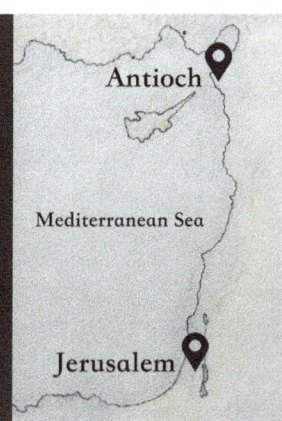

Luke was from Antioch in Syria also known as Syrian Antioch. Today this city is known as Antakya in southern Turkey. It was an early center of Christianity. Jews and Gentiles lived in Antioch. It was a large and very important city in the Roman Empire during the 1st century AD. It was where the Apostle Paul began all of his missionary journeys. It is about 440 miles from Jerusalem to Antioch.

(As a comparison, it is 403 miles from Tulsa, OK to Memphis, TN. It's 384 miles between Los Angeles and Sacramento, CA.)

(Archaeological Study Bible, 2005)

Define the following:

New Testament – (Including the four types of writings)

Hebrew Bible –

TANAK –

Jew –

Hellenistic Jew –

Diaspora –

God-Fearer –

Synagogue –

Parchment –

Papyrus –

Codex –

Who was Luke? –

Who was Theophilus? –

Answer the following questions:

Luke was well educated in _____ and had a thorough understanding of the _____ (Old Testament) (_____).

More and more scholars today believe that Luke was a _____

Where was Luke from? _____

What is the name of Syrian Antioch today? _____

Name two ways that Antioch was important in early Christianity? _____
_____

Where was the Gospel of Luke written? _____

When was the Gospel of Luke written? _____

To whom was the Gospel of Luke written? _____

What was the purpose of the Gospel of Luke? _____
_____

How did Luke write his "Gospel"? _____
_____

How did he gather his information? _____
_____

Is the Gospel of Luke reliable? _____

Why? _____
_____

What was the Gospel of Luke originally? _____
_____

Did they intend to share Luke's letter to Theophilus with other people? _____

How do we know? _____

GOSPEL OF LUKE

What does "Gospel" mean?

What does Theophilus mean?

What does Yedidyah mean?

What language is Yedidyah?   Are the meanings similar?

How do you think the Gospel of Luke is important to the Christian faith?

Write a summary paragraph about what you learned in this chapter:

Write a sentence summarizing your summary paragraph:

Research Luke and write something interesting that you discovered about him:

Discuss and compare your summary and research with others.

What was the most interesting thing that you learned in this chapter?

What was the most important thing that you learned in this chapter?

Write and answer three of your own questions from this chapter:

Research the climate and geography of Antakya, Turkey.

What is the average temperature there in the summer and winter? _____

Is Antakya mountainous? _____ Is there a river? _____

What is interesting about that city?

Discuss and compare your answers with others.

Questions for thought and/or discussion:

Who was Marcion?

What did Marcion teach?

How could Marcion's teachings have led to Jews being persecuted?

If Marcion's teachings were false, how could anybody believe or follow them?

Have you ever been affected by somebody saying something not true about you or someone you know?

What can people do to stand up against false rumors or lies?

How can studying the Bible help us stand up against things that are wrong?

Discuss and compare your answers with others.

i. *Archaeological Study Bible* (2005)
ii. *The ESV Archaeology Study Bible* (2017)
iii. Stern (1992)
iv. Wilson (1989) p. 44
v. Gundry (2003)
vi. Stern (2016)
vii. Wilson (1989)
viii. *Archaeological Study Bible* (2005)
ix. Stern (2016)
x. Gundry (2003)
xi. *The ESV Archaeology Study Bible* (2017)
xii. Bruce (1988)
xiii. Gundry (2003)
xiv. Bruce (1988)
xv. Stern (2016)
xvi. Young (2019)
xvii. *Cultural Backgrounds Study Bible* (2016)
xviii. *Archaeological Study Bible* (2005)
xix. Bruce (1988)
xx. ibid
xxi. Stern (2016)
xxii. *Cultural Backgrounds Study Bible* (2016)
xxiii. Lindsey (2017)

HISTORY OF THE JEWS

Lesson 2

Historical Background

Knowing the "culture, history, and physical setting" of the Gospels is extremely important for the reader to properly understand their meaning. It is also important to understand that Jesus was a Jew who remained within the Jewish Faith, and he lived and ministered in the time of the Second Temple period in Judea.[i]

What does "Second Temple period" mean?
The Second Temple period means the time that the Second Temple stood in Jerusalem. The Second Temple was built by Zerubbabel after the Jews returned to Judea from their exile in Babylon. The Second Temple was dedicated in 516 BC. Herod the Great "remodeled" the Second Temple and increased the size of the Temple Mount during his reign. Altogether, the Second Temple stood for 586 years – from 516 BC until AD 70 when it was destroyed by the Romans.

> "Even though I grew up in church, I never really understood or cared about what I was being 'taught.' Sermons always consisted of a generic message paired with a few out-of-context verses. Actually studying the context and culture surrounding the Bible is a much-needed reminder that these aren't just isolated stories; they're a record of an entire culture and religion. Needless to say, the Bible is a much more interesting book now."
> Carly Welch – Class of 2020

Herod the Great's most ambitious building project was the Temple Mount complex in Jerusalem. Work began in 20 BC, and it took decades to finish, but when Herod finished construction of the Temple Mount, it was the largest manmade platform on earth. It covered an area roughly equal to 24 football fields (about 40 acres). The retaining wall of the Temple Mount is approximately one mile in circumference. Each stone weighs an average of 9,000 pounds. Over 18,000 people worked on its construction, and over 1,000 priests were trained as stone masons. Craftsmanship – not mortar – held the wall together.

(*Lost Worlds: Herod the Great*, History Channel)
(*Jesus' Jerusalem*, *History* Channel)

Photo of the model of the Second Temple. Israel Museum, Jerusalem.

The fact that Jesus was a Jew is seldom questioned today, but the importance of understanding his culture is frequently overlooked. His society was rooted deeply in the faith experiences of his people. Jesus' teachings about God's love and the dignity of each human being were based upon the foundations of Jewish religious thought during the Second Temple period. "The more that is learned about this fascinating period in history, the more will be known about Jesus. Jesus worshipped in the synagogue. He offered prayers in the Temple in Jerusalem. The Jewish religious heritage of Jesus impacted his life in every dimension of his daily experience. Jesus must be understood as a Jewish theologian. His theology is Jewish to the core."[ii]

> Jesus worshipped in the synagogue. He offered prayers in the Temple in Jerusalem. The Jewish religious heritage of Jesus impacted his life in every dimension of his daily experience.

What was it like to live as a Jew in the 1st Century AD in Judea under the reign of the Roman Empire?

To comprehend more fully the teachings of Jesus, the complexity of his environment must be explored. To grasp the meaning of the Gospel of Luke (and even the entire New Testament), one must attempt to enter into an understanding of what it was like to be a Jew living in Judea during the 1st century AD under the reign of the Roman Empire.[iii]

- **What does "AD" mean?** The term AD is an abbreviation of the Latin *Anno Domini* which means "in the year of the Lord" – the year of Jesus' birth and the time after.
- **What does "BC" mean?** The term BC is an abbreviation for the English "Before Christ."
- **What does 1st century AD mean?** First Century AD represents years AD 1 through 100.
- **Where is Judea?** The region of Judea was located where the tribe of Judah was given land when the Israelites entered the Promised Land under the leadership of Joshua after the Exodus. It is called Yehudah in Hebrew. It was called Judea during the time of the Roman Empire. Jerusalem was located in Judea, and it was in the southern part of modern-day Israel.

The time frame for Jesus' ministry was most likely between AD 27 and AD 30.[iv] The Gospels of Matthew, Mark, and Luke were probably written between AD 45 and AD 80.[v] The Gospel of Luke was most likely written between AD 61 and AD 65.[vi,vii]

The political, economic, and religious climate of the times was one of Roman occupation and oppression. The Romans had invaded and conquered Judea in 63 BC under general Pompey. Roman power and control increased over the people and the land every year during Jesus' ministry and Luke's writing. This was a time filled with great challenges and turmoil for the Jews.[viii] One of these challenges was the economic hardship of the Jewish people. The "downtrodden and oppressed Jews could look forward to nothing but a miserable existence. With the enormous taxation and a small yield of the soil, the peasant population (the poor) was being reduced to grinding poverty" under Roman occupation.

> Roman power and control increased over the people and the land every year during Jesus' ministry and Luke's writing.

The lifestyles of the upper-class Jews and upper-class Romans were similar, but their religions were completely different. The middle-class lifestyle was quite different from the very rich. The number of Jews who lived a middle-class lifestyle was small and decreased considerably during the first century, while the number of Jews who lived in absolute poverty dramatically increased.[ix]

Fun Fact

The survey tool (groma) used by the Romans to build their roads could only survey in a straight line. So, Roman roads were only constructed in straight lines and 90-degree angles.

(*Rome: Engineering an Empire*, The History Channel)

> By the 1st century AD, Rome was the world's lone superpower. In the city of Rome, many middle and upper-class homes had running water. Aqueducts carried 200 million gallons of water a day into the city of almost one million people. By the end of the 1st century AD, the Roman empire reached from England to Egypt and Portugal to Persia with 50 million people under its rule. Around AD 107, Emperor Trajan expanded the borders of the Roman empire to its greatest size, and the city of Rome became the capital of the world.
>
> (*Rome: Engineering an Empire*, The History Channel)

When Augustus Caesar was emperor (ruler) in Rome (27 BC-14 BC), he established a system to collect taxes from all the territories that Rome had conquered. These taxes supported the Roman military, the royal household, government salaries, road maintenance, public works, and free grain (food) for the people living in the city of Rome. In Judea, the Jews had to pay an income tax and a poll tax. A poll tax was a tax that every person, women over the age of 12 and men over the age of 14, had to pay regardless of their income, even if they didn't have a job or any resources. There were toll taxes collected for traveling on the roads, commercial taxes collected from businesses, licenses, and harvest taxes. The tax collectors even invented taxes for a variety of reasons. For example, there were bridge taxes that had to be paid to cross a bridge and axle taxes that were charged depending on how many axles were on a person's cart. The job of collecting taxes was contracted to private individuals (known as publicans) who collected the required taxes for Rome. The publicans (tax collectors) collected set taxes, invented some of their own taxes, and kept all profits for themselves. Taxes were heavy and unfair. Tax collectors, like Matthew and Zacchaeus (who were Jewish), were almost always dishonest, frequently abusive, and were hated by the Jewish people.

> "Studying the book of Acts this last year has offered a lot of insight into the lives and culture of those we read about in the Bible. I've spent nearly my whole life hearing these stories and having no clue what they really mean. The historical and geographical context I learned has been the most interesting and most helpful learning technique for studying the Bible."
> Ben Easley – Class of 2020

Fun Fact

The secret weapon of Rome's building success was waterproof concrete.

(*Rome: Engineering an Empire*, The History Channel)

> In Judea, the Jews had to pay an income tax and a poll tax. A poll tax was a tax that every person, women over the age of 12 and men over the age of 14, had to pay regardless of their income, even if they didn't have a job or any resources.

The Roman occupiers not only oppressed the Jews economically, they also suppressed them religiously. The Jews felt humiliated by being treated as a conquered province. Rome not only wounded the political sensibilities of the Jews but also their religious feelings. For example, for a number of years during the Second Temple period, the Romans would keep the "official robes of the high priests under lock and key." If the Jews behaved themselves, the high priest would receive his robe in time to officiate in the Temple during the Jewish high holy day of Yom Kippur. The Romans were responsible not only for humiliating the Jews, but also for murdering tens of thousands of Jews for religious and political reasons during the Second Temple period.[xi]

> The Romans were responsible not only for humiliating the Jews, but also for murdering tens of thousands of Jews for religious and political reasons during the Second Temple period.

Because of this economic, political, and religious oppression, some Jews were looking for a military Messiah to deliver them from the hands of their Roman oppressors.[xii] This anticipated deliverance at the hands of a Jewish Messiah caused internal conflict among the Jews themselves and created violent conflicts with their Roman rulers.[xiii] The Jewish Sadducees, who were powerful and often wealthy, were not looking for a Messiah. They were often quite content with the Roman government the way it was. The Zealots, on the other hand, were Jews fiercely determined to rid the land of the Roman idol worshippers. This division led to unrest within the Jewish community, as many Jews, except for the very rich and powerful, were looking for a Messiah to deliver them from their Roman oppressors. Along with the internal economic tensions between the Jewish classes, "the actions of the messianic teachers and the failure of Judean and Roman leaders to deal effectively with them propelled the nation into open revolt."[xiv]

The tensions within the Jewish community, between the Jews and the Romans, and the messianic atmosphere (an atmosphere anticipating a Jewish military deliverer) were all present during the time of Jesus' earthly ministry and continued through the time of the writing of Luke's Gospel. The result of all of the religious, political, and economic oppression created such stress

> "I was born into a Christian family and went to church daycare with my grandmother. I grew up never understanding the Bible because I would never speak up. Use context when you read. If you don't understand what you are reading, research. It will truly change your life, like it did mine."
> Bre Henderson – Class of 2021

> "Before I came to a Christian school, I went to church every Sunday, but I would never open my Bible. I am a senior in high school and am now studying the Bible every day. I never knew I enjoyed history so much until I started going through the book of Acts in-depth. Now I want to read the Bible, learn about the history, and question the scholars who wrote the books and made their own translations. I think that Jesus wanted things to be a certain way, and I want to find out why the ways have changed. I have never been more fascinated with anything else as much as I am with the Bible right now."
> Avery Tucker – Class of 2020

that the Jews mounted a military uprising against the Romans in AD 66. This was known as the First Jewish Revolt against Rome. As a result of the Revolt, the Second Temple was destroyed by the Romans in AD 70, and hundreds of thousands of Jewish people lost their lives.[xv]

> Because of this economic, political, and religious oppression, some Jews were looking for a military Messiah to deliver them from the hands of their Roman oppressors.

The attitude of the average Jewish person was that Rome might destroy their cities and kill their people, but there were some portions of Jewish life which Rome could not touch. The part Rome could not touch was the Jewish idea of God's unity and the Jewish concept of human brotherhood.[xvi] "Though politically split, the Jews of the Holy Land were one spiritually and any wave of religious feeling rising in one community could sweep them all." Their religion bound them together.[xvii] Even though the Jews were surrounded, occupied, and influenced by many cultures and civilizations, the Jews reflected a Hebrew way of looking at life.[xviii] They had survived centuries of conquests and persecutions. They remembered God's deliverance and celebrated his goodness. As God's covenant people, they had survived.

What was the Jewish religion and culture like in the first century?

It is difficult to differentiate between the historical, cultural, and religious histories of the Jewish people at the time of Jesus' ministry and the writing of the Gospels. For the Jews of the Second Temple period living in Judea they were so intricately woven together that it is virtually impossible to separate them. Their culture is defined by their religion, and their history is replete with both.

The basis of Judaism is a faith – but that faith is only the starting-point for a way of life and a complete culture. The foundation of the faith is the concept of God, and from this stems the entire ideology.[xix] God was the center of life for the Second Temple period Jew, and the worship of God was fundamental to their existence. "The Temple was the center of Jewish life, and the synagogues all faced the Jerusalem Temple."[xx]

Although the Jews living inside the land of Israel fiercely embraced their Jewish faith and identity, they were affected by the Greek culture. For example, synagogue is "a Greek word that means 'gathered together' …for religious purposes."[xxi] And, even though synagogues were built for Jewish study and worship, their architecture was influenced by the Greeks.[xxii]

> God was the center of life for the Second Temple period Jew, and the worship of God was fundamental to their existence.

During the first century, the Jewish synagogue was a place of formal teaching and acted as the activity hub of the community.[xxiii] At the time of Jesus, synagogues were everywhere in Israel.[xxiv] The synagogue was built for the reading of the Law (Torah) and for the teaching of the commandments, and it had a guest room which served as an inn for those who needed a place to stay when they were on a journey.[xxv] Itinerant (traveling) Jewish rabbis, such as Jesus, would travel and teach in various synagogues throughout Judea and Galilee. During Jesus' ministry, the Temple in Jerusalem was the center of worship for the Jewish nation, but the synagogue was the center of worship, study, and assembly for the local community.

During Jesus' ministry, the Temple in Jerusalem was the center of worship for the Jewish nation, but the synagogue was the center of worship, study, and assembly for the local community.

During the Second Temple period, many of the foundational Jewish religious teachings and traditions were established in the home and continued learning occurred in the synagogues.[xxvi]

During the first century, the Jews considered education as important as prayer, and as early as the midcentury, most synagogues housed an elementary school for the Jewish youth.

A rabbi is a teacher of the Torah.

"Study of the Bible has impacted me in incredible ways. Without deep exploration of the text, my beliefs would feel hollow. The Bible has led me to desire not just knowledge, but also understanding. This desire for understanding has infiltrated every aspect of my life. The study of scripture has made me who I am, someone who doesn't just want to know a word, but understand it; someone who doesn't want to just know God, but to understand him. I have found through my studies that it's much easier to love someone when you try to understand them."
David Calvert – Class of 2020

During the first century, the Jews considered education as important as prayer, and as early as the mid-century most synagogues housed an elementary school for the Jewish youth.

Messiah means "anointed one." The word is "Mashiach" in Hebrew, meaning a "savior or liberator."

Not only was early childhood education important, almost all adults studied. The Jews had a horror of ignorance and looked down upon the uneducated man.[xxvii] "For the Jews "the primary purpose of education in biblical times was to train the whole person for lifelong, obedient service in the knowledge of God.

The aim of learning was holiness in living." For first-century Jews, "study as well as prayer was worship."[xxviii]

"Jewish life in the Second Temple period revolved around halakhah (the path that one walks) or Jewish law, and this was a natural component of Jewish life in the land of Israel. The halakhic framework was a self-evident reality where the yoke of Torah and commandments was part of the very fabric of the daily spiritual life of the Jewish people."[xxix]

> For the Jews "the primary purpose of education in biblical times was to train the whole person for lifelong, obedient service in the knowledge of God. The aim of learning was holiness in living." For first-century Jews, "study as well as prayer was worship."

The rabbis of Jesus' day emphasized that the study of the Torah led to practice. The Hebrew text of the Torah was the common cultural background of the Jews, and the life of the Jewish community revolved around Torah study. For the Jews, reverence for God required a commitment to education so that individuals would understand and ultimately obey God's teachings in the Torah. On the other hand, the Greeks learned in order to comprehend.[xxx]

The role of education and the quest for knowledge were viewed quite differently in the Jewish and Greek (Hellenistic) cultures. The object or aim of the Hebrew system was to gain knowledge of God. The object or aim of the Greek system was to know thyself. The Hebrew system started with God. The Greek system started with the knowledge of man. "The Greek world did not understand education to be tied to holiness of life. Rather, teaching primarily involved the transference of knowledge in the intellectual and technical areas." For the Jews, knowledge began and ended with God. "Furthermore, in the ancient Greek society, only the wealthy and leisure classes were enlightened through education, while Jewish education was for all people and concerned the whole person."[xxxi] "So important was a knowledge of God's law, that the study of Torah had first claim to a man's time. A man should dedicate his entire life to the study of Torah and not occupy himself with secular learning."[xxxii]

> "There is no adequate wording in the English dictionary to describe the impact studying the 'Breath of God' has had on my life. It was a humbling moment when I realized how 'poor in Spirit' I am, and yet He has given me a guide to help me 'grow in Spirit,' when by no means do I deserve it. I'm a naturally curious person, so it goes without saying, I like questions...a lot. Studying the Bible and asking for wisdom and clarity has given me the ability to grow in my faith; it has turned words on a page to a light which guides my way."
> Beka Woods – Class of 2020

> "In the ancient Greek society, only the wealthy and leisure classes were enlightened through education, while Jewish education was for all people and concerned the whole person."

The first century historian Josephus wrote, "God is one and the Hebrew race is one." Before the destruction of Jerusalem and the Temple "there were three singular entities: one God, one city, and one people."[xxxiii] Although the Jews were bound together as a people by their religion, they underwent internal turmoil.

During the late Second Temple period, the Jews experienced schisms (divisions) among themselves that resulted in the emergence of several religious Jewish sects (groups) that included the Sadducees, the Pharisees, the Essenes, the Herodians, and the Zealots.[xxxv]

> During the late Second Temple period, the Jews experienced schisms (divisions) among themselves that resulted in the emergence of several religious Jewish sects (groups) that included the Sadducees, the Pharisees, the Essenes, the Herodians, and the Zealots.

The "Sadducees were heirs of the intertestamental (the time between the "Old" and "New" Testaments) Hasmoneans. Though fewer in number than the Pharisees, they wielded more political influence because they controlled the priesthood," and they controlled the Temple worship.[xxxvi]

> The Hasmoneans were Jews from a priestly family who ruled Judea for about 80 years before the Romans invaded the land.
> (Jewish Virtual Library)

The Pharisees made up the largest of Jewish religious sects,[xxxvii] and they "promoted the faithful observance of Jewish law (or TANAK). The exact meaning of the term Pharisee remains uncertain. The name comes from the Hebrew verb meaning 'to separate' or 'distinguish'."[xxxviii] The Pharisee sect began shortly after the Maccabean Revolt (about 165 BC) from a group of Jews who had objected to the Hellenization of Jewish culture.[xxxix] The Pharisees were the only Jewish religious sect to survive the destruction of the Temple and were the forerunners of modern Judaism.[xl] The "Pharisees represented one of the most significant reform movements in Judaism at the close of the Second Temple period."[xli] The rabbis were Pharisee Torah scholars.[xlii]

> The Pharisees were the only Jewish religious sect to survive the destruction of the Temple and were the forerunners of modern Judaism.

The Essene sect began in the late second century BC, probably because of strong disagreements that involved various Temple matters. The Essenes withdrew from the Jewish community and established an isolated settlement near the Dead Sea.[xliii]

The Herodians were probably a small but influential group of Jews whose community was centered in Galilee. They apparently supported the Herod family and the Romans.[xliv] Little is known about the Herodians.

The "Zealots were radical Jews who sought the violent overthrow of the Roman regime (government control) in Judea under the rallying cry 'No king but God!' They came to importance during the Jewish Revolt against Rome, but their beginnings can be traced back to the first century BC."[xlv] All of these sects were Jewish, but with profound differences in their interpretation (understanding) of the Torah and their reaction to the occupation of the Romans and the Hellenization of the culture. Eventually, however, in AD 66, each sect would be drawn into the First Jewish Revolt with many of them fighting side-by-side.[xlvi]

> All of these sects were Jewish, but with profound differences in their interpretation (understanding) of the Torah and their reaction to the occupation of the Romans and the Hellenization of the culture. Eventually, however, in AD 66, each would be drawn into the First Jewish Revolt with many of them fighting side-by-side.

What were some of the historic events that shaped the Jewish people of the first century?

A brief history of the Jews begins with Abraham and includes the discussion of the interaction of the Jews with the many cultures and civilizations of the Middle East and Mediterranean region over the span of thousands of years.

> The great civilizations that conquered Israel included the Assyrians, Babylonians, Persians, Greeks, and Romans.

Below is a brief outline of the major events that shaped Judea and the Jews leading up to the first century AD and the Roman occupation:

2000 BC – Abraham: the father of the Jewish people lived around the year 2000 BC.

- God called Abraham to leave where he lived (Mesopotamia) and go to a place that God would show him.

Abraham's father was an idol worshipper.

- Abraham lived in Ur of the Chaldeans and was told to settle in the land of the Canaanites (Israel).
- The land of the Ur of Chaldeans was in the ancient civilization of the Sumerians in Mesopotamia. The Sumerians were a very advanced society.
- Abraham's father was an idol worshipper. (Joshua 24:2)
- The land that Abraham was to settle (Israel) is a land-bridge between Africa, Asia, and Europe. In this location, because the major trade routes passed through it, Abraham could be a witness to the world about God.

> The land that Abraham was to settle (Israel) is a land-bridge between Africa, Asia, and Europe. In this location, because the major trade routes passed through it, Abraham could be a witness to the world about God.

- God made a covenant with Abraham (Genesis 15:1-20) (Genesis 17:1-13).
- The land was part of an area known as the Fertile Crescent: an area of fertile land in the Middle East extending from the Tigris and Euphrates Rivers through the land of Israel to the Nile River in Egypt.

> The **Fertile Crescent** is an area of fertile land in the Middle East extending from the Tigris and Euphrates Rivers (in modern Iraq) to the Nile River (in Egypt) including the land of Israel. Its name comes from the fact that area is shaped like a crescent. It is a region that has enough water to support agriculture such as the production of crops and the raising of livestock. It is also known as the "Cradle of Civilization."

1400-1200 BC – Moses and Joshua: The Exodus of the Israelites from Egypt.

- Most scholars state that Moses led the Israelites out of Egypt sometime between 1400-1200 BC.

> **Moses** wrote the first five books of the Bible – Genesis, Exodus, Leviticus, Numbers and Deuteronomy. The first five books are called the **Torah**. They are also called the **Pentateuch** (Greek word) which means "five books".

1000 BC – King David.

- King David lived around 1000 BC.

1000 BC – King David (continued).

- He was the great warrior king.

- He defeated Israel's greatest enemy – the Philistines.

> The **Philistines** were also known as the "Sea Peoples" and had come to the land of Canaan because their homeland had probably suffered a famine. They were originally from the Aegean (Greek) island of Crete.
>
> (*Archaeology of the Bible*, Hoffmeier, 2008)

- David was the first to conquer Jerusalem and made it the capital of the United Monarchy (kingdom) of Israel.

- God made a covenant with David. The Messiah would come from the line of David. (2 Samuel 7:1-13)

> **King David** was a "man after His [God's] own heart" (1 Samuel 13:14, NIV; Acts 13:22, HH). **David** wrote many of the **Psalms**. The book of **Psalms** is a collection of 150 poems – most of them are hymns – to God.

966-959 BC – King Solomon built the First Temple.

- Solomon built, prayed over and dedicated the Temple, and the glory of the LORD filled the Temple. (2 Chronicles 6:40-7:3)

- Solomon was the great builder king.

- Solomon fortified defense cities.

- The United Kingdom of Israel was in a time of peace and prosperity under the rule of Solomon.

931 BC – King Solomon died and the Kingdom split.

- Shortly after King Solomon died, the United Kingdom of Israel split.

- The northern kingdom with ten tribes became "Israel."

- The southern kingdom with two tribes – Benjamin and Judah – became "Judah."

- The border between the two kingdoms was just north of Jerusalem.

- Jerusalem was part of the southern kingdom of Judah.

- **King Solomon** was **King David's** son. **Solomon** wrote **Song of Songs (The Song of Solomon)**, **Ecclesiastes**, and **Proverbs**.
- The book **Amos** was written between 760-750 BC. The book **Jonah** was written between 785-750 BC.

722 BC – The northern kingdom "Israel" was destroyed by the Assyrians.

The **Assyrian** empire (870 BC – 630 BC) began in Mesopotamia (modern-day Iraq) and expanded to become the largest empire of its time. In 722 BC, when the Assyrian army defeated the northern kingdom of Israel, the Assyrian army had 200,000 soldiers who fought using chariots and on horseback. They had an enormous advantage over their enemies because they used weapons made out of iron. They utilized siege warfare to destroy cities. The Assyrians were especially brutal as their own records depicted them beheading and impaling enemy troops.

(*Archaeology of the Bible*, Hoffmeier, 2008)

- The northern kingdom (called Israel, where ten tribes lived) was warned to turn from their wicked ways, but they did not.
- The great Assyrian army invaded and destroyed Israel and carried off some of the people who lived in the northern kingdom of Israel. People from Assyria moved into the territory. (2 Kings 17:7-12)
- The descendants of the intermarriages between the people from the northern tribes of Israel and the Assyrians became the Samaritans.

The **Samaritans** are descendants of the intermarriages between the people from the ten northern tribes of Israel and the Assyrians.

The book **Micah** was written between 740-710 BC. The book Hosea was written in 715 BC.

701 BC – The Assyrians invaded Judah.

- The fortified city of Lachish was destroyed. Many Jews were murdered. Many Jews were carried into captivity. The King of Assyria decorated his palace with huge reliefs that told the story.

- The Assyrians marched toward Jerusalem. God delivered Jerusalem. (2 Kings 17:13) (2 Kings 19:32-37)

- Hezekiah was the King of Judah during this time.

- Hezekiah built his water tunnel in Jerusalem while the Assyrians advanced against Jerusalem.

> The book **Isaiah** was written by the **Prophet Isaiah** between 700-681 BC. He witnessed the Assyrian destruction of the northern kingdom of Israel and parts of Judah. He warned of God's judgment and told of God's promises. **Isaiah** lived in Jerusalem. He prophesied about **Cyrus the Great**, the king of Persia, about 150 years before **Cyrus** lived and prophesied about the coming **Messiah** about 700 years before Jesus' (Yeshua's) ministry began.

> The **Babylonians** defeated the **Assyrians** and became the superpower of the ancient world. Like the Assyrians, the Babylonians originated in Mesopotamia. In 586 BC, the Babylonians conquered Jerusalem and destroyed the First Temple that had been built by Solomon in 959 BC.
>
> (*Archaeological Study Bible*, 2005)

586 BC – The Babylonians destroyed Jerusalem and the Temple.

- The Temple was destroyed.

- The Presence of the LORD had already left the Temple.

- The Ark of the Covenant was gone.

- The people had sinned by worshiping false gods and idols.

- The strong, smart, wealthy, and educated Jews were carried into captivity in Mesopotamia.

- Mesopotamia means "between the rivers" (Tigris and Euphrates) in modern-day Iraq.

- Some Jews escaped to Egypt and other areas.

- This was the first great dispersion of the Jews.

- Because most of these people were refugees or deportees of Judah, or Yehud, the name "Jew" became the generic name given to all the Israelites after the exile in Babylon.

Mesopotamia ("meso" meaning "between" and "potamia" meaning "the rivers") is a specific area between the Tigris and Euphrates Rivers, mostly located in modern-day Iraq, although it also includes some areas of Syria and Turkey. It is in the northern part of the Fertile Crescent. It was the home of the Sumerians, Assyrians, and Babylonians of antiquity.

The name **"Jew"** described a person from the tribe of Judah. After the destruction of the First Temple, most of the refugees were from the tribe of Judah, or Yehud. **Jew** became the generic name given to all the Israelites after the exile in Babylon.

- Diaspora is a term used of the scattered Jewish community who are away from the land of Israel.
- The people "sat by the rivers and wept" as they lamented the loss of their homes and Temple.
- Many books in the Hebrew Bible or TANAK (Old Testament) were written during this time, and the Jews developed a better understanding of who God is during this time.

Books of the Bible written around the time leading up to and including the destruction of the First Temple in Jerusalem by the Babylonians include:
- **Nahum**, written 663-609 BC
- **Zephaniah**, written 635-630 BC
- **Habakkuk**, written 610-605 BC
- **Jeremiah**, written 626-585 BC
- **Ezekiel**, written 593-571 BC
- **Obadiah**, written 586 BC
- **Lamentations**, written 586-516 BC
- **Daniel**, written 536-530 BC

- **Diaspora** is a term used to describe the scattered Jewish community who are away from the land of Israel.
- The term **theology** means "the study of God," coming from the combination of "Theo" which means "God" and "logy" which means "study of."

539 BC – The Persians under Cyrus the Great defeated the Babylonians.

- The Jews were allowed to go home (to Judah).

- The Persians allowed many of the people they had conquered to return to their own lands and reestablish their kingdoms under the rule of the Persian authority. They were "little kings" and Cyrus was the "king of kings."

- Many of the Jews went back to Judah, but many chose to remain in Mesopotamia. Many also remained in Egypt and other areas to which they had fled.

- The land of Judah was in ruins. Only the elderly, sick, and poor had remained.

520-516 BC – The Second Temple was built.

- The Second Temple was built with much difficulty under the leadership of Zerubbabel.

- It was dedicated, but the people who remembered the glory of Solomon's Temple wept.

444 BC – Nehemiah.

- Nehemiah returned to Judah with a group of Jews to rebuild the walls around Jerusalem that had been destroyed by the Babylonians.

> The **Persians** defeated the **Babylonians** and allowed the Jews to return home in 539 BC. During the time of Ezra (458 BC) the **Persian** empire saw its peak – controlling land from Greece to India.
>
> (*ESV Archaeology Study Bible*, 2017)

> The books known as **Ezra** and **Nehemiah** were written about the Jews returning to Judah after the **Persians** defeated the **Babylonians**. The Jews returned (after the exile) and began building the Second Temple in Jerusalem. Later, they rebuilt the wall around the city. Other books of the Bible that are set around this time include: **1 and 2 Chronicles, Esther, Haggai, Zechariah,** and **Malachi**.

Sometime shortly after the time of **Nehemiah**, the canon is closed and the "Old Testament" it complete. The time of prophecy and activity of the Holy Spirit is finished until the Messiah comes. The TANAK (Torah – Prophets – Writings) is also known as the "Old Testament" or the Hebrew Bible.

333 BC – Alexander the Great established the largest kingdom that the world had ever seen.

- Alexander the Great's vision was to make everything "Greek" – this is known as Hellenism.

- Alexander the Great died at a young age, and his kingdom was divided among his generals.

Hellenism means adopting or embracing ancient Greek culture, language, ideas, art, and religion.

> The **Greeks** defeated the **Persians** and became the dominant civilization in the world under the leadership of Alexander the Great. In 333 BC, Alexander the Great began his conquest of Asia Minor and marched nearly unopposed down the Mediterranean coast toward Egypt, capturing Palestine and Judea on his mission to civilize the world. Alexander the Great's vision was to make everything "Greek." This is known as **Hellenism** – Greek language, Greek culture, Greek theater, Greek philosophy, and Greek religion. Even though Alexander the Great died at a young age, his vision was fulfilled as the Greek language, culture, philosophy, and religion spread across the land he conquered in the Middle East, parts of Europe, Asia, and Africa.
> (*Archaeology of the Bible*, Hoffmeier, 2008, pp. 125-126)

167-160 BC – The Maccabean Revolt.

- Under the Greek ruler Antiochus of the Seleucid dynasty, the Jews face the first religious persecution in history. They could not celebrate their Shabbat nor circumcise their baby boys. It was forbidden for them to worship God. The Greeks desecrated the Temple Mount.

- Judea (the Jews) under Judas Maccabeus (Judas "The Hammer") revolted against the Greeks.

- The Jews won and rededicated the Temple.

- The land of Judea was under Hasmonean rule (the dynasty of the Maccabees) until 63 BC when Rome invaded.

> Shabbat or Sabbath or Shabbos is the seventh day of the week. Shabbat begins at sunset on Friday evening and ends at sunset on Saturday evening. It is the day of rest as commanded by God in the Ten Commandments.

> Under the Greek ruler of the Seleucid dynasty, the Jews faced the first religious persecution in history. They could not celebrate their Shabbat nor circumcise their baby boys. It was forbidden for them to worship God. The Greeks desecrated (defiled) the Temple Mount by worshiping and sacrificing to Greek gods. They also forced the Jews to worship the Greek gods. The Jews revolted against the Greeks, and the Jews won. The Jews regained control of the Temple, and they immediately began to remove all items associated with pagan idol worship. They purified and rededicated the Temple and celebrated. The holiday that commemorates this event is called Chanukah. Chanukah is the Hebrew word that means "dedication."
> (Aharoni et al. (2002)

Fun Fact

Chanukah is also called the Festival of Lights. It is an eight-day holiday that was celebrated by the Jews of Jesus' day and continues to be celebrated by Jews today. It is always celebrated in the winter (usually December). Jesus was in Jerusalem during Chanukah as recorded in the Gospel of John 10:22-23, *"At that time the Feast of Chanukah (Dedication) took place in Yerushalayim. So it was winter, and Yeshua (Jesus) was walking in the Temple under the porch of Shelomo (Solomon)"* (Hebrew Heritage Bible, 2019).

Fun Fact

The Jewish day begins at sunset and ends the next day at sunset. Why? Because in the creation story in Genesis 1:5, the Bible says that the first day began in the evening, and every day after that began in the evening – and then the morning...

63 BC – Rome Conquered Jerusalem.

- The Roman army under general Pompey took Jerusalem. The assault on Jerusalem came on Shabbat. "The towers and the wall gave way, and the Romans invaded the Temple, but the priests continued the service as if nothing had happened. According to Josephus, 12,000 people died on this one day."[xlvii]

During the time of Jesus, the worship of Greek and Roman gods and idols occurred everywhere. The Romans brought their detestable idol worship with them when they invaded Israel. Temples to the major deities of the Greek and Roman cultures and worship of local spirits dominated the landscape and the atmosphere throughout the Roman empire. Household gods and personal shrines were found in the homes of the Gentiles. The Romans even carried small god and goddess figurines in their uniforms to give them victory. This was an abomination to the Jews who believed in and had been commanded to worship only one invisible God and no idols.

37 BC – Herod appointed ruler of Judea.

- Rome appointed Herod the Great (King Herod) as the ruler of Judea, but he had to fight for control.

Sometime between 6 BC to 4 BC – Jesus was born in Bethlehem.

4 BC – Herod the Great (King Herod) died in Jericho.
- Augustus divided Herod's kingdom among his sons Herod Antipas and Herod Philip.

AD 30 – Jesus' death, burial, resurrection, and ascension in Jerusalem.

AD 66 – First Jewish Revolt.
- The First Jewish Revolt began and continued until AD 70.

AD 70 – The Temple in Jerusalem was destroyed by Rome under the command of Titus.
- Thousands of Jewish men were enslaved and deported to Rome.
- Vespasian became emperor in Rome.
- Vespasian's son Titus continued the campaign against the Jews and in AD 72/73 Masada was destroyed.
- The loot from the destroyed Temple in Jerusalem was used to pay for the building of the Colosseum in Rome.
- Emperor Vespasian commissioned the making of a Roman coin "Judea Capta" (meaning "Judea Captured") to celebrate the capture of Judea and the destruction of the Temple in Jerusalem.

Here are two pendants with the images of the two Egyptian gods Isis and Harpocrates that were worn by Roman soldiers. The soldiers believed these "personal idols" would protect them from danger. These were found at Masada from about AD 70. (Photo: Masada Museum, Israel)

Inside the Colosseum in 2019

Exterior of the Colosseum as it looked in 2019

Construction of the Colosseum in Rome began in AD 72 and was financed by the sale of the loot taken from the Jerusalem Temple. Thousands of Jewish captives brought from Judea were used to build the Colosseum. It took eight years to complete and at 160 feet, it was the tallest ancient Roman structure ever built. It held some 70,000 spectators. Each had a ticket with a number that corresponded to a number above the entry gate to the section where they were to sit. The Colosseum had a retractable canvas roof called a velarium that could be unfurled to shade spectators from the sun. It also had water fountains and restrooms (Rome: Engineering an Empire).

Define the following:

Second Temple period –

"AD" –

"BC" –

Poll tax –

Toll tax –

Messiah –

Sadducees –

Pharisees –

Essenes –

Herodians –

Zealots –

Fertile Crescent –

Philistines –

Assyrian Empire –

Samaritans –

Babylonians –

Mesopotamia –

Jew –

Theology –

Persians –

TANAK –

Greeks –

Hellenism –

Answer the following questions:

Knowing the _____ , _____ and _____ of the Gospels is extremely important for the reader to properly understand their meaning. Jesus was a _____ who remained within the _____, and he lived and ministered in the time of the _____ period in Judea.

Jesus' teachings about God' love and the dignity of each human being were based upon the foundations of

When (what years) was the Second Temple period?

Who built the Second Temple?

Describe Herod's most ambitious building project:

What faith did Jesus practice?

Where did Jesus worship and pray?

Where is Judea?

During what years did Jesus have His ministry?

When was Jesus born?

What year did the Romans conquer Judea?

Who was the general that led the Romans in that victory?

What was it like economically for the Jews who lived in Judea during Jesus' ministry?

How was life different for the upper-class Jews compared to the upper-class Romans?

Who established a system to collect taxes from all the territories that Rome had conquered?

_____

Who were publicans and what did they do?

_____

Were Jews ever tax collectors? _____ Give two examples: _____

_____

Why did the Romans murder tens of thousands of Jews?

_____

Why were many Jews looking for a military messiah?

_____

Describe the conflict between the Zealots and the Sadducees:

_____

_____

Describe the "Messianic atmosphere" during the time of Jesus:

_____

_____

The result of all the _____ , _____ , and _____ oppression created such a stress that in AD 66 the Jews mounted a _____ against the _____ .

As a result of the Revolt, the _____ was destroyed by the _____ in AD 70, and _____ of people lost their lives. The _____ in Jerusalem was the center of _____ for the Jewish nation, but the _____ was the center of _____ , and _____ for the _____ community.

What does a rabbi do?
___
___
___
___

For first-century Jews, "_____ as well as _____ was worship."
What was the primary purpose of education for the Jews in Bible times?
___
___
___
___

What was the goal of Greek education?
___
___

Compare the availability of education between the Jews and Greeks:
___
___
___

Who were the Hasmoneans?
___
___

List the great civilizations that conquered Israel:
___
___

Who was Abraham and when did he live?
___
___

Who was Moses and when did he live?
___
___

What kind of king was David and when did he live?
___
___
___

GOSPEL OF LUKE 41

Who was the first king of Israel to conquer Jerusalem?

Who was Solomon and what was his great achievement?

When did Solomon die and what happened after he died?

What was the "northern kingdom" called and who were the people that lived in that kingdom?

What was the "southern kingdom" called and who were the people that lived in that kingdom?

What happened in 722 BC?

Who are the descendants of that event?

What events happened in 701 BC in Judah?

Who was Hezekiah and what did he do in 701 BC?

What did the Babylonians do in 586 BC?

What does diaspora mean?

What did the Persians allow the Jews to do in 539 BC, and what did the Jews do when they returned?
_____
_____
_____

What did Nehemiah do and when did he do it?
_____
_____

What did Alexander the Great do?
_____
_____

What was Alexander the Great's vision?
_____
_____

The Jews were the recipients of the first _____
_____ in history. They could not _____
_____ nor _____ their baby boys.

What did the Greeks do to the Temple Mount?
_____
_____

What holiday celebrates the victory of the Maccabean Revolt?
_____
_____

What happened in 63 BC?
_____
_____

What two civilizations brought their idol worship to Israel during the Second Temple period?
_____
_____

What is the Sabbath?
_____
_____

Why does the Jewish day begin at sunset?
_____
_____

Who appointed Herod the Great as ruler of Judea?

What began in AD 66?

What happened in AD 70?

What happened to thousands of Jewish men?

Who destroyed the Temple in Jerusalem?

How did Rome pay for the Colosseum in Rome?

Who was emperor in Rome in AD 70?

How long did it take to build the Colosseum in Rome?

Digging deeper: For discussion, projects, and research

Read out loud and discuss as a group the story of Abraham from Genesis 12:1-7, Genesis 15:1-19, and and Genesis 17:1-14. What is happening in these stories and why is it important? Who wrote Genesis? When was it written? How many years after Abraham lived was the story written about him?

Read Exodus 1:1-3:22. Discuss how it is related to Genesis. Are there any similarities between the stories of Moses' birth and Jesus' birth? Discuss these similarities. Why do you think this is important? Who wrote Exodus?

Read 1 Samuel 13:14 and Acts 13:22. What do these verses say about David? Why do you think this is important?

Read 2 Samuel 7:1-17 and discuss God's covenant with David. Why is this covenant so important?

Read about the dedication of the First Temple by Solomon in 2 Chronicles 6:40-7:3.

Read Ezekiel 10:1-22 and discuss the vision God gave to Ezekiel of the Glory of the LORD leaving

Solomon's Temple before it was destroyed by the Babylonians in 586 BC. How does this story relate to the story you just read in 2 Chronicles?

As a group project make a giant timeline using dates mentioned in this chapter.

Illustrate your timeline.

After reading this chapter, write and discuss what do you think it was like living in Judea as a Jew during the time of Jesus.

_____

Write and discuss the favorite thing you learned in this chapter.

_____

Write and discuss the most important thing you learned in this chapter.

_____

Write and discuss why it is important to understand the history and context of the Bible.

_____

Write and discuss how the Greek and/or Roman cultures influenced the Jews living in Judea during Jesus' ministry.

_____

Write a summary paragraph about what you learned in this chapter:

_____
_____
_____
_____
_____
_____
_____
_____
_____
_____
_____
_____

Write a summary sentence from your paragraph:

_____
_____

How can you apply what you learned from this chapter to your life?

_____
_____
_____

For further research and context:

Research and discuss more about Herod the Great's Temple Mount and/or his other building projects.

Research and discuss the Colosseum in Rome.

Research and discuss one ancient Roman or Greek god or goddess.

---

i. Flusser (2001) pp. 9, 13
ii. Young (1995) p. xxxiv
iii. Flusser (2001) pp. 27-28
iv. ibid
v. *Archaeological Study Bible* (2005)
vi. Gundry (2003)
vii. Bruce (1988)
viii. Grayzel (1947)
ix. Grayzel (1947) p. 159
x. Edersheim (1994)
xi. Grayzel (1947) p. 155
xii. Grayzel (1947)
xiii. *Archaeological Study Bible* (2005)
xiv. Ibid, p. 1632
xv. Grayzel (1947)
xvi. Grayzel (1947) pp. 192-193
xvii. Aharoni et al. (2002) p. 171
xviii. Wilson (1989)
xix. *Israel Pocket Library: Jewish Values*) 1974, p. 1
xx. Flusser (2001) p. 21
xxi. Edersheim (1994) p. 229
xxii. Schama (2013)
xxiii. Wilson (1989)
xxiv. Edersheim (1994)
xxv. Hoffmeier (2008) p. 145
xxvi. Wilson (1989)
xxvii. Grayzel (1947)
xxviii. Wilson (1989) pp. 275, 310
xxix. Flusser (2009) p. 16
xxx. Young (1998)
xxxi. Wilson (1989) pp. 289-291
xxxii. Belkin (1960) p. 26
xxxiii. Flusser (2001) p. 44
xxxiv. Gundry (2003)
xxxv. Ibid p. 65
xxxvi. *Archaeological Study Bible* (2005)
xxxvii. Gundry (2003)
xxxviii. *Archaeological Study Bible* (2005) p. 1566
xxxix. Gundry (2003) p. 63
xl. *Archaeological Study Bible* (2005)
xli. Young (2007) p. 8
xlii. Buxbaum (2004)
xliii. Roitman (2009)
xliv. Gundry (2003)
xlv. *Archaeological Study Bible* (2005) p. 1576
xlvi. Grayzel (1947)
xlvii. Aharoni et al. (2002)

THE GOSPEL OF LUKE CHAPTER ONE

Lesson 3

Before you begin your study, read Luke Chapter 1 out loud (as a group) from your Bible.

In your own words, summarize Luke Chapter 1 in one paragraph and write at least two questions that you had about the chapter as you read the biblical text: (Discuss)

_____
_____
_____
_____
_____
_____
_____
_____
_____
_____
_____
_____
_____
_____
_____
_____

Luke Chapter 1 begins with Zecharyah (Zechariah) serving as a priest in the Temple in Yerushalayim (Jerusalem) and the angel Gavriel's (Gabriel's) appearance to him in the Temple. After Zecharyah serves in the Temple, he travels home. Tradition says that he lived with his wife Elisheva (Elizabeth) in a village (modern-day Ein Karem) just a little over five miles west of the Old City of Yerushalayim (Jerusalem) and the Temple where he served as priest. Also, in chapter one is the story of the angel Gavriel's visit with Miryam (Mary) in the village of Natzeret (Nazareth) which is located about seventy miles north of Yerushalayim (Jerusalem). Miryam (Mary) travels from Natzeret (Nazareth) to visit Elisheva (Elizabeth). Yochanan (John the Baptist) is born in Ein Karem.

Take a visit online to Ein Karem (BibleWalks.com) and Nazareth (BiblePlaces.com) and see what they look like today. Find the churches dedicated to the events in this chapter, and learn more about the history of these sites. Write and discuss interesting things that you learned:

_____
_____
_____
_____
_____
_____
_____
_____
_____
_____
_____

Chapter 1

1:1) Since many have undertaken the writing for a record of the events which transpired among us, 1:2) like those who from the beginning were eyewitnesses and servants of the teachings, who have passed them down to us, 1:3) it seemed appropriate for me as well, having investigated everything carefully from the beginning, to write for you, in sequential order, most noble Theophilus, 1:4) so that you might know the exact truth concerning everything that you have been taught.

- The author of the Gospel of Luke is never named in the Gospel, but very early church tradition and most scholars agree that Luke wrote the Gospel that bears his name (*Archaeology Study Bible*, 2005).
- Luke wrote like a historian. He spoke with eyewitnesses and traveled to the sites where events occurred. Spoken stories were usually very accurate because the people who lived in these ancient cultures had memories that were carefully trained (*Cultural Backgrounds Study Bible*, 2016).
- It is also quite likely that Luke had access to a written record about the Hebrew life of Jesus (Lindsey, 2017).

1:5) It happened during the days of Herod, the King of Yehudah,

- "It happened during the days of Herod..." This is Herod the Great or King Herod.
- The probable date for the events mentioned here was around 6 BC.
- Herod the Great was born in southern Palestine in 73 BC and died in 4 BC at Jericho. He began his reign in 37 BC when the Romans made him King of Judea. He was of Arab origin on both sides of his family. Although he was a practicing Jew, he was known as an "Idumean 'half-Jew'" (Rozenberg & Mevorah, 2014, p. 31).
- Herod was "married at least ten times, he fathered a host of children, and potential heirs."
- Herod murdered many in his family including wives and sons.
- Caesar Augustus said this about Herod's brutality, "I would rather be Herod's pig than his son" (Rozenberg & Mevorah, 2014, p. 31).
- Herod the Great ruled over Judea for 33 years and was responsible for several immense building projects that completely changed the landscape of the ancient land of Israel.
- In addition to his greatest achievement – the expansion and reconstruction of the Temple in Jerusalem – he also conceived and realized elaborate palaces, fortresses, public buildings, pagan temples, and even entire cities (Rozenberg & Mevorah, 2014).

Hebrew Names and their English Equivalents

Hebrew	English
Yehudah	Judea
Zecharyah	Zechariah
Aviyah	Abijah
Aharon	Aaron
Elisheva	Elizabeth
Yochanan	John
Eliyahu	Elijah
Gavriel	Gabriel
Galil	Galilee
Natzeret	Nazareth
Miryam	Mary
Yaakov	Jacob
Yosef	Joseph
Yeshua	Jesus
Yisrael	Israel

Hebrew Names

Yedidyah – "Friend of the LORD" was Theophilus' name in Hebrew.

Zecharyah – "The LORD has remembered." From zakhar to remember and Yah referring to the Hebrew name of God – YAHWEH – or LORD.

Elisheva – "My God is an oath." From sheva which means oath and El which refers to God.

Aviyah – "My Father is Yah or God."

Yochanan – "God or Yah is gracious."

Herod imported significant quantities of fish sauce, fruit, and wine from Italy. These items were shipped in jars like the ones pictured here. (Photo: Pompeii, Italy)

Masada was one of Herod's massive palace fortresses. It was built on the top of a mesa near the Dead Sea in the middle of the Judean Desert. Covering about 18 acres, this complex had a palace that hung on the edge of the northern face of the mesa. (Photo: Northern palace at Masada, Israel. Photo credit: David Anderson)

Take a visit online to one or more of King Herod's palace fortresses in Israel at Caesarea Maritima, Masada, or Jericho, or visit the place where he was buried at Herodium. Check out his most impressive project of all at the Temple Mount in Jerusalem. Write about and/or discuss the innovative technology and architecture that he used in design and construction:

_____
_____
_____
_____

that there was a priest whose name was Zecharyah from the course of Aviyah. His wife was also from among the daughters of Aharon and her name was Elisheva. 1:6) Both of them were righteous people before God, walking in all the commandments and ordinances of the LORD, being blameless. 1:7) But they did not have a child because Elisheva was barren. They were well on in years.

- From the time of David, the priests were organized into 24 divisions, and Aviyah was one of the heads of the priestly families (*Archaeological Study Bible*, 2005).
- Priests could marry any Israelite, but most preferred to marry daughters of priestly families (as here) (*Cultural Backgrounds Study Bible*, 2016).
- Luke stresses the piety of Zecharyah and Elisheva and shows that it gains reward from God. They were religiously pure in regard to God's commands and went beyond a merely external legal righteousness (Marshall, 1978).

1:8) Then it happened that as he was performing his priestly service before God when his division was on duty, 1:9) he was selected by lot to burn the incense when he went into the Temple of the LORD in accordance with the practices of the priesthood. 1:10) All the throng of the people were praying outside during the time of the incense offering. 1:11) An angel of the LORD appeared to him standing at the right side of the altar of incense. 1:12) When he saw him, Zecharyah was troubled and fear fell upon him.

1:13) But the angel said to him, "Do not fear, Zecharyah, for your prayer has been heard, and your wife Elisheva will give birth to a son, and you shall call his name Yochanan. 1:14) You will be filled with joy and gladness. Many will rejoice at his birth. 1:15) He will be great before the LORD. He will drink neither wine nor fermented drink. He shall be filled with the Holy Spirit even from his mother's womb.

1:16) "Many among the children of Israel will repent, returning to the LORD their God. 1:17) He will go before the LORD in the spirit and the power of Eliyahu, turning the hearts of the fathers to the children, and the disobedient to the wisdom of the righteous, preparing for the LORD a people who are ready."

1:18) Zecharyah said to the angel, "How can I acknowledge this word? I am an old man and my wife is well advanced in her days!" 1:19) The angel answered and said unto him, "I am Gavriel who serves in the presence of God, and I have been sent to give you this message. 1:20) See, from now on you will be silent and unable to speak until the day when these events shall happen, because you did not believe my words which shall be fulfilled in their own time."

1:21) All the people waited for Zecharyah and were feeling anxious because he was delayed for so long in the Temple. 1:22) When he came out, he was unable to speak to them and they knew that he had seen a vision in the Temple. He could only make signs to them because he remained speechless. 1:23) After his time of service was completed, he returned to his home.

- The various daily Temple duties were assigned to the priests by lot.
- Since there were about 18,000 priests, no priest was permitted to offer incense more than once in his lifetime.
- The daily ritual at the Temple included the offering of the morning and evening sacrifices; in both cases, a burnt offering was made.
- Before the morning and after the evening sacrifices, incense was offered on the altar of incense in the Holy Place.
- While Zecharyah was performing his duty inside the temple structure, the crowd of people who regularly gathered to share as spectators in the daily sacrifices were waiting outside.
- This event was occurring in the evening.
- The offering of incense was symbolic of prayer.
- The people prayed during the offering: "May the merciful God enter the Holy Place and accept with favor the offering of his people."
- Zecharyah's task was to place incense on the heated altar and then prostrate himself in prayer.
- It was during this time that the angel of the LORD appeared to him standing at the right side of the altar of incense. The right side is significant as the side of favor and honor and indicating that the angel brings good news.
- It is unlikely that Zecharyah was praying for a personal request at the time he was performing his priestly duties.
- Prayer for salvation for the people of Israel was associated with the evening sacrifice.
- Zecharyah is not to fear because the angel brings him good news. His prayer has been heard (Marshall, 1978).

1:24) After these days, his wife Elisheva conceived and kept herself secluded for five months saying, 1:25) "Thus the LORD has worked [this miracle] for me in these days when He looked upon me and removed this shame from me before the people."

The Holy Place was located inside the Temple. This is where the Golden Menorah, the Table of Shewbread, and the Altar of Incense were located. This is where Zecharyah was serving when Gavriel appeared to him. (The Holy Place: Illustration by Debbie Willey)

- It was normally the father's privilege to choose the son's name.
- The fact that God commanded Zecharyah to call his son by a particular name indicated his son's unique position (Marshall, 1978).
- Yohanan was to be the source of joy and gladness to a far wider circle than just the family (Edersheim, 1993).
- The name Yohanan particularly indicates the joy and happiness that arise from the experience of God's saving action.
- Zecharyah's joy was not only for the birth of his son but also the work his son would do in preparing the people for the coming of the Lord.
- Zecharyah lost his ability to speak because of his unbelief, and it was also a way to preserve the information he had received from Gavriel.
- The crowd expected Zecharyah to come out of the Holy Place and pronounce the Aharonic (priestly) blessing.
- When he was unable to speak, the crowds drew the conclusion that he had seen a vision (Marshall, 1978).
- Zecharyah was a "common" priest (Edersheim, 1993) and therefore lived outside of Jerusalem in the hill country and probably had a secular job (Marshall, 1978).
- Similar to the story about Hannah who conceived a son after her visit to the Tabernacle (1 Sam. 1:19), Elisheva conceived a son in fulfilment of God's promise after Zecharyah's visit to the Temple (Marshall, 1978).
- Being childless was considered an indication of divine disfavor and often brought social shame (Archaeological Study Bible, 2005).

1:26) In the sixth month the angel Gavriel was sent out by God to a village in the Galil named Natzeret, 1:27) to a virgin engaged to a man named Yosef from the family of David. The virgin's name was Miryam. 1:28) When he came to her, he said, "Greetings! Exceedingly favored one, the LORD is with you." 1:29) But she was deeply distressed by this blessing and wondered what this greeting could mean. 1:30) Then the

- Nazareth was a very small agricultural village during the time of Jesus, and very little is known about it from ancient sources. It is not mentioned in the Hebrew Bible.
- Engagement often lasted for about one year during which time the couple would not be left unchaperoned.

- Engagement involved a financial agreement between families and could only be ended by divorce or death.
- The Messiah was to come from the lineage of David (2 Samuel 7:1-13) (Cultural Backgrounds Study Bible, 2016).
- "Exceedingly favored one" means that Miryam has been given grace, strength, and empowerment. God Himself has bestowed immense blessing upon Miryam.
- Elisheva declares that Miryam is the most blessed among women. The Semitic pattern begins with the positive and makes a comparison (see BDF, paragraph 245, p. 128). From among all women, she is the most favored (Young, 2019).
- For Miryam to be greeted as "highly favored" was unusual for her low status as a teenager who lived in an obscure village (Cultural Backgrounds Study Bible, 2016).

angel said to her, "Have no fear, Miryam, for you have found favor before God. 1:31) Listen: you shall conceive and give birth to a son. You must call His name Yeshua. 1:32) He shall be great and shall be called the Son of the Most High and the LORD God will give unto Him the throne of David His father. 1:33) He shall reign in the house of Yaakov forever and of His kingdom there shall be no end." 1:34) Then Miryam said to the angel, "How shall this be, since I am a virgin?" 1:35) And the angel said to her, "The Holy Spirit will come upon you and the power of the Most High will overshadow you; hence the Child born to you shall be called holy, the Son of God. 1:36) Now look, your kinswoman Elisheva has also conceived a son even in her advanced age. This is her sixth month of pregnancy with her who was called barren. 1:37) For nothing is impossible with God." 1:38) Miryam responded, "Here I am, the handmaiden of the LORD. Let it be to me according to your word." The angel departed from her.

Hebrew Names

Yeshua – "Yah or God saves"

- The child's name was given by God.
- The Hebrew name Yeshua was a common Jewish name until the beginning of the second century AD. It means "Yahweh saves."
- The "Son of the Most High God" – "El Elyon" – the child's greatness is to be seen in the lofty title assigned to Him.
- The messianic nature of the child's rule over Yisrael is confirmed by the prophecy that it will be eternal – the Messiah Himself will rule forever.
- The son of Miryam is the Son of God – the promised Messiah (Marshall, 1978).

1:39) Miryam arose in those days and went to the hill country with great urgency to a city of Yehudah. 1:40) She entered the house of Zecharyah and greeted Elisheva. 1:41) Then it happened just as Elisheva heard Miryam's greeting, the baby kicked in her womb. Elisheva was filled with the Holy Spirit 1:42) and she exclaimed in a loud voice saying, "Most blessed are you among women and blessed is the fruit of your womb! 1:43) Why should I be privileged to have the mother of my Lord come to me? 1:44) Take notice of this! As the voice of your greeting came to my ears, the baby kicked for joy in my womb. 1:45) Blessed is she who believed that there would be a fulfillment from what was spoken to her by the LORD."

- Miryam has been bestowed with divine grace over and beyond normal expectations (Young, 2019).
- Verse 46 begins what is known as "Mary's song" of praise. The words that Miryam (Mary) speaks are reminiscent of Hannah's praise as recorded in 1 Samuel 2:1-10 (Archaeological Study Bible, 2005).

1:46) Then she exclaimed, "My soul does magnify the LORD, 1:47) and my spirit does rejoice in the God of my salvation, 1:48) because He has seen the humble state of His servant and behold now all generations will call me blessed; 1:49) because He who is powerful has done great miracles and holy is His name. 1:50) From one generation to another, His mercy is showered upon those who revere Him. 1:51) He has done strong miracles with His arm; He has scattered the proud in the imagination of their hearts. 1:52) He has abased the mighty from their thrones and has exalted the humble. 1:53) He has filled the hungry with good things and the rich He has sent away empty handed. 1:54) He has helped his servant Yisrael remembering His mercies 1:55) as He promised to our forefathers, to Avraham and His descendants forever." 1:56) Miryam remained with her for three months and then returned home.

1:57) The time arrived for Elisheva to give birth and a son was born. 1:58) So her neighbors and relatives magnified the LORD for His mercy unto her. 1:59) When the time came on the eighth day for the child to be circumcised, they named him Zecharyah after his father. 1:60) But his mother intervened, "Not so! His name must be called Yochanan." 1:61) They argued with her, "But none of his relatives is called by that name." 1:62) They made signs to his father, asking what he wanted to call him. 1:63) He requested a writing tablet and wrote, "His name shall be called Yochanan!" At that they all were astonished. 1:64) Suddenly his mouth was opened—the fetters holding his tongue had been loosed. Being able to speak, he began to recount his blessings to God. 1:65) All the neighbors were overwhelmed with awe as these events were discussed throughout all the hill country of Yehudah.

- Circumcision occurs on the eighth day. It is a community event, and it is traditionally the time when the child is named. It is more common to name the son after his father or grandfather (more commonly the grandfather).
- The neighbors refused to accept the word of a woman, especially since she went against the custom of naming the child after the father or grandfather.
- Zecharyah wrote Yochanan's name, and immediately Zecharyah was able to speak and began to praise God.
- This miraculous recovery and everything else that has been witnessed by the community produced awe (Marshall, 1978).

1:66) Everyone who heard [about these happenings] laid them up in their hearts saying, "What kind of child will he be? Surely the hand of the LORD is upon him!"

1:67) His father Zecharyah was filled with the Holy Spirit, and he prophesied, saying, 1:68) "Blessed be the LORD God of Yisrael because He has visited and redeemed His people. 1:69) He has raised up a horn of salvation for us in the house of David His servant. 1:70) As He promised by the mouth of His holy ones, His prophets of old, 1:71) salvation will be granted unto us from our enemies and we will be delivered out of the hands of those who hate us. 1:72) In showing mercy for our fathers, He will remember to keep His holy covenant, 1:73) the promise which He pledged to our father Avraham, to save us from our enemies, 1:74) granting us the ability to serve Him without fear, 1:75) in holiness and righteousness before Him all the days of our lives. 1:76) But you, child, shall be called prophet of the highest, who will go before the LORD to prepare His ways, 1:77) to give knowledge of salvation to His people for forgiveness of their sins, 1:78) according to the tender mercies of our God, when the sunrise of a new day has dawned upon us from on high, 1:79) to give light to those living in darkness under the shadow of death, and to guide our feet unto the way of shalom." 1:80) So the child grew, became strong in spirit, and lived in the wilderness until the time he appeared publicly among Yisrael.

- This Holy Spirit-inspired prophecy spoke about the saving work of God which had already begun with the birth of John and the conception of the Messiah; but the content of the verbs indicate that Zecharyah was looking forward to the redemption which had not yet been accomplished but could be said to be "as good as accomplished" now that the "divine train" of events had been set in motion (Marshall,1978, p. 90).

Questions for review and discussion

Study and compare the Hebrew names in this chapter with their English equivalents. What do these names mean in Hebrew? Do you notice similarities? From the information given in this chapter, what do you think the name Eliyahu means in Hebrew?

Who was Eliyahu (Elijah)? Compare who he was with his Hebrew name. Look up Elijah on chabad.org or jewishvirtuallibrary.org or jewsforjesus.org

What did you discover about Elijah?

How was Yochanan (John the Baptist) similar to Elijah?

_____
_____
_____
_____

Map work:

This map uses the modern-day outline of Israel. Natzeret (Nazareth) is located in the northern district of Galil (Galilee). Ein Kerem is located just west of Yerushalayim (Jerusalem).

Use Google maps or MapQuest to plot a route from Natzeret to Ein Kerem.
How far is it? _____ How long does it take? _____

Discuss the logistics of your trip. What do you think the trip was like 2,000 years ago for Miryam?

GOSPEL OF LUKE   58

Summarize the study notes from this chapter and discuss:

_____
_____
_____
_____
_____
_____
_____
_____
_____
_____
_____
_____
_____
_____
_____
_____
_____
_____
_____
_____
_____
_____

Summarize in one or two sentences the most important or the most interesting thing you learned in this chapter from your study:

_____
_____

What makes it important or interesting to you?

_____
_____
_____
_____
_____

Re-read Luke Chapter 1 from the *Hebrew Heritage Bible* translation used in this book. Discuss.

Summarize Luke Chapter 1 in one paragraph and discuss:

_____
_____
_____
_____
_____
_____
_____
_____
_____
_____
_____
_____

Choose one verse from Luke Chapter 1 that you think is the most important and write it here. Discuss why you think it is the most important verse:

_____
_____
_____

How did your understanding of Luke Chapter 1 change after you studied it and read it again? Discuss.

_____
_____
_____

How can you apply what you learned from Luke Chapter 1 to your life? Discuss.

_____
_____

What question or questions do you still have about Luke Chapter 1 that you don't understand or want to know more about? Discuss.

_____
_____
_____
_____

THE GOSPEL OF LUKE CHAPTER TWO

Lesson 4

Before you begin your study, read Luke Chapter 2 out loud (as a group) from your Bible.

In your own words, summarize Luke Chapter 2 in one paragraph and write at least two questions that you had about the chapter as you read the biblical text: (Discuss)

_____
_____
_____
_____
_____
_____
_____
_____
_____
_____
_____
_____
_____
_____

Luke Chapter 2 begins with the birth of Yeshua (Jesus). An order has been given by Caesar Augustus that requires Yosef (Joseph) and Miryam (Mary) to travel from Natzeret (Nazareth) to Beit Lechem (Bethlehem). Yeshua is born in Beit Lechem. An angel of the LORD appears to the shepherds in the fields. The shepherds visit Miryam and Yosef. When Yeshua is eight days old, He is circumcised. Miryam and Yosef present Yeshua in the Temple in Yerushalayim and meet Shimeon (Simeon) and Chanah (Anna). When Yeshua is 12 years old, He visits the Temple on Pesach (Passover) with His family. Yeshua lives in Natzeret with His family.

Take a visit online to Beit Lechem (Bethlehem) and see what it looks like today. Find the Church of the Nativity, and learn more about the history of this site. Write and discuss interesting things that you learned:

_____
_____
_____
_____
_____
_____

Hebrew Names and their English Equivalents

Hebrew	English
Yosef	Joseph
Beit Lechem	Bethlehem
Shimeon	Simeon
Chanah	Anna
Yerushalayim	Jerusalem
Pesach	Passover
Paniel	Phanuel

Hebrew Names

Beit Lechem – "Beit means "house" and "Lechem" means "bread."

Chapter 2

2:1) In those days an order from Caesar Augustus went forth that a census should be taken in the entire domain. 2:2) This census was the earlier [census, taken] before Quirinius was governor in

Syria. 2:3) So everyone went to be enrolled, each to his own town. 2:4) Thus also Yosef arose out of the Galil, from the town of Natzeret, to Yehudah, to the city of David, which is called Beit Lechem, because his family descended from David,

- The literal translation says "This census was before the census which Quirinius, governor of Syria, made."
- "Family descended from David" is translated more literally, "the household and patriarchy [ancestry] of David" (Young, 2019).
- Beit Lechem was the birthplace of King David, and the promised Messiah was to come from his line (2 Samuel 7:1-13).
- In Jesus' day, Beit Lechem was a village of fewer than 1,000 people (today's population is about 25,000). It is located about six miles south of Yerushalayim.
- Miryam, also of the house of David, was probably required to enroll. Women 12 years old and older were required to pay a poll tax and therefore to register (Archaeological Study Bible, 2005).
- Newborn babies had their navels cut, and were washed with water, salted, and wrapped in swaddling clothes (Archaeological Study Bible, 2005). The infant's limbs were wrapped in long strips of cloth to help them grow straight. The wraps could be used until the infant's limbs became strong or for as long as two months (Cultural Backgrounds Study Bible, 2016).
- A manger was the feeding trough for the animals. They were carved into a stone block. Both water and feed would be placed in the troughs (Hoffmeier, 2008). Very early tradition suggests that Yeshua's birthplace was a cave (or grotto) that was being used as a stable (Archaeological Study Bible, 2005).
- The Church of the Nativity in Beit Lechem has a very long tradition as marking the place where Jesus was born.
- The very early followers of Yeshua (Jesus) had constructed a martyrium where they believed He had been born. A martyrium is an octagonal-shaped structure that is built to mark a holy site. "Martyrium" is from the Greek word for "witness."
- In AD 136, Roman Emperor Hadrian converted that site above the grotto (small cave) where Yeshua was born into a shrine dedicated to Hadrian's favorite Greek god.
- In the fourth century AD Emperor Constantine constructed the first church over this site. It was commissioned by Constantine and his mother Helena.
- Because of the antiquity of the tradition connecting the birth of Jesus to this church, and the fact that no alternatives have been suggested, most New Testament scholars accept this location as authentic.
- The grotto located inside the Church of the Nativity is the oldest site of continuous worship in Christianity, and the church is the oldest major church in the Holy Land (Hoffmeier, 2008).

2:5) to be registered along with Miryam, his betrothed. She was expecting a child. 2:6) While they were there, the time arrived for her to give birth. 2:7) She delivered a son, her first born, and wrapped Him in a swaddling baby blanket. She laid Him in a feeding trough because there was no room for them to lodge in the inn. 2:8) Some shepherds were staying in that same region out in the open fields keeping watch over their flocks during the night. 2:9) An angel of the LORD suddenly stood before them, and the glory of the LORD blazed around them. They were terrified.

- "They were terrified" is translated more literally to "they feared with great fear." In both Greek and Hebrew, the text stresses being overwhelmed with awe-inspiring terror. The Hebrew language is fond of using both a noun and a verb from the same three letter root, in this case "yara" which means "fear" (Young, 2019).
- Despite Biblical traditions about Moses and David being shepherds, most people viewed shepherds as lowly, rough, unclean, and even dangerous (*Cultural Backgrounds Study Bible*, 2016).
- The flocks reserved for Temple service were kept in the fields near Bethlehem throughout the year.
- The shepherds were keeping watch against thieves and predatory animals (*Archaeological Study Bible*, 2005).

Shofar is a Hebrew word that is often translated as "ram's horn" in the Bible. It is an ancient instrument used by the Jewish people on holy days. In antiquity it was used to announce important news, summon worshipers to Jerusalem, and call warriors to battle (*Archaeological Study Bible*, 2005).

2:10) The angel said to them, "Do not fear! Take notice of this! I bring you good news of a great joy which shall be for all people. 2:11) Because today, in the city of David, a Savior is born who is the Anointed One of the LORD. 2:12) This shall be a sign for you: you will find the baby wrapped in a swaddling blanket, lying in a feeding trough." 2:13) Suddenly there appeared with the angel, a multitude of the heavenly host, praising God and saying,

2:14) "Glory belongs to God in the highest, Shalom is given on earth, Goodwill is granted to [all] people!"

2:15) When the angels had gone away from them into heaven, the shepherds said one to the other, "Let us go straight to Beit Lechem right now and witness this event which has happened, which the LORD has made known to us." 2:16) Then they hurried off and found Miryam and Yosef and the baby, who was lying in a feeding trough. 2:17) When they had seen Him, they made known the message telling everyone about the Child. 2:18) Everyone who heard about Him was filled with wonder at what the shepherds told them. 2:19) But Miryam treasured all these things, pondering over them in her heart. 2:20) Moreover, the shepherds returned glorifying and praising God for all the things they had heard and seen. Everything had happened just as it had been told to them.

2:21) When eight days had passed, the time arrived for His circumcision. He was named Yeshua, the name given to Him by the angel before He was conceived in the womb.

> "Through the years, as I learned more about the Bible, I had questions come up that tested my faith to the point of disbelief. If you were to come to me a few years ago, I would not have called myself a Christian. I had so many questions and knew so little about everything. My questions felt impossible to answer. I found someone, my Bible teacher, and I went to him with a broken faith, and he showed me that the answers I was looking for were right in front of me the whole time. Studying, he showed me that these hard-to-answer questions can be answered – you just have to ask the right person – God. Later, as I studied with my other Bible teachers, I was able to learn and find answers to my questions. Studying the Bible saved my faith. I urge you, if you have questions that seem impossible, study the word and ask God."
> Kaden Cannon – Class of 2020

- On the eighth day, when it was time to circumcise Him, He was named Yeshua. Circumcision is the sole condition for a Jew to be under the covenant God made with Abraham (Genesis 17:10-14). It is to be done on the eighth day of a boy's life.
- This probably happened with the community in Natzeret (Nazareth).
- The etymology of the name Yeshua is a contraction of the Hebrew name "Y'hoshua" (Joshua), which means "YHVH saves." It is also the masculine form of the Hebrew word "yeshu'ah" which means "salvation" (Stern, 1992).

2:22) Then the time came for their purification according to the Torah of Moshe. They took Him to Yerushalayim to present Him to the LORD. 2:23) As it is written in the Torah of the LORD, "Every male that opens the womb will be called holy to the LORD" (Exodus 2:2, 12), 2:24) and to offer sacrifice according to what is prescribed in the Torah of the LORD, "A pair of turtle doves or two young pigeons" (Lev 12:8).

- These verses record the observance of two Jewish laws:
  - Redemption of the first-born son.
  - Purification of the mother after childbirth (Stern, 1992).
- The ceremony of redeeming the first-born male reminds the Jewish people of their redemption from slavery in Egypt (Exodus 13:2-16) and the death of the first-born sons of Egypt.
- Each family dedicates their first-born son to God's service but then redeems the boy for a payment of five sanctuary shekels (Numbers 18:16). As a result, God accepts the Levites for service in the Tabernacle or Temple (Numbers 3:12-13,45; 8:14-19).
- This ceremony takes place after the son is 30 days old.
- The text suggests that Miryam and Yosef went up to Jerusalem when Yeshua was 30 days old and remained in Jerusalem for 10 days until it was time for Miryam's purification.
- The mother of a son remains ceremonially unclean for 40 days after childbirth. On the 41st day a sacrifice is offered (Leviticus 12:1-8) (Stern, 1992).
- If he could not afford both a lamb and a pigeon (or a dove), then two pigeons (or doves) were acceptable (*Archaeological Study Bible*, 2005).

2:25) Now there was a man in Yerushalayim named Shimeon and this man was righteous and devout, seeking the consolation of Yisrael, and the Holy Spirit was upon him. 2:26) It had been revealed to him by the Holy Spirit that he would not see death before he had seen the Anointed One of the LORD. 2:27) Being led by the Spirit, he came into the Temple when the parents brought the child Yeshua in order to do what is commanded in the Torah concerning Him. 2:28) Then he took Him in his arms, and blessed God, saying, 2:29) "Now, LORD, You may let Your servant depart in shalom, according to Your word, 2:30) because my eyes have seen Your salvation, 2:31) which You have prepared in the presence of all the peoples, 2:32) a light of revelation will shine among the Heathens and the glory of Your people Yisrael."

2:33) His father and mother were filled with wonder at what he said about Him. 2:34) Shimeon blessed them and said to Miryam His mother, "Listen, this Child is destined to cause the fall, in order to cause the rising of many in Yisrael, for a sign which will be spoken against. 2:35) A sword will pierce [[her]] soul in order that the thoughts of many will be revealed."

2:36) In addition, there was a prophetess, Chanah, a daughter of Paniel, out of the tribe of Asher.

She was advanced in age, having lived with her husband for seven years after her marriage. 2:37) She remained a widow until the age of eighty-four. She did not leave the Temple, worshiping [God] night and day with fastings and prayers. 2:38) At that moment, she came up to them and began giving thanks to God, speaking about Him to all who were longing for the redemption of Yerushalayim.

> To this day, when one thinks of Jerusalem as it was before the Romans destroyed it, they think of it as the religious capital of the Jews. The palaces of its kings and procurators, the stalls of its merchants, its political parties, its soldiers, its rabble and its visitors, all fade into insignificance before the majestic institution which crowned the city's heights and around which Jewish life revolved. It had never been as beautiful as after Herod had rebuilt it and after the Jewish people had finished embellishing it only a few years before it was destroyed. Its simple grandeur impressed every visitor, and it became known far and wide as one of the wonders of the ancient world.
>
> If any Jew of that time, not only in Judea but anywhere in the world, were asked what they considered most important as an institution in Jewish life, they would have answered that the Temple was most sacred to them, and that for it, above all, they were ready to give their life. No wonder it was the ambition of every Jew, no matter where they lived, whether in far-off Spain or deepest Asia, to visit the Temple at least once during their lifetime, or if they could afford it, to spend their declining years under the shadow of its sacred walls. Hundreds of thousands of visitors would crowd into Jerusalem during the three major festivals of the Jewish year: Passover, Shavu'ot, and Sukkot. There was never enough room for them all. On such occasions the suburbs of Jerusalem would be covered with tents, as though an army were besieging the city. The proud natives of Jerusalem would look down on these provincials who went gaping through the city's streets, admiring its marvels, paying their respects to the relics of the past...and above all, hurrying to the Temple whose atmosphere they wanted to breathe deeply before returning to their distant homes (Grayzel, 1947, pp. 115-116).

2:39) Hence, they fulfilled all the requirements according to the Torah of the LORD, and returned to the Galil unto their own village of Natzeret. 2:40) So the child continued to grow and become strong, ever increasing with wisdom, as the grace of God was with Him.

2:41) Now His parents went up every year to Yerushalayim for the feast of Pesach. 2:42) When He was twelve years old, they made the pilgrimage for the feast according to custom. 2:43) While they were returning after the days of observing Pesach were ended, the boy Yeshua stayed behind in Yerushalayim. His parents did not realize this. 2:44) Supposing that He was with others in the caravan, they traveled a day's journey. They looked for Him among His relatives and friends. 2:45) When they did not find Him, they returned to Yerushalayim earnestly looking for Him. 2:46) After three days had passed, they found Him in the Temple sitting among the rabbis, listening to them and asking them questions. 2:47) Everyone who heard Him, was marveling at His wisdom and the way He answered questions. 2:48) When they saw Him, they were astonished, and His mother said

For the Jew living during the Second Temple period, the worship of God was fundamental to their existence, and the Temple was the center of Jewish life (Flusser, 2001). (Illustration "Court of the Women" Debbie Willey, 2020)

to Him, "Son, why have You treated us this way? Look at how Your father and I have been frantic searching for You everywhere!" 2:49) But He said unto them, "Why have you been looking for Me? Did You not understand that I must be about My Father's work?" 2:50) They did not understand the saying which He spoke to them. 2:51) Then He went with them, and they came to Natzeret where He continued to be obedient to them. His mother was treasuring all these things in her heart. 2:52) Yeshua kept growing in wisdom, in stature, and in favor before God and people.

- The three pilgrim festivals on the Hebrew calendar are Pesach (or Passover, in the spring), Shavu'ot (in the spring), and Sukkot (or Feast of Booths or Tabernacles, in the fall). Being observant and pious Jews, Yeshua's family went every year.
- When he was 12 years old, this single event from Yeshua's "silent years" took place near the age at which a Jewish boy today (age 13) undergoes his Bar Mitzvah ceremony and becomes a "son of the commandment" (Stern, 1992).
- On the Feast of Pesach (Passover), the pilgrims were required to stay in Jerusalem at least two days. Yeshua stayed longer.
- His family would have been traveling in a large caravan.
- The first day was their outward journey. The second day was their return to find him, and the third day was when they found him sitting among the rabbis (teachers) (Marshall, 1978).

Questions for review and discussion

The study notes in this chapter talk about the position in society that shepherds had during biblical times. Discuss their position. How did people view them?

How do you think people treated them?

How did God treat the shepherds in this story?

Write and discuss why you think it was important that the angel of the LORD appeared to the shepherds:
_____
_____
_____
_____

How does that make you feel about how God cares for people? Or for you?
_____
_____
_____

What is a shofar? _____ How is it used? _____
_____

What do you think the name Chanah means in Hebrew (refer to "Hebrew Names" in the previous chapter:
_____

Read the story about Jerusalem and the Temple on page 67 out loud. What do you think about Shimeon and Chanah after reading this information? Were they devout Jews? Write and discuss:
_____
_____
_____
_____

How do you think Shimeon and Chanah felt when they saw Yeshua?
_____

How important was the Temple to the Jews of Yeshua's time?
_____
_____
_____

How could you compare its importance to something today in society?
_____
_____
_____
_____

What could you compare (the importance of the Temple) to in your life? Is there anything that important to you? What would it be? What makes it so important to you? Write and discuss:

Summarize the study notes from this chapter and discuss:

Summarize in one or two sentences the most important or the most interesting thing you learned in this chapter from your study:

What makes it important or interesting to you?

Re-read Luke Chapter 2 from the *Hebrew Heritage Bible* translation used in this book. Discuss. Summarize Luke Chapter 2 in one paragraph and discuss:

_____
_____
_____
_____
_____

Choose one verse from Luke Chapter 2 that you think is the most important and write it here. Discuss why you think it is the most important verse:

_____
_____
_____

How did your understanding of Luke Chapter 2 change after you studied it and read it again? Discuss.

_____
_____
_____
_____

How can you apply what you learned from Luke Chapter 2 to your life? Discuss.

_____
_____
_____

What question or questions do you still have about Luke Chapter 2 that you don't understand or want to know more about? Discuss

_____
_____
_____

For a deeper cultural experience, research and discuss what a "bar mitzvah" or a "bat mitzvah" is. What did you learn?

_____
_____
_____
_____

THE GOSPEL OF LUKE CHAPTER THREE

Lesson 5

Before you begin your study, read Luke Chapter 3 out loud (as a group) from your Bible.

In your own words, summarize Luke Chapter 3 in one paragraph and write at least two questions that you had about the chapter as you read the biblical text: (Discuss)

_____
_____
_____
_____
_____
_____
_____
_____
_____
_____
_____
_____
_____
_____

Luke Chapter 3 begins with a list of the political rulers of the Roman Empire, Galil, and Yehudah (Judea). This chapter introduces Yochanan's ministry in the wilderness where he was preaching a message of repentance and baptism. Yochanan was preparing the way of the LORD. Yeshua is baptized in the Yarden (Jordan) River. The genealogy of Yeshua is listed in this chapter.

Genealogies were very important in the biblical world. They were a person's identity. They certified a person's right to inherit property or a position of authority (*ESV Archaeology Study Bible*, 2017). Ancestry websites and DNA testing are very popular today. Have you ever checked into your family tree? What do you know about yourself and your heritage? Write and discuss:

_____
_____
_____
_____
_____
_____
_____
_____
_____
_____

Hebrew Names and their English Equivalents

Hebrew	English
Chanan	Annas
Kayafa	Caiaphas
Yarden	Jordan
Yehudah	Judea
Avraham	Abraham
Yeshayahu	Isaiah

Chapter 3

3:1) In the fifteenth year of the reign of Tiberius Caesar,

Tiberius became emperor in Rome when Caesar Augustus died in AD 14. Tiberius ruled until his death in AD 37. Tiberius appointed Pontius Pilate as Prefect of Yehudah in AD 26. Herod Antipas (Herod the Great's son and Tetrarch of Galil) built a new capital city around AD 17-20 on the western shore of the Sea of Galil and named it "Tiberias" in honor of the emperor. Tiberias was built on the site of an ancient cemetery, so many Jews considered it "unclean" and would not live there. However, after the Temple was destroyed, Tiberias became a center of Jewish learning. Several archaeological discoveries have been made at Tiberias. Just south of the city are many hot springs. These hot springs were used medicinally during the first century (*ESV Archaeology Study Bible*, 2017). Tiberias is mentioned in the Gospel of John 6:23.

 Take a trip online to Tiberias, Israel. It is the Sister City of Tulsa, Oklahoma. Check out the modern city and the ancient archaeological sites. It is an important city in the history of Judaism. Write and discuss what you learned:

_____
_____
_____
_____
_____

when Pontius Pilate was Prefect of Yehudah,

- Pontius Pilate was the Roman governor of Judea from AD 26-36. His official residence was in Caesarea on the Mediterranean Sea.

- In 1961, archaeologists excavated a stone step in an amphitheater at Caesarea that had this engraved in Latin: "Pontius Pilatus, the prefect of Judea, (erected) a (building dedicated) to the emperor Tiberius"

GOSPEL OF LUKE 75

and Herod was Tetrarch of the Galil, and Philip his brother was Tetrarch of the region of Ituraea and of Trachonitis, and Lysanias was Tetrarch of Abilene, 3:2) during the high priesthood of Chanan and Kayafa,

- Herod the Great died in 4 BC. When Herod died, three of his sons Archelaus, Herod Antipas, and Herod Philip were given jurisdiction over his divided kingdom.
- Herod Antipas became tetrarch of Galil and Perea.
- Chanan (Annas) was high priest from AD 6 until he was deposed in AD 15. He was followed by his son Eleazar, his son-in-law Kayafa (Caiaphas) and then four more sons.
- Even though Rome had replaced Chanan (Annas), the Jews continued to recognize his authority (Archaeological Study Bible, 2005).

the word of God came to Yochanan the son of Zecharyah in the wilderness. 3:3) So he went into all the surrounding area of the Yarden, proclaiming an immersion for people in water, resulting from repentance for the forgiveness of sins.

Yochanan was in the desert at the Yarden River preaching the baptism of repentance for the forgiveness of sins. The traditional baptismal site of Yeshua is known as Qasr al-Yehud. This site is full of history. Tradition says that it was at this location on the Yarden River where the Israelites entered the Holy Land under the leadership of Yehoshua (Joshua) after their 40 years of wandering in the desert (Josh. 3:13). This is also the place where tradition says that Eliyahu (Elijah) ascended to heaven in the fiery chariot (2 Kings 2:8).

Take a trip on-line to Qasr al-Yehud, Israel. Find its location on the Yarden River and read about its vast history covering thousands of years (including the more modern history of land mines at this site). Write and discuss what you learned from this investigation. One good source for Qasr al-Yehud is parks.org.il (Israel Nature and Parks).

_____
_____
_____
_____
_____
_____
_____

Christians from all over the world travel to Yisrael and are baptized in the Yarden River at Qasr al-Yehud.

3:4) As it is written in the book of Yeshayahu the prophet, "The voice of one crying in the wilderness, prepare the way of the LORD, make straight paths for him, 3:5) every valley shall be raised, every mountain and hill shall be made low, and crooked trails will be made straight, the rough roads smooth. 3:6) All flesh will see the salvation of God" (Isa 40:3-5). 3:7) He said to the multitudes of people who gathered to ritually immerse themselves in water under his supervision, "You swarm of vipers! Who warned you to escape from the anger which is to come? 3:8) Bring forth fruits that are fitting for repentance. Do not begin saying to yourselves, 'We have Avraham as our father!' I tell you that from these stones God is able to raise up children to Avraham. 3:9) Already the axe is laid to the root to cut the trees; every tree which does not produce fruit will be cut down and thrown into the fire."

3:10) The crowds of people began to ask him, "What shall we do?" 3:11) He answered and said unto them, "The one who has two coats must share with someone who has none, and the one with food must do the same." 3:12) The tax collectors came to immerse themselves in water, and they said to him, "Rabbi, what shall we do?" 3:13) He told them, "Collect no more than what is the assessment." 3:14) The soldiers asked him saying, "What shall we do?" He said to them, "Do not extort, do not accuse falsely, make do with your wages."

- Luke describes this event in a style typical of the call of the prophets (Marshall, 1978).
- Yochanan is the last of the "Old Testament" prophets (Young, 1995).
- Before a king made a journey to a distant country, the roads he traveled were improved. Similarly, moral and spiritual preparation for the Messiah was made by the ministry of John the Baptist (Archaeological Study Bible, 2005).

- A tax collector (publican) was employed by Roman tax contractors to collect taxes – collecting enough taxes to meet the demands of the state and line their own pockets. They worked for Rome and often demanded unreasonable payments. They were hated and considered traitors.

- The profession of tax collector and soldier were not condemned by Yochanan, but the common unethical practices associated with them were (*Archaeological Study Bible*, 2005).

- When the tax collectors asked Yochanan, "What shall we do?" they were seeking a true relationship with God through repentance. They wanted to renew a proper relationship with their Father in Heaven. Yochanan said to them, "Collect no more than you are authorized to do."

- The soldiers asked the same. He challenged them with the appeal, "Rob no one by violence or by false accusation, and be content with your wages." Yochanan did not ask them to leave their questionable occupations and drop out of society.

- Instead, his prophetic message pleaded with the people to live a holy life in the mainstream of society. As a prophet, Yochanan wanted everyone to repent.

- Yochanan the Immerser preached divine goodness for all who would reform their lives before the coming judgment (Young, 1995).

- Yochanan encouraged those who accepted his message to be active in the mainstream of society by living a life of holiness and bringing redemption in everyday life (Young, 1995).

- Since forgiveness was unthinkable without repentance, Yochanan summoned the people to express their repentance in baptism (Marshall, 1978).

- Yochanan's activity is regarded as fulfilling "Old Testament prophecy."

- He is making the paths straight for the Messiah – a poetic way of saying that the way of the LORD is made easier by having people already repentant of their sins and prepared to meet Him.

- Yochanan outlines the practical meaning of repentance in terms of love and justice for his hearers, including tax collectors and soldiers.

- His answer is very Jewish – the command to love one's neighbor.

- Yochanan's call to repentance was the significance of his baptism and the need to submit to it.

- Baptism was regarded as an outward ritual signifying the washing away of sin.

- The mention of repentance shows that, like other Jewish ritual washings, it was understood as a symbolic action that was ineffective without the appropriate inward attitude. A change had to occur in the heart (Marshall, 1978).

3:15) All the people were waiting expectantly. They questioned in their hearts concerning Yochanan, whether he could be the Anointed One or not. 3:16) Yochanan answered them saying, "Surely I cause you to immerse yourselves in water, but He who is more powerful is coming after me. I am unworthy to loosen the thong of His sandals. He Himself will immerse you with the Holy Spirit and with fire. 3:17) His winnowing fork is in His hand to clear out His threshing floor and to gather His wheat into the storehouse. But He will burn the chaff with unquenchable fire.

3:18) With many other exhortations he preached to the people. 3:19) Yochanan sharply reproved Herod the Tetrarch for taking Herodias his brother's wife, and the many wicked things that Herod had done. 3:20) At that, he added this evil act also to them all, he threw Yochanan into prison.

- To tie or carry someone's sandals was the lowly task of a slave. Yochanan considers himself unworthy as a statement of humility.
- Jewish baptisms consisted of immersion in water, but the Jews were looking forward to the day in the future when the Holy Spirit would be poured out (in divine fire). This fire could also refer to the coming judgement.
- For political reasons, Herod the Tetrarch (Antipas) had married the daughter of the powerful Nabataean king Aretas IV. However, Antipas wanted to marry Herodias, his brother's wife. So, Antipas divorced his Nabataean wife and married Herodias. The Nabataean princess fled to her father Aretas IV, who later defeated Antipas in battle.
- Josephus states that Antipas imprisoned Yochanan in his palace fortress of Machaerus. The ruins of Machaerus have been excavated on the east side of the Yarden River near the Dead Sea in modern-day Jordan (*Cultural Backgrounds Study Bible*, 2016).

3:21) So it happened that as all the people were immersing themselves in water that Yeshua also immersed Himself. While He was praying, the heaven opened 3:22) and the Holy Spirit descended upon Him in the bodily form like a dove. A voice from heaven declared, "You are My Son; this day I have brought You forth" (Ps 2:7).,

- The translation "Yeshua immersed Himself" is preferred since Jewish baptism or ritual immersion in water was self-administered under the supervision of a spiritual leader who would make certain that the whole body (including the hair) was immersed (Young, 2019).
- The NRSV reads "You are my Son, the Beloved; with you I am well pleased" which is based on strong textual witnesses. It is also the message of the transfiguration (Matt 17:5; Mark 9:7; Luke 9:35). The *Hebrew Heritage Bible* is based upon other manuscript evidence which presents Yeshua as the Son for the messianic task. Compare Moffatt, "Thou art my Son, the Beloved, to-day I have become thy father." The translation, "I have brought You forth" *(HHB)* stresses the presentation of the Anointed One like the royal king's coronation in Ps 2:7 which also was interpreted as referring to the future messiah. In a Jewish context, the Sonship is coronation or presentation and cannot be viewed as adoptionist (B. Young, *Jesus the Jewish Theologian*, 13-26).

- At the baptism, Yeshua is presented to the people empowered to fulfill His difficult mission.
- Luke suggests that the baptism of Yeshua occurred after that of the people: It was the climax of the activity of Yochanan, and after the Messiah had come, there was no place left for the ministry of Yochanan (Marshall, 1978).
- Yeshua must fulfill all righteousness.
- In Yeshua's identity of the totality of human need, He submitted to baptism in order to affirm the process of redemption which was a result of Yochanan's prophetic career.
- Luke's portrayal drives home the message. Yeshua is with all the people, thus demonstrating his total identification with all humanity.
- The most distinctive feature of Luke's description of the baptism is the "Divine voice."
- A voice from heaven was well known during this period (Young, 1995).
- Sometimes the "voice from heaven" or "divine voice" was likened to the sound of a chirping bird or the cooing of a dove. Some thought it was the "voice" of God Himself.
- The people were dependent upon guidance from the "voice from heaven."
- It was believed that when the prophet of the final redemption appeared, the Holy Spirit would return and prophecy would be renewed for the people. Then the redemptive process would be put forward with powerful force.
- The rabbis associated the bestowal of the Spirit with the coming Messiah.
- Yisrael (Israel) believed that the prophetic time when the Holy Spirit spoke through the prophets and worked miracles of deliverance had ended. When the TANAK (Old Testament) was completed (when the latter prophets of the Bible died) the Holy Spirit was taken away. The "heavenly voice" was thought to replace prophetic inspiration.
- The Jews taught that the Holy Spirit had been removed until the proper time for the renewal of prophecy. When the time is right, and the people are prepared, the prophetic ministry of the Holy Spirit will be renewed – at the time of the Messiah. A new prophet like Moses would renew the Spirit and bring about the redemption of the people.
- "Divine voices" were not an uncommon phenomenon among the Jews of those days, and frequently these voices were heard to utter verses from Scripture.
- The message of the "divine voice" at Yeshua's baptism focuses attention on the special mission of Yeshua. He is God's Son, the empowered servant of the LORD (Young, 1995).

3:23) When Yeshua began His ministry, He was thirty years of age,

- Thirty was the age at which the Levite undertook his service and at which a man was considered mature (*Archaeological Study Bible*, 2005).
- The age of thirty corresponds with the age that David began to reign (Marshall, 1978).

being the son (as supposed) of Yosef, the son of Eli, 3:24) the son of Matat, the son of Levi, the son of Melki, the son of Yanai, the son of Yosef, 3:25) the son of Matityahu, the son of Amotz, the son of Nachum, the son of Chesli, the son of Nagai, 3:26) the son of Machat, the son of Matityahu, the son of Shemi, the son of Yosef, the son of Yoda, 3:27) the son of Yochanan, the son of Resha, the son of Zerubavel, the son of Shealtiel, the son of Neri, 3:28) the son of Malki, the son of Adi, the son of Kosam, the son of Elmadan, the son of Er, 3:29) the son of Yose, the son of Eliezer, the son of Yorim, the son of Matat, the son of Levi, 3:30) the son of Shimeon, the son of Yehudah, the son of Yosef, the son of Yonam, the son of Elyakim, 3:31) the son of Malah, the son of Mana, the son of Matatah, the son of Natan, the son of David, 3:32) the son of Yeshai, the son of Oved, the son of Boaz, the son of Salmon, the son of Nachshon, 3:33) the son of Aminadav, the son of Aram, the son of Chetzron, the son of Peretz, the son of Yehudah, 3:34) the son of Yaakov, the son of Yitzchak, the son of Avraham, the son of Terach, the son of Nachor, 3:35) the son of Serug, the son of Reu, the son of Peleg, the son of Ever, the son of Shalach, 3:36) the son of Kenan, the son of Arpachshad, the son of Shem, the son of Noach, the son of Lamech, 3:37) the son of Metushelach, the son of Chanoch, the son of Yered, the son of Mahallalel, the son of Kenan, 3:38) the son of Enosh, the son of Shet, the son of Adam, the son of God.

- Ancient biographers often listed well-known ancestors.
- Jewish genealogies often began with earlier ancestors and ended with the descendent listed.
- The scholarly explanations of Matthew and Luke's genealogies vary in their interpretations (*ESV Archaeology Study Bible*, 2017).

"The Bible is made up of the history of God's people, His commands, and examples of how we should live. It is necessary to study the Bible so that we can live according to the way God wants us to. It is a resource given by Him to us, to use in our walk of life."
Weston Moore – Class of 2020

The Nabataean king Aretas IV ruled his kingdom from about 9 BC to AD 40. His daughter was married to and then divorced by Herod Antipas. This resulted in a battle between Antipas and Aretas IV with a resulting victory for Aretas IV. The Nabataeans were a very wealthy civilization whose capital is known as Petra in modern-day Jordan. Petra has been featured in many movies including "Indiana Jones and the Last Crusade" and "Transformers 2."

Take a trip on-line and visit fascinating Petra, Jordan. Explore its rich history and learn about the people who lived there – the Nabataeans. Also, visit what archaeologists believe is the tomb of Aretas IV (Al-Khazneh). Write and discuss what you learned:

_____
_____
_____
_____
_____
_____
_____
_____
_____

Locate and become familiar with where the following sites are on the map: Tiberias, Sea of Galil, Qasr al-Yehud, Yarden River, Petra, Dead Sea, Machaerus.

Briefly describe on the map what happened at each of these sites as discussed in this chapter:

Qasr al-Yehud: _____
_____

Petra: _____
_____

Machaerus: _____
_____

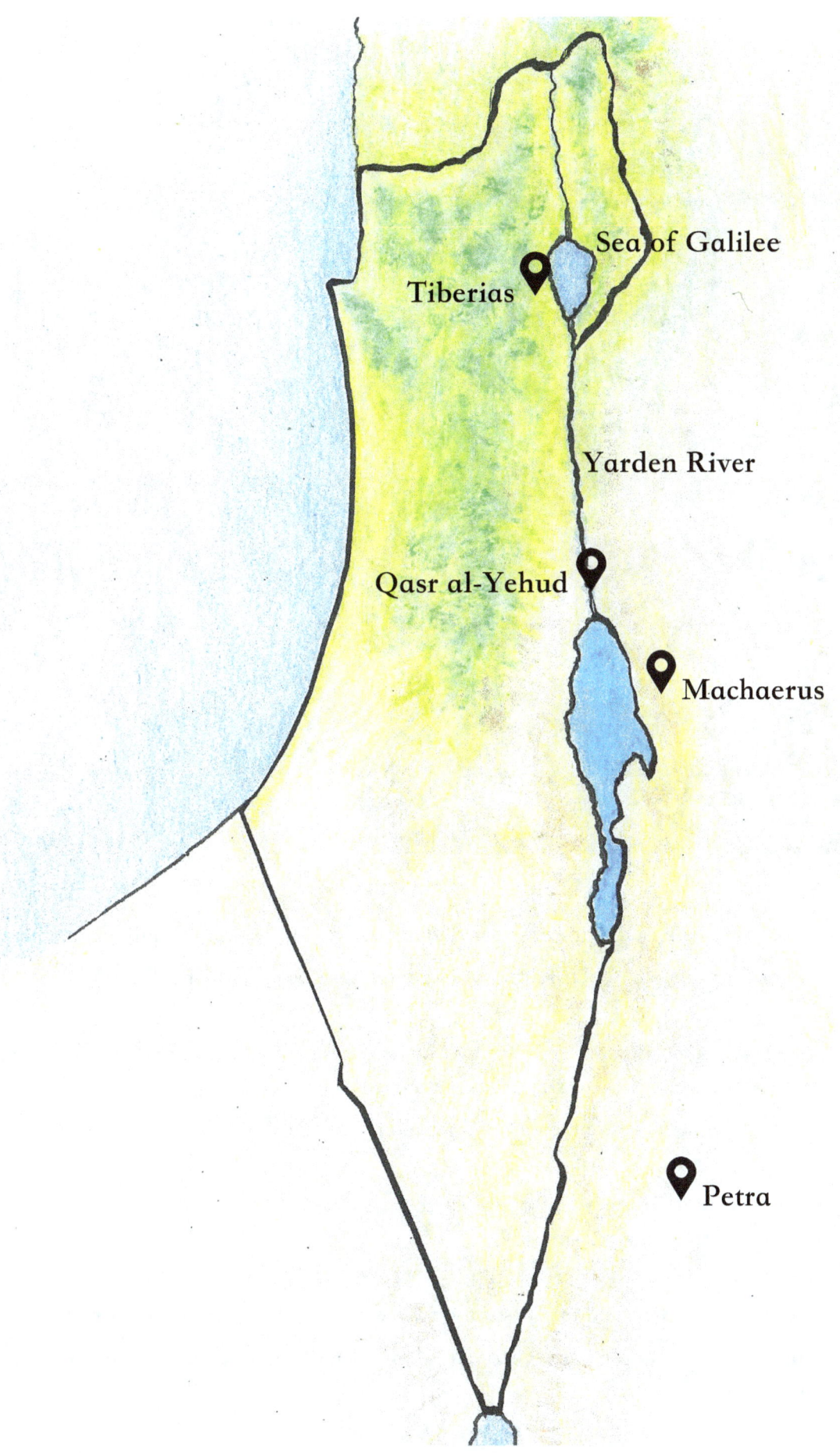

Pictured left is a mikveh (ritual immersion bath) from the time of Yeshua that was excavated just south of the Temple Mount in Yerushalayim. A person would enter the water in the mikveh going down the steps on the right. They would completely immerse and then exit going up the steps on the left.

(Photo credit: David Anderson)

- To baptize means to "dip, soak, or immerse" and is rooted in the Jewish ritual of immersion.
- A Jew had to be "ritually pure" before they could enter a synagogue or the Temple to worship God.
- In antiquity a Jew would immerse in mikveh (ritual immersion bath) that was full of "living water" or they would immerse in a river to wash away their impurity.
- Mikva'ot (plural of mikveh) were located at synagogues and at the southern stairs of the Temple Mount.
- There were many ways that a person could lose their ritual purity and the foremost way to restore purity was through immersion.
- Gentiles would immerse themselves to fulfill part of the requirements of conversion to Judaism (remember that Christianity was not a religion yet at this point in history).
- In Luke Chapter 3, Yochanan is supervising an immersion of repentance, a cleansing from a lifetime of sin (Stern, 1992).

Questions for review and discussion

What was Yochanan's ministry and why was it important?

How did he baptize?

What did Yochanan's baptism mean?

What happened when Yeshua was baptized? What do you think it meant?

Summarize the study notes from this chapter and discuss:

Summarize in one or two sentences the most important or the most interesting thing you learned in this chapter from your study:

What makes it important or interesting to you?

Re-read Luke Chapter 3 from the *Hebrew Heritage Bible* translation used in this book. Discuss. Summarize Luke Chapter 3 in one paragraph and discuss:

_____
_____
_____
_____
_____
_____
_____
_____

Choose one verse from Luke Chapter 3 that you think is the most important and write it here. Discuss why you think it is the most important verse:

_____
_____

How did your understanding of Luke Chapter 3 change after you studied it and read it again? Discuss.

_____
_____
_____
_____

How can you apply what you learned from Luke Chapter 3 to your life? Discuss.

_____
_____
_____

What question or questions do you still have about Luke Chapter 3 that you don't understand or want to know more about? Discuss

_____
_____
_____
_____
_____

THE GOSPEL OF LUKE CHAPTER FOUR

Lesson 6

Before you begin your study, read Luke Chapter 4 out loud (as a group) from your Bible.

In your own words, summarize Luke Chapter 4 in one paragraph and write at least two questions that you had about the chapter as you read the biblical text: (Discuss)

_____
_____
_____
_____
_____
_____
_____
_____
_____
_____
_____
_____
_____
_____

Luke Chapter 4 begins with Yeshua entering the wilderness after His baptism in the Yarden River. He is tempted by the devil for forty days. Yeshua returns to Galil and goes to Natzeret where He had been brought up. He reads from the scroll of Yeshayahu (Isaiah) the prophet in the synagogue on Shabbat. Yeshua then travels to Kefar Nachum (Capernaum), a city of the Galil where He drives out an unclean spirit and heals many people.

Take a trip online using Google maps or MapQuest. Plan a trip from Jericho (Jericho is near where tradition says that Yeshua was tempted in the wilderness) to Natzeret (Nazareth) to Kefar Nachum (Capernaum). How far is it between each location? How is the climate different at each site? How far is the total trip? What did you learn? Write and discuss:

_____
_____
_____
_____
_____
_____
_____
_____
_____
_____
_____
_____

Hebrew Names and their English Equivalents

Hebrew	English
Yeshayahu	Isaiah
Kefar Nachum	Capernaum
Tzarfat	Zarephath
Tzidon	Sidon
Eliyahu	Elijah
Shimon	Simon

Hebrew Names

Yeshayahu – "Yahweh is salvation" from "yesha" which means "salvation" and "yahu" or "yah" for Yahweh.

Shimon – means "to hear", "to be heard" from the root word "shama."

GOSPEL OF LUKE

Chapter 4

4:1) Yeshua, being full of the Holy Spirit, returned from along the Yarden River being led by the Spirit into the desert. 4:2) For forty days He was being tempted by the devil. He ate nothing in those days, and when they were ended, He was hungry. 4:3) The devil said to Him, "Since You are the Son of God, speak to this stone that it should be turned into bread."

4:4) Yeshua answered him, "It is written, 'A person does not live by bread alone…'" (Deut. 8:3).

- "Since you are the Son of God," is the preferred translation over the rendering, "If you are the Son of God" (NRSV). The *HHB* translation conveys the "condition of reality" meaning from the Greek text. The better translation demonstrates that the temptation is to misuse the power and the authority of the Son of God. Jesus does not have to prove the fact (Young, 2019) that He is the Son of God.
- The temptation was real. Yeshua is led into the wilderness and fasted for 40 days like Moses and Eliyahu. When Yeshua is physically weak, the devil came to tempt Him with food (Young, 1995, p. 28).

4:5) Then the [[devil brought Him to a high mountain]] and showed Him all the kingdoms of the world in a moment of time.

- The textual reading, "And the [[devil brought him to a high mountain]]," for the words of the translation in double brackets do not have strong textual support. Nevertheless, the context and the Jewish background support their authenticity. They may have been deleted by a scribal error when the copier's eyes moved ahead a few words in the line. The story reminds the listener of the experience of Moses upon Mount Nebo when he was shown all the land of Israel in a moment of time (Deut. 31:1). Some scholars will argue that the better manuscript reading is, "Then he brought Him and showed Him…" (Young, 2019).

4:6) The devil said to Him, "I will give You all this power and their grandeur because it has been handed over to me and I can give it to anyone I please. 4:7) If You will just worship before me, all of it will be Yours." 4:8) But Yeshua answered Him, "It is written, 'You shall worship the LORD your God and Him only shall you serve'" (Deut. 6:13). 4:9) So he brought Him to Yerushalayim, and he caused Him to stand up on the wing of the Temple. He said to Him, "Since you are the Son of God, jump off! 4:10) After all, it is written, 'He will cause his angels to watch over you to protect you,' 4:11) moreover, 'They will carry you on their hands, so that your foot may not even hit a rock'" (Ps 91:11, 12). 4:12) But Yeshua answered him, saying, "It is said, 'You shall not test the LORD your

God'" (Deut. 6:16). 4:13) When the devil had gone through every temptation, he left Him until an opportune time.

Yeshua was led into the Judean Desert after His baptism. The Judean Desert is an area that begins just east of Yerushalayim and continues east to the Yarden River and the Dead Sea. Yeshua's baptism probably occurred in the area of the Yarden River that is in the Judean Desert. Photo: The Judean Desert near the site of Yeshua's baptism in the Yarden River. Photo credit: David Anderson

- At the very beginning of His ministry, Yeshua is depicted as overcoming the devil who stands in opposition to the kingdom of God.
- In each event, Yeshua replies to temptation with a quotation from Scripture, and overcomes the devil by His superior knowledge of Scripture.
- The point is that Yeshua as the Son of God is obedient to God's will.
- The Scriptures that Yeshua chooses are significant.
- These Scriptures come from passages that relate to Yisrael in the wilderness during the Exodus.
- Yeshua (Jesus) is not to follow the example of Yisrael when they were in the wilderness by faithlessly putting God to the test.
- Again, it is the devoted and loving relationship of trust in the Father which is the object of the devil's attack against Yeshua – and the attack has failed (Marshall, 1978).
- It is interesting that these events begin near where tradition says that the Israelites crossed the Yarden River under the leadership of Joshua. In verse 5, the story reminds the listener of the experience of Moses upon Mount Nebo when he was shown all the land of Yisrael in a moment of time. Mount Nebo is located near this site, just east of the Yarden River.

📍 Take a trip online to Mount Nebo in Jordan. Find Mount Nebo on the map and explore the archaeological excavations and discoveries that have been made at this ancient location. What did you learn? Write and discuss:

_____
_____
_____
_____
_____

In verse 9, Yeshua is at the Temple in Yerushalayim. The Temple Mount complex was the largest man-made structure in the ancient world. It covered approximately 35-40 acres. The Temple itself was located on top of the Temple Mount complex. The Temple was about 150 feet tall, and the southeast corner of the Temple Mount complex was about 164 feet in height. It was 250 feet from the top of the Royal Stoa (red roofed structure) to the ground below the complex (Ritmeyer.com, 2016).
Photo: Model of the Second Temple, Jerusalem.

4:14) In the power of the Spirit, Yeshua returned unto the Galil, and His fame was reported throughout the entire region. 4:15) He taught in the Jewish learning centers, being highly regarded by everyone.

GOSPEL OF LUKE   91

- The translation "...highly regarded by everyone," is rendered more literally, "glorified by all." Here Luke's text stresses the point that Yeshua was highly "esteemed," "honored," or "praised." He was guided by the Spirit. His teachings were very well received (Young, 2019).
- "Jewish learning center" means "Synagogue." One of the primary purposes of the synagogue is to serve as a learning center.

4:16) Then He came to Natzeret where He had been brought up. As was His custom, He attended the Jewish learning center on the day of Shabbat. He stood up to read. 4:17) The scroll of Yeshayahu the prophet was handed to Him. He unrolled the scroll and found the place where it is written, 4:18) "The Spirit of the LORD is upon me because He has anointed me to proclaim good news to the poor, He has sent me to proclaim the release of the prisoners and the recovering of sight for the blind; to activate deliverance for the oppressed, 4:19) to announce the year of God's favor" (Isa 61:1, 2; 58:6).

4:20) He rolled up the scroll and handed it back to the attendant. He sat down. The eyes of everyone in the Jewish learning center were fixed upon Him. 4:21) He began to say to them, "Today, this Scripture has been fulfilled in your hearing."

- While the Temple stood, all synagogues were oriented in its direction.
- The main purpose of the synagogue was the teaching of the people – "the Jewish learning center."
- The teaching part of the service consisted mainly of
  - Reading a section from the Torah
  - Reading a section from the Prophets
  - Teaching
  - The ritual elements of the service included
    - Prayer
    - The Aharonic blessing, "The LORD bless you and keep you..." (Numbers 6:24-26)
    - Public worship began with the "Shema" (Deut. 6:4-5) and benedictions. All males were bound to repeat the Shema twice every day.
- The person who read the selection from the Prophets was also expected to say the Shema and offer the prayers which have just been quoted.
- In all likelihood, Yeshua had led the devotions on that Shabbat in Nazareth when He read the selection from Isaiah (Edersheim, 1994).

- The Torah was divided and arranged into sections. It took three years to complete the cycle and read the entire Torah from Genesis to Deuteronomy.
- Today the reading is arranged into 54 sections, one section is read on each Shabbat of the year beginning immediately after Sukkot. (More than one portion is read during certain weeks) (Edersheim, 1994, p. 252).
- Shabbat is the Sabbath and is observed from sunset on Friday night to sunset on Saturday night.
- The "books" of the TANAK ("Old Testament") were written on scrolls and kept in the "Ark" (Aron HaKodesh) in the synagogue. Just as ("The Holy Ark") the ark of the covenant was kept in the Holy of Holies behind the curtain, the Torah scrolls are kept in the Holy place in the synagogue behind the curtain (parokhet). The "Ark" where the Torah scrolls are kept is usually similar to an upright cabinet.
- A special attendant would take the scrolls out of the Ark (or cabinet) and hand them to the reader.
- The passage that Yeshua read was one that was already assigned as part of the reading cycle.
- It was customary to stand while reading Scripture and sit while teaching (*Archaeological Study Bible*, 2005). Therefore, Yeshua stood to read from the scroll of Yeshayahu (Isaiah) and then sat down to teach or explain the verses He had just read.
- Fulfilled in your hearing...People expected this text to be fulfilled only in the Messianic era, the time of the coming kingdom (*Cultural Backgrounds Study Bible*, 2016).

Reading the Word of God

Since the time of Moses, reading the Scriptures has been a community event. The Hebrew word for reading assumes speaking out loud "before an audience: qra means literally 'to cry out', and miqra means a 'gathering of listeners and readers.' That reading obligation would become the characteristic practice of Jewish observance. 'Gather the People, men, women, and children...that they may hear and learn'" (Schama, 2013, p. 33).

4:22) Everyone bore witness against Him but marveled at the grace-filled message which poured forth from His mouth. They asked, "Is not this the son of Yosef?" 4:23) But He said unto them, "Surely you will quote to Me the proverb, 'Doctor, heal yourself! That which we have heard was done in Kefar Nachum, do here in Your home town as well.'" 4:24) But He responded, "No prophet is recognized at home! 4:25) In truth, I say to you that in the days of Eliyahu, there were many widows in Yisrael. Although there was a great famine throughout the earth when [rain] from heaven was shut off for three years and six months, 4:26) Eliyahu was not sent to them, but rather to Tzarfat in the land of Tzidon, to a woman who was a widow (1 Kgs 17:8-16). 4:27) There were many lepers in Yisrael during the time of Eliyahu the prophet, yet they were not healed, but rather Naaman the Syrian" (2 Kgs 5:1-14). 4:28) Upon hearing these words, everyone attending the meeting was filled with anger. 4:29) They rose up and escorted Him outside the city to the brow of the hill upon which their town had been constructed. They intended to push Him down. 4:30) But He walked right through the midst of them all and went on His way.

The Torah that is used in the synagogue service is written in Hebrew on scrolls. The Hebrew language is written and read from right to left.

- Yosef (Joseph) was Yeshua's earthly father. Tradition says that Yosef was a carpenter. Carpenters were considered particularly learned. If a difficult problem was under discussion, people would ask, "Is there a carpenter among us and/or the son of a carpenter?" (Flusser, 2001, p. 33)
- Although in this case, the crowd may have been criticizing this "local lad" for putting on airs and claiming to be a prophet (Marshall, 1978, p. 186).
- The area of Tzidon is located in modern-day Lebanon.
- Similar to Eliyahu (Elijah), Yeshua's ministry will include raising the dead and curing leprosy (Cultural Backgrounds Study Bible, 2016).

4:31) He came to Kefar Nachum, a city of the Galil.

Interior of a typical synagogue from the time of Yeshua. Notice the Ark where the Torah scrolls were kept (with the curtain) and the platform in the center of the room where the rabbi would read from the Scriptures and teach.
Illustration: Synagogue by Debbie Willey

- Located along the northwestern shore of the Sea of Galilee, Kefar Nachum (Capernaum) was where Shimon (the Apostle Peter) lived.
- Jesus established His ministry base at Kefar Nachum (Capernaum) for approximately three years.
- Seventy-five percent of Jesus' ministry took place around the Sea of Galilee.
- Kefar Nachum's (Capernaum's) location near major trade routes helped to spread Yeshua's message.
- The Gospels record that many miracles happened at Kefar Nachum.
- The Bible refers to Kefar Nachum as Yeshua's "own town."
- The road to Damascus passed nearby, providing a commercial link with regions to the north and south.
- Shimon (Peter) and his brother Andrew, John and James, the sons of Zebedee, and Matthew were from this area (*Archaeological Study Bible*, 2005).
- Kefar Nachum is located over 90 miles north-northeast of Jerusalem and slightly more than 20 miles northeast of Natzeret (Nazareth) in the region of Galilee in northern Yisrael.
- During the time of Jesus' ministry, the population of Kefar Nachum may have been around 2,000 people.
- It was probably a relatively prosperous community located in the rolling hills and fertile land next to the Sea of Galilee.

He taught the people on the Shabbat days. 4:32) They were greatly impressed with His teachings, for His word was delivered with authority. 4:33) There was a man in the Jewish learning center who had an unclean demon spirit. He shouted with a loud voice, 4:34) "Hey! What do you have to do with us—Yeshua of Natzeret? Have you come to destroy us? I know who you are—the Holy One of God." 4:35) But Yeshua rebuked him saying, "Shut up! Come out of him!" After the demon threw him down into their midst, he came out of the man without harming him. 4:36) They were amazed. They all marveled one to another, saying, "What miraculous action is this that with authority and power He commands the unclean spirits and they obey?" 4:37) So His fame went forth into every place in the entire region.

Hebrew Names

Kefar Nachum – "Kefar" means "village."

Nachum is a Hebrew personal name. Kefar Nachum was probably not named after the Prophet Nachum.

4:38) He arose and went out of the Jewish learning center coming to the home of Shimon. But Shimon's mother-in-law was sick with a high fever. He asked Yeshua to help her. 4:39) Yeshua stood beside her and rebuked the fever. It left her. Immediately she rose up and served them.

4:40) While the sun was setting, people brought to Him all those having various kinds of sickness. He laid hands upon each one of them and healed them. 4:41) Demons came out of many crying and saying, "You are the Son of God!" But He rebuked them and would not allow them to speak. They knew that He was the Anointed One.

4:42) When the day came, He left and went into a secluded place. But the people searched for Him and came to Him, compelling Him not to leave them. 4:43) He said to them, "I must proclaim the good news of God's sovereignty in other cites as well—for this purpose I have been sent." 4:44) Thus He preached in the Jewish learning centers located in the Galil.

The Synagogue at Capernaum was the center of activity for the community. It was the place where the people gathered for worship and the reading of the Torah.
Photo: Looking at the ancient synagogue from Peter's house.

- High fever…Fevers were common; one of the most common causes of fevers in the ancient Mediterranean world was malaria, which could be serious and did not normally disappear suddenly (*Cultural Backgrounds Study Bible*, 2016).
- Because healing on Shabbat could have been considered a violation of the laws regarding work on Shabbat, the people waited until Shabbat was over that evening to bring the sick to be healed (Stern, 1992).
- Peter's house was only a few feet from the shore of the Sea of Galilee and 84 feet from the synagogue.
- Archaeologists believe that the ruins of Peter's house have been properly identified.
- The structure identified as Peter's house or Peter's mother-in-law's house was a first century house built out of basalt that had received special treatment at an early date:
  - First, the walls and the floor of one room measuring 19x21 feet were plastered in the first century, and later were re-plastered (no other homes excavated in Capernaum were plastered.)
  - This indicates that this home had an exalted status.
  - It is believed that the early Christians worshiped here.
  - Very early in Christian history it became a place of pilgrimage.
  - A baptistery was discovered, which indicated that the home had become a functioning church.
  - In the fourth century AD, the house's structure was expanded and surrounded by a wall (Hoffmeier, 2008).

Kefar Nachum (Capernaum) is one of the most visited sites in Yisrael. Two very important archaeological discoveries are located at Capernaum – the ancient synagogue and Peter's house.

Take a trip online to Capernaum in Israel, and visit the ancient site. What did you learn about the ancient synagogue? Write and discuss:

_____
_____
_____
_____
_____
_____
_____

continued on pg. 100

Kefar Nachum with Peter's house and the Synagogue. Kefar Nachum was a busy fishing village along the shore of the Lake of Kinneret. Black basalt rock was used to construct the synagogue.
Illustration: Kefar Nachum by Debbie Willey

continued from pg. 98

📍 What did you discover about Peter's house at Capernaum?

_____
_____
_____
_____
_____

📍 When was Capernaum first excavated and by whom?

_____
_____

📍 What else did you learn about this site?

_____
_____
_____

Questions for review and discussion

What happened to Yeshua in the desert and why was it important?

_____
_____
_____

What is another name for "Jewish learning center?"
_____

What did Yeshua do in the learning center in Natzeret and why was that important?

_____
_____
_____

Explain "Reading the Word of God"
_____
_____

Map work:

Identify and become familiar with the following locations that are mentioned in this chapter. Write and discuss what happened at each site:

Tzidon

Kefar Nachum

Natzeret

Qasr al-Yehud

Mount Nebo

Yerushalayim

Judean Desert

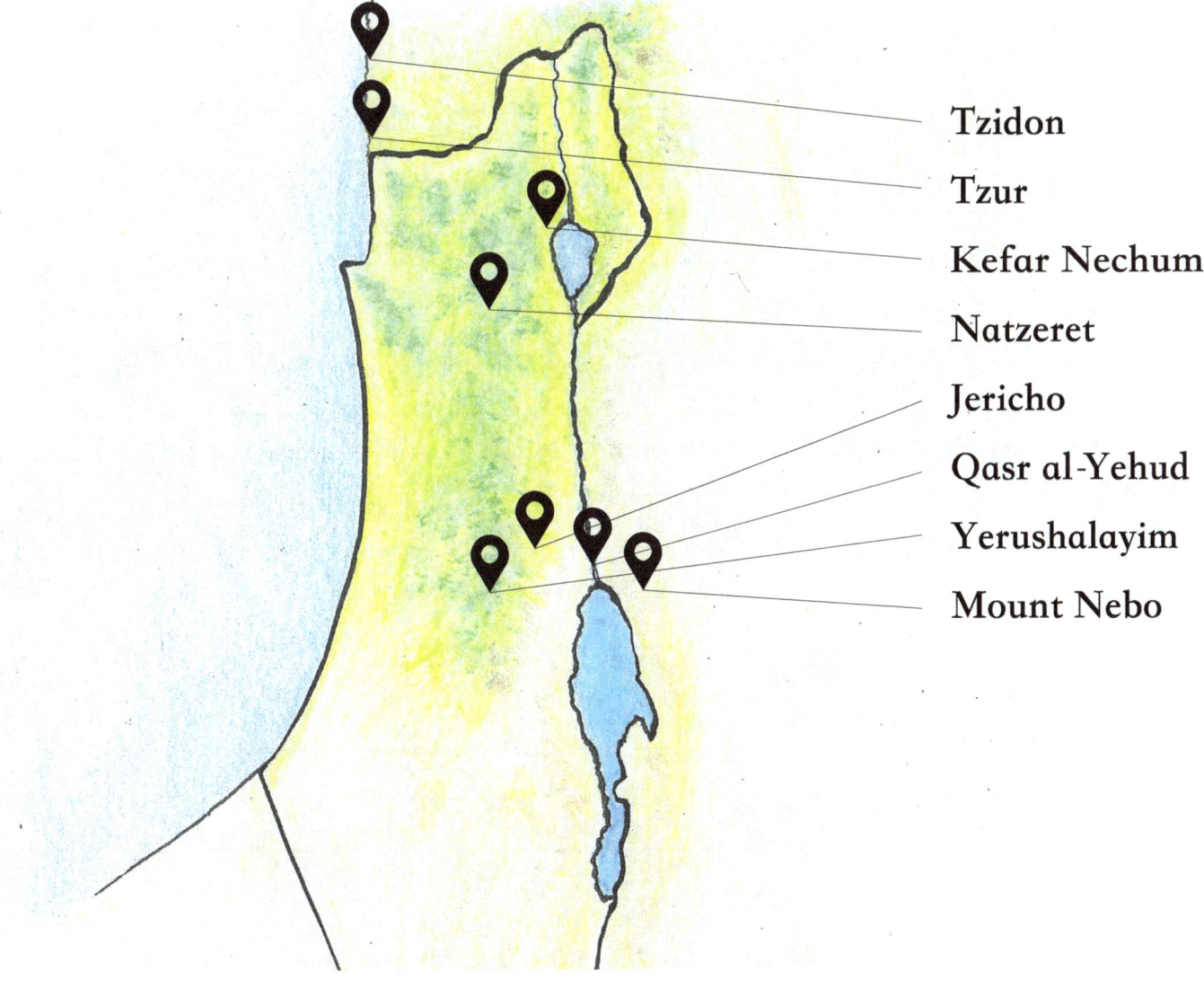

Summarize the study notes from this chapter and discuss:

_____

_____

_____

_____

_____

_____

_____

_____

_____

_____

_____

_____

_____

_____

_____

_____

_____

_____

_____

_____

_____

_____

_____

_____

Re-read Luke Chapter 4 from the *Hebrew Heritage Bible* translation used in this book. Discuss. Summarize Luke Chapter 4 in one paragraph and discuss:

_____

_____

_____

_____

_____

_____

_____

_____

Choose one verse from Luke Chapter 4 that you think is the most important and write it here. Discuss why you think it is the most important verse:

_____
_____
_____
_____
_____
_____

Summarize in one or two sentences the most important or the most interesting things you learned in this chapter from your study:

_____
_____
_____
_____

What makes it important or interesting to you?

_____
_____
_____
_____

How did your understanding of Luke Chapter 4 change after you studied it and read it again? Discuss.

_____
_____
_____
_____
_____
_____
_____
_____
_____

How can you apply what you learned from Luke Chapter 4 to your life? Discuss.

What question or questions do you still have about Luke Chapter 4 that you don't understand or want to know more about? Discuss

THE GOSPEL OF LUKE CHAPTER FIVE

Lesson 7

Before you begin your study, read Luke Chapter 5 out loud (as a group) from your Bible.

In your own words, summarize Luke Chapter 5 in one paragraph and write at least two questions that you had about the chapter as you read the biblical text: (Discuss)

___
___
___
___
___
___
___
___
___
___
___
___
___
___

The setting for Luke Chapter 5 is around the Lake of Kinneret (Sea of Galilee). Yeshua calls His first disciples by the lake. He causes Shimon (Simon) to have a miraculous catch of fish and declares to him, "Do not be afraid! From now on you will be catching people." Yeshua heals the man with leprosy and the man who was crippled. Yeshua calls Levi to follow Him. Yeshua teaches by telling a parable.

Take a trip online and visit the Lake of Kinneret (Sea of Galilee) in northern Yisrael. In the TANAK ("Old Testament"), the Sea of Galilee is called the" Lake of Kinneret" because the lake is shaped like a harp. The Hebrew word "kinnor" means harp or lyre (*Archaeological Study Bible*, 2005). At 700 feet below sea level, it is the lowest freshwater lake on earth. Write and discuss five interesting things that you learned about the Sea of Galilee:

_____
_____
_____
_____
_____
_____
_____
_____
_____
_____
_____
_____

Hebrew Names and their English Equivalents

Hebrew	**English**
Shimon	Simon
Kefa	Peter
Yaakov	Jacob (James)
Yochanan	John
Zavdai	Zebedee
Moshe	Moses
Yehudah	Judea
Yerushalayim	Jerusalem

Chapter 5

5:1) So it happened, the crowds of people pressed in close to Him so they could hear the word of God. He stood by the Lake of Kinneret.

5:2) He saw two boats in the lake. The fishermen had left them to wash their nets. 5:3) After climbing on board one of the boats which belonged to Shimon, He asked him to put Him out a little way from the shore. He sat down in the boat and taught the crowds of people. 5:4) When He had finished speaking, He said to Shimon, "Launch out into the deep water and let down your nets for a catch." 5:5) But Shimon explained to Him, "Master, we have worked hard all night and have not caught anything. Nonetheless, because of Your word, I will let down the nets." 5:6) When they had done this, they netted an enormous haul of fish and their nets began to break. 5:7) They called their partners in the other boat to come and help them. They came and loaded up both boats until they began to sink. 5:8) But when Shimon Kefa saw it, he fell on his knees saying to Yeshua, "Go away from me, O Lord. I am a sinful man." 5:9) Wonder gripped him as well as all those who were with him, because of the haul of fish they had taken. 5:10) Yaakov and Yochanan, the sons of Zavdai who were partners with Shimon, felt the same way. At that, Yeshua said to Shimon, "Do not be afraid! From now on you will be catching people." 5:11) After they brought their boats to shore, they left everything and followed Him.

The Lake of Kinneret is about 14 miles long and about 8 miles wide. The Yarden River flows into the northern end of the lake and exits out of the southern end of the lake. At the time of Yeshua's ministry there were many fishing villages around the lake.

Photo: Near the northwestern shore of the Lake of Kinneret looking south.

- Fishing was an important part of the Galilean community. The major types of fish would have been tilapia, carp, and sardines.
- Much of the catch would have been dried for sale or manufactured into fish sauce and exported throughout the Mediterranean.
- The fishing boats would have held about one ton (crew plus cargo).
- The nets they used might have been large dragnets that were hundreds of feet long, or a circular casting net that was 6 - 8 yards in diameter. They also might have used a hook and line.
- The Galilean fishermen were most often employees or partners in small, family-run businesses *(Archaeological Study Bible, 2005)*.

- After a dry season in the Galilee in 1986, two fishermen discovered an ancient fishing boat from the time of Yeshua.
- Scientists from all over the world traveled to Yisrael to help safely move this boat from the mud where it had been preserved for 2,000 years.
- The dimensions of the boat are 27 feet long, 7.5 feet wide, and 4.3 feet deep. It would carry a crew of about 12-13 men.

Take a trip online to Kibbutz Ginnosar in Yisrael and discover more about the fascinating history of the "Jesus Boat." What did you learn? Write and discuss:

_____
_____
_____
_____
_____
_____
_____
_____
_____
_____
_____
_____

5:12) While visiting one of their cities, suddenly a man full of leprosy caught sight of Yeshua. He fell on his face begging Him, "Lord, if You will; You can make me clean!" 5:13) At that, Yeshua stretched out his hand and touched him saying, "I will, be made clean!" Immediately the leprosy left him.

- Leprosy – (not modern leprosy or Hansen's disease) refers to a group of infectious conditions under the category of "scaly" skin diseases.
- Affliction with a skin disease meant that an individual was ritually unclean (Archaeological Study Bible, p. 171).
- By the first century, Judaism had developed a list of major signs the true Messiah could be expected to give as proof of his identity. Healing a leper was one of them (Stern, 1992).

5:14) He charged him not to speak to anyone, but to "go and show yourself to the priest, and make an offering for your cleansing, as Moshe commanded, as a witness to them." 5:15) But so much the more the news concerning Him kept spreading. Large crowds of people gathered to hear and to be healed of their sicknesses. 5:16) But He withdrew into the wilderness areas and prayed.

- Based on the laws that applied to lepers in Leviticus 13-14, Yeshua told the man to show himself to the priest in Yerushalayim and offer the sacrifices that Moses had commanded for his cleansing. This would also send a message to the religious establishment that the Messiah has come and is at work doing only what the Messiah can do (Stern, 1992).
- According to the law of Moses, when the leper was healed, he had to bring offerings to the Temple, and he was shaved completely. During the next seven days, he was not allowed to enter into his own home or have marital relations. On the eighth day he had to bring additional sacrifices to the Temple. Then he had to immerse himself in a mikveh in the Chamber of the Lepers at the Temple Mount, after which he went to Nicanor's Gate closer the Temple itself. At the gate, the leper thrust his hand into the Court of the Israelites. After the performance of certain rituals, during which blood (of a sacrificed animal) and olive oil were put on his body and his sin offering and burnt offering were presented, the leper was considered cleansed from the disease (Ritmeyer, 2006, pg. 352).
- Jesus healed without charge or the fanfare associated with the pagan temples, and He did not follow prescribed rituals (regarded as the key to tapping into magical, healing power) associated with pagan temple practices (Cultural Backgrounds Study Bible, p. 1752).
- Yeshua healed like no other. He healed by "the finger of God."
- He is the Messiah with supernatural character and power, proven by his healing and confrontation of evil, and the happiness of those who were healed or those who watched others as they were healed (Lindsey, 2017, p. 67).

Court of the Israelites — Chamber of the Lepers
Nicanor's Gate

- In obedience to Yeshua and the commands of Moses, the leper would have traveled to Yerushalayim to present himself to the priests. Above is a diagram of the various areas on the Temple Mount complex that he would have visited to fulfill all the requirements of the Torah.

- The news of Yeshua had spread. This next scene follows the healing of the man with leprosy.

- Where valuable medical resources were lacking, people flocked to what they believed might cure them. In antiquity people flocked to the hot springs in Tiberias. (*Cultural Backgrounds Study Bible*, 2016, p. 1688).

- Ancient medical tradition included a mixture of observed cures and superstition.

- Various schools of medicine existed, and there was no standard certification.

- Greeks, women, and well-educated slaves were doctors.

- Temples of the Greco-Roman god of healing were found all over the Roman empire, including Judea.

- Religion played a major role in medicine (*Cultural Backgrounds Study Bible*, 2016).

- The pagan temples of healing were more like spas, where the treatment consisted of "incubation" as the person slept inside the temple hoping to receive a "dream-revelation" from a god.

- Those who were "healed" made special contributions to the pagan temple. This often included a plaster reproduction of whatever body part had been healed. These were put on display as testimonies (*Cultural Backgrounds Study Bible*, 2016).

5:17) One day as He was teaching, there were spiritual leaders and teachers of Torah who were sitting nearby, who had come from every village of the Galil and Yehudah and Yerushalayim. The power of the LORD was with Him to heal. 5:18) Take notice of this, there were men carrying a crippled man on a stretcher. They wanted to bring him inside to lay him before Yeshua, 5:19) but they could not find a way because of the crowd. They went up to the roof. They lowered him, stretcher and all, through the roofing tiles into the middle of the people, right before Yeshua. 5:20) With that, He saw their [chutzpah style] faith. He said, "Man, your sins are forgiven you." 5:21) The scribes and spiritual leaders began to think in their hearts saying, "Who is this? He speaks blasphemies. No one is able to forgive sins except God alone." 5:22) Yeshua knew what they were thinking. He answered and said unto them, "What is this you are thinking in your hearts? 5:23) What is easier to say, 'Your sins are forgiven you' or 'Stand up and walk'? 5:24) However, so that you may know that the Son of Man possesses the authority upon earth to forgive sins"—He said to the crippled man—"I say to you, stand up and pick up your stretcher and go to your house." 5:25) Immediately he stood up before them. Picking up what he had been lying on, he went to his home glorifying God. 5:26) Sheer amazement seized one and all, and they glorified God. They were overcome with awe and said, "We have seen incredible things today."

- More than belief, faith is unyielding persistence – called "[chutzpah style] faith." This "bold-faced assertiveness means unyielding tenacity or strong persistence.
- Faith must be faithfulness with actions that accompany belief (Young, 2019).
- Yeshua was teaching in Kefar Nachum (Capernaum) "His own town." When the people heard that He had come home, they gathered in such large numbers that there was no room left, not even outside the door.
- Some tried to take him in the house (probably Peter's house). It was not a small house. It was one of the better dwellings of the middle class (Edersheim, 1994).
- Logs were used as roof beams to support most Galilean roofs; reeds or branches were laid across the logs, then the entire roof was covered with packed mud and clay. However, some had tile roofs (*Cultural Backgrounds Study Bible*, 2016).
- Often the cause of sickness was wrongly attributed to sin (Young, 1995, p. 41).
- The common belief was that recovery to the sick couldn't happen until sins were forgiven.
- The inner paralysis of guilt must be removed before the outward could be taken away (Edersheim,1993).
- Yeshua speaks a word as the power of forgiveness and acceptance begins a process of healing.
- In Jewish texts, true faith, like that of the paralytic and his friends, must be based on the sovereignty of God.
- Healing faith in the Gospels focuses, not upon the problem but upon God, by recognizing God's goodness and mercy (Young, 1995, p. 42).
- In Jewish tradition, when someone benefits in any way from God's creation, that one is required to give thanks to God. One receives God's grace with thanksgiving and praise.
- Early Jewish tradition stated that when God worked a miracle, or when God blesses, the people were to respond, "Blessed be God who has done so great wonders for the children of men" (Young, 1995, p. 42).

"Yeshua was seated in the covered gallery that ran around the courtyard and opened to various areas of the home. The scribes and pharisees were seated around him. The area was packed with people out into the street. All were absorbed listening to the Master. Suddenly those appeared who were carrying the paralyzed man in his pallet. It was such a common scene to see the sick being brought to Yeshua. It didn't warrant any special attention. You would have thought that someone would move and make room. But, with the courtyard crowded all the way out into the street, this was out of the question. Access to Yeshua was impossible. Should they wait for the crowd to disperse? Or wait for another day? No. The need was too great. Now was the opportunity. They knew He could heal. Perhaps in the heart of the paralytic was fear, however, that his sins might hinder his healing. Imagine the digging – the unroofing – the disturbance and surprise of the crowd as the opening appeared. It must have been a marvelous sight – when the marvelous became an everyday occurrence" (Edersheim, Messiah, pp. 347-349, 1993).

Most houses, including Peter's had flat roofs.
Illustration: Kefar Nachum by Debbie Willey

5:27) After these happenings, He went outdoors and saw a tax collector named Levi sitting at the tax office. He said to him, "Follow Me." 5:28) Abandoning everything, he arose and followed Him. 5:29) Levi prepared a great banquet for Him in his house. A large company of tax collectors and many others who were with them joined in the banquet. 5:30) The spiritual leaders and their scribes complained to His disciples, saying, "Why do you eat and drink with tax collectors [[and sinners]]?" 5:31) Yeshua answered and said unto them, "It is not the healthy that need a doctor, but the sick. 5:32) I have not come to call the righteous, but rather sinners to repentance."

> "The Bible is a light to my life. No matter the circumstances, there is always a passage that can get you through life, even in the hardest times. It can help every area of life and ultimately it is a path to grow closer to God."
> Gage Barham – Class of 2020

- Roman Emperor Augustus Caesar had established the system to collect taxes from conquered territories such as Judea. The taxes supported the Roman army, the imperial household, Roman government salaries, road maintenance, public works, and the dole of grain for the Roman masses (free bread for people who lived in Rome – about 1 million people in AD 70).
- Taxes were in the form of land (or income) tax and poll tax (a tax on every person regardless of income). A poll tax was collected from every man 14 years old and older and women 12 years old and older.
- Gathering taxes was contracted to private companies. The tax collectors (publicans) collected the required amount for Rome and kept the profit for themselves.
- Taxes were heavy and unfair, and tax collectors were often abusive and brutal. They were hated traitors.
- Levi was collecting tolls from commercial traffic (or taxes for fish), a heavy toll for struggling Galileans.
- Sitting at his tax booth, Levi (Matthew) was not only a publican, he was the worst kind. He was a "Mokhes" (a custom-house official): the type notorious for extracting the harshest and most unfair tax collection (Edersheim, 1993). The root meaning associated with "Mokhes" is oppression and injustice – literally "an oppressor."
- Repentance for people who held positions like Levi was especially difficult if not impossible.
- But how many stories had Levi heard about Yeshua's miracles? How many times had he overheard Yeshua's teaching? How many healings had he seen while he sat collecting taxes on the road near Kefar Nachum? (Edersheim, 1993)

- Levi-Mattityahu (Levi-Matthew). It was common to have more than one name (Stern, 1992).
- Maybe Levi changed his name from Levi to Mattityahu when he became a disciple of Yeshua. Mattityahu means "gift from Yah" (*Archaeological Study Bible*, 2005).
- Levi responded quickly. Maybe he was already familiar with Yeshua's teaching.
- Levi-Mattityahu's background and talents were important to ministry. He was skilled at writing and keeping records (*Archaeological Study Bible*, 2005).
- Follow Me...Levi rose up and left his custom house where he had been collecting taxes and followed Yeshua.
- That day was a gain, not just for Levi-Matthew, but for all the poor and needy in Israel – all the sinners among men and women – to whom the door of heaven was now open (Edersheim, 1993).
- In verse 29, This phrase, "many others who were with them," most certainly refers to friends of the tax collectors who would be despised by the outwardly pious (religious) who could not sense the spiritual need of others or recognize the opportunity for change (Young, 2019).
- In verse 29, the translation, "joined in the banquet," is literally, "reclined." The posture of the guests may indicate the nature of the banquet. In the Passover Seder meal, the participants recline as was the ancient custom at feasts. The reclining is translated, "joined in the banquet" which captures the idea of eating together at a festive occasion.
- In verse 30, in the phrase, "tax collectors [[and sinners]]," the word "sinners" is missing in a number of manuscripts. David Flusser believed that it was an addition to the Gospels because it has no meaning in Jewish halakhah. Here the word has been retained because of its manuscript support. It probably further clarifies the others who had come to the banquet with the tax collectors. In all probability they were secular-minded Jews and were non-observant of traditional Jewish ritual practices (Young, 2019).
- Big meal! Big house! Big guest list!
- Tax collectors and others were regarded as sinful "people with whom no respectable Jew would have anything to do."
- Levi was the host, and Yeshua was the guest of honor.
- People were sitting at the table with them. Yeshua disregarded the standards according to which they were both sinful and ritually unclean because of their contact with Gentiles as they conducted their businesses.
- This meal was clearly intended for the business associates of Levi-Matthew to meet Yeshua – to welcome the outcast of Jewish society and summon them to repent (Edersheim, 1993).

- Matthew was giving up a lucrative trade to follow Yeshua.
- Jesus calls the sinners to himself/to the Kingdom – and the beginning of repentance.
- A person might throw a banquet in another's honor – table fellowship established a covenant relationship – therefore it could be understood as indicating or signifying acceptance (Edersheim, 1993).

5:33) They said to Him, "Yochanan's disciples fast and pray often, much like the disciples of our spiritual leaders, but Yours go on eating and drinking." 5:34) But Yeshua said unto them, "Can the guests of the bridegroom fast as long as the bridegroom is with them? 5:35) The days are coming, however, when the bridegroom will be taken from them. In those days, then, they will fast."

5:36) He told them a parable, "No one makes a patch to sew on an old garment by tearing a new garment. If he does, the new garment will have been torn and the fabric of the new patch will not match the old garment. 5:37) No one, moreover, pours new wine into old wineskins. If he does, the new wine will burst the old wineskins. The wine will be spilled out and the wineskins destroyed. 5:38) New wine must be poured into fresh wineskins. No one after drinking old wine desires new. He says, 'The old is better.'"

- Fasting is not the main focus in these verses. Yeshua was telling them something about his purpose. He came to bring renewal and redemption through the power of the kingdom of heaven. His purpose was not to destroy the significance of the Torah but to fulfill it. The "old wine" of the Torah was best (p. 158).
- The rabbis of Yeshua's day related the study of the Torah with wine. The more a person studies the Scriptures, the more capable they will become.
- Knowledge of the Scripture will change a person's life.
- Yeshua wanted to see "new wineskins." He wanted to see revitalized and renewed people enjoying the best of the Torah ("old wine"). "Men and women of God must be renewed in order to hold the 'old wine' of the Torah" (p. 157).
- Yeshua is saying that this is not the time for fasting. He is bringing renewal. "Renewed wineskins for the finest old wine" (p. 159)
- Yeshua speaks about the rich Hebrew heritage of Judaism with the highest esteem.
- But the day will come for His disciples when He (the bridegroom) will be taken, and they will fast. He was speaking about His death on the cross (Young, 1995).

Questions for review and discussion

With what you know about Kefar Nachum, do you think that there were only two boats in the lake? How did you come to this conclusion?

_____
_____
_____

Why do you think Yeshua just picked these two boats?

_____
_____

What happened in the story with Shimon and his boat?

_____
_____

Why is this story important?

_____
_____

Do you think Shimon and Levi knew each other before Yeshua called Levi to follow Him? Why do you think that?

_____
_____
_____

Do you think they liked each other? Why or why not?

_____
_____
_____

Why did Yeshua tell the leper to show himself to the priest?

_____
_____

What did the man have to do?

_____
_____
_____

Summarize the study notes from this chapter and discuss:

_____

Summarize in one or two sentences the most important or the most interesting thing you learned in this chapter from your study:

_____

What makes it important or interesting to you?

_____

Re-read Luke Chapter 5 from the *Hebrew Heritage Bible* translation used in this book. Discuss. Summarize Luke Chapter 5 in one paragraph and discuss:

_____
_____
_____
_____
_____
_____
_____
_____

Choose one verse from Luke Chapter 5 that you think is the most important and write it here. Discuss why you think it is the most important verse:

_____
_____
_____

How did your understanding of Luke Chapter 5 change after you studied it and read it again? Discuss.

_____
_____
_____
_____

How can you apply what you learned from Luke Chapter 5 to your life? Discuss.

_____
_____
_____
_____

What question or questions do you still have about Luke Chapter 5 that you don't understand or want to know more about? Discuss.

_____
_____
_____
_____
_____

THE GOSPEL OF LUKE CHAPTER SIX

Lesson 8

Before you begin your study, read Luke Chapter 6 out loud (as a group) from your Bible.

In your own words, summarize Luke Chapter 6 in one paragraph and write at least two questions that you had about the chapter as you read the biblical text: (Discuss)

_____
_____
_____
_____
_____
_____
_____
_____
_____
_____
_____
_____
_____
_____

In Luke Chapter 6, Yeshua is traveling with and teaching His disciples. He is a master teacher using His surroundings and the disciples' own knowledge of the Scriptures to help them understand the concepts of the "Kingdom of Heaven." The setting for this chapter is around the Lake of Kinneret.

Look at verses 20-26 in the translation offered in this chapter and two other translations. After looking at all of the translations, write and discuss your own devotional based on your understanding of verses 20-26:

_____
_____
_____
_____
_____
_____
_____
_____

Hebrew Names and their English Equivalents

Hebrew	English
Shimon	Simon
Kefa	Peter
Yaakov	Jacob (James)
Yochanan	John
Bar Talmai	Bartholomew
Matityahu	Matthew
Toma	Thomas
Yaakov the son of Chalfai	Jacob (James) the son of Alphaeus
Yehudah the son of Yaakov	Judas the son of Jacob (James)
Yehudah man of Kariyot	Judas Iscariot
Tzur	Tyre
Tzidon	Sidon

Chapter 6

6:1) On the second Shabbat day [after the counting of the omer], Yeshua was going through the wheat fields. His disciples picked some heads of grain, rubbed them in their hands, and ate some of the kernels. 6:2) But some of the spiritual leaders asked, "Why are your disciples doing what is forbidden on the Shabbat day?" 6:3) Yeshua, however, answered them saying, "Have you never read what David and his companions did when they were hungry? 6:4) He entered the House of God, took the bread of the presence, and gave it to his companions. They ate bread which is forbidden because only the priests are permitted to eat it" (1 Sam 21:1-6). 6:5) He said to them, "The human being is master of the Shabbat day."

Fun Fact

The only day on the Hebrew calendar that has a name is "Shabbat" or "Sabbath." All the other days are called, "day one", "day two", "day three", etc. Shabbat is the seventh day of the week and it begins at sunset on Friday evening. It is commanded that no work is done on Shabbat. It is a day that is supposed to be different from all the other days of the week. It is a day Holy unto the LORD. It is a day of rest. The Jews were the only people in antiquity who observed the Sabbath.

- In verse 1, the text says that "On the second Shabbat day [after the counting of the omer], Yeshua was going through the wheat fields. His disciples picked some heads of grain, rubbed them in their hands, and ate some of the kernels."
- The time of year for this story is late spring after Pesach (Passover) near the time of Shavu'ot.
- The Biblical command to count the omer is found in Leviticus 23:15-16…They are to count seven weeks from the time that the omer, the new barley offering, was brought to the Temple, and recite a blessing each day (Chabad.org).
- From the information given here in the text, it is clear that this event is happening in the spring, around the time of the barley and wheat harvests, when the grains are ripe.
- It was only a few years before this event that the Jews began to develop their ideas about what they could and could not do on Shabbat. They were not supposed to work on Shabbat, but what was the definition of "work?"
- Can grain be picked on Shabbat? Some of the Pharisees said "no". There were 39 categories of "work" that were prohibited on Shabbat including reaping and picking, threshing and rubbing.
- When Yeshua's disciples picked some heads of grain, rubbed them in their hands and ate some of the kernels, they had violated the rabbis' interpretation of two of the laws regarding work on Shabbat (ESV Archaeology Study Bible, 2017).

GOSPEL OF LUKE

Oral Torah

- The questions that the spiritual leaders asked Yeshua were a real concern for those who wanted to obey what the Bible was telling them to do.
- The Jewish people, in an effort to remain true to the biblical faith, tried to understand or interpret the commandment of the Sabbath rest with the Oral Torah.
- The Oral Torah is a body of orally transmitted traditions which were believed to have been given to Moses by God on Mount Sinai at the same time that God gave Moses the written Torah.
- The Oral Torah clarified points in the Torah that were unclear or difficult to understand. This helped the people to obey what the Torah said.
- What is the need for an oral law? The written record of the Bible should be interpreted properly by the Oral Torah in order to give it fresh life and meaning in daily living (Young, 1995, p. 105).
- The Oral Torah places great emphasis on the preservation of life.
- All commandments of the Bible must be suspended to save a human life.
- The Pharisees emphasized saving a life at all costs.
- The only exceptions to this rule are idolatry, incest, and murder.
- The preservation of life takes priority over observing the Sabbath (Young, 1996, p. 107).

- Yeshua pointed to the event in David's life when he and his companions ate the bread of presence. This event in David's life happened on Shabbat. David and his friends' lives were at risk because of great hunger.
- Yeshua's listeners would have been very familiar with this story from the TANAK
- The preservation of life takes precedence over Shabbat (Young, 1995, p. 107).

> "Studying the Bible has brought me closer to the person of Christ than anything else ever has. I've never understood my place in the world better than when I'm reading and studying God's word."
> Nathan Huskins – Class of 2020

6:6) On another Shabbat day, He entered the Jewish learning center to teach. There was a man present there who had a shriveled right hand. 6:7) The scribes and spiritual leaders watched Him to see if he would heal on the Shabbat day in order that they might find a reason to test Him. 6:8) But He knew what they were thinking and said to the man who suffered with the shriveled hand, "Get up and stand in the middle of the people." He got up and stood there. 6:9) Yeshua said to them, "I ask you, is it permitted to do good on the Shabbat day or to do wrong? Is it allowed to save a life or to lose it?" 6:10) He looked around at them all. Then He said to the man, "Stretch out your hand!" When he did so, his hand was fully healed. 6:11) But they were filled with bewilderment and questioned among themselves what they might do with Yeshua.

> In verse 11, the NRSV states, "But they were filled with fury" should be translated more literally as here, "But they were filled with bewilderment." Sadly, in Luke 6:11 the Greek word anoia has often been mistranslated "fury," "rage," or "anger" when the actual meaning of the term is "folly," "lack of understanding," or even "bewilderment." It is only in Luke 6:11 that some scholars have attempted to translate this word as "fury." In classical and Hellenistic Greek, the word is almost always rendered "folly" or "lack of understanding" (Young, 2019).

- Again, on Shabbat, here is the cry of a man in need. Was he a plasterer and depended on his right hand for his livelihood? Was there muscular atrophy? Paralysis? It does not say, but he desperately needed to be healed.
- The Greek word used to describe his hand is lifeless – shrunken.
- Sabbath was given for the good purpose of God, and the principle of love for each other should characterize the use of it.
- The contrast is not between doing good and doing nothing – but between doing good and purposefully doing evil – to fail to do good is the same as doing harm.
- To fail to heal is to do harm to the sufferer who must continue to suffer.
- The man's act of faith is rewarded by a cure (Marshall, 1978).
- Yeshua never broke a Torah commandment.

6:12) During these days, He went up to the mountain to pray. He continued in prayer through the night. 6:13) When it was morning, He called His disciples and chose twelve whom He designated to serve as emissaries,

- Reminiscent of the scene of Mount Sinai where Moses ascended the mountain to commune with God and receive His Torah and then descend to bring the Torah to the people (Marshall, 1978).
- In verse 13, The word for "emissaries" in Greek is apostolos and in Hebrew, it comes from sheliach. As emissaries, they receive delegated authority from their master. As authoritative delegates they represent their master. Their word is the word of the one who sent them (Young, 2019).
- In verse 17, the three groups of people present include
  - Apostles
  - Disciples who have committed themselves to Him
  - Wider group of people who are not yet committed (Marshall, 1978).

6:14) Shimon who was nicknamed Kefa, Andrew his brother, Yaakov, Yochanan, Philip, Bar Talmai, 6:15) Matityahu, Toma, Yaakov the son of Chalfai, Shimon nicknamed the Zealot, 6:16) Yehudah the son of Yaakov, and Yehudah man of Kariyot who betrayed him.

Hebrew Names

How did the Jewish name **Yaakov** (Jacob) become **"James"** in the New Testament? It is a mistranslation issue found in the New Testament that goes back centuries, and it was never corrected (Wilson, *James or Jacob in the Bible?* Biblicalarchaeology.org, November 12, 2019).

6:17) He went down with them and stood on a level place. A large company of His disciples and an enormous crowd of people from Yehudah, Yerushalayim, and even the region of Tzur and Tzidon all had come together to hear Him and to be healed of their sicknesses. 6:18) Those troubled by unclean spirits were healed. 6:19) Many in the crowd wanted to touch Him because power was coming out of Him to heal them all.

6:20) He lifted up His eyes on His disciples and said, "O what great blessing God shows to the poor, for you make up the kingdom of heaven. 6:21) O what great blessing God shows to you who hunger now, for you shall be satisfied. O what great blessing God shows to you who weep now, for you shall laugh. 6:22) O what great blessing God shows to you when people hate you, when they exclude you, when they insult you, and when they condemn your name as evil, on account of the Son of Man! 6:23) Rejoice in that day and leap for joy, look and [understand] because your reward in heaven is immense. That is the way their fathers treated the prophets. 6:24) Indeed, divine retribution threatens you who are rich, for you have received your consolation. 6:25) Retribution threatens you who are full now, for you shall hunger. Retribution threatens you who laugh now, for you shall mourn and weep. 6:26) Retribution threatens you when all the people speak well of you, for this is the way their fathers praised the false prophets.

6:27) "But for all who will listen, I say unto you, love your enemies and do good to those who hate you.

> Tzur (Tyre) and Tzidon (Sidon) are located just north of Yisrael along the Mediterranean Sea in modern-day Lebanon. In antiquity these cities were home to a very wealthy seafaring people who had explored much of the Mediterranean. Tzur was known for its production of purple dye and the coins that were made there.
>
> 📍 Take a trip online to Sidon and Tyre, Lebanon and explore the depth of history found at these two sites. Write and discuss what you discovered:
>
> _____
> _____
> _____
> _____
> _____
> _____
> _____
> _____

> In verse 27, the word "enemies" may well refer to the Romans. The Roman soldiers were everywhere in first-century Israel. The people longed for freedom from Roman oppression (Young, 2019).

6:28) Bless those who curse you; pray for those who victimize you. 6:29) To the one who strikes you on the cheek, turn to him the other as well. To the one who takes your coat, do not stop him from taking your shirt as well.

> In verse 29, the translation "shirt" is a long under-garment or tunic and "coat" is an outer cloak or robe (Young, 2019).

6:30) Give to everyone who asks from you. Do not demand from someone who takes away your goods to pay you back as restitution. 6:31) Treat others the way that you want to be treated.

6:32) "What merit is it to you, if you love only those who love you? Even the sinners love those who love them! 6:33) What merit is it to you, if you do good only to those who do good to you? Even the sinners do good to those who do good to them! 6:34) What merit is it to you, if you lend to those from whom you expect to receive repayment? Even the sinners lend to sinners expecting a return. 6:35) Love your enemies; do good and lend without expecting repayment. Then your reward will be abundant. You will be children of the Most High because He shows kindness even to those who are not grateful and to those who are evil. 6:36) Show mercy to others, just like your Father shows mercy.

6:37) "Do not judge others so that [God] will not pronounce judgment against you. Do not condemn, so that [God] will not condemn you. Forgive others so that [God] will forgive you.

> In verse 37, the translation, "Ask and [God] will give you brings out the true meaning of the divine passive. Because of the sanctity [holiness] of God's name, faithful Jewish leaders sometimes used the passive form of the verb, 'it will be given you' to describe God's decisive actions, 'God will give you.' The passive voice means that God will act" (Young, 2019).

6:38) Give to others so that [God] will give to you, in abundant measure, pressed down, shaken together, and running over. It will be heaped into your lap. Because with the measure you give, [God] will give back to you."

- The theme of these passages is love.
- This is the type of love that must be shown by the disciples – Love to those who hate and persecute.
- Love will gain heavenly reward.
- Love is not emotional affection, but it is willing service and the desire to do good (Marshall, 1978).
- It is Christ flinging open the gates of His kingdom and its righteousness. It is going deeper than the letter of the law.
- The Ten Beatitudes reflect the Ten Commandments presented to us, not in the observance of the Law written on stone, but the realization of the Law, which by the Spirit, is written on the fleshly tablets of the heart. It is calling the disciples to a deeper, more sincere, heart-felt commitment to what the Torah is demanding.
- The question is not the literal concerns of the Law – but the piety, spirituality and sanctity – alms, prayers, and fasting.
- It is, moreover, absolute and undivided self-dedication to God (Edersheim, 1993).
- Yeshua is teaching a foundational Jewish concept – The disciples show themselves to be God's children by their imitation of His character.

- In everyday conduct, disciples are forbidden to take the place of God in judging and condemning other people.
- Judging is different than discernment.
- Judging is a critical, criticizing, condemning, rigid, or severe attitude.
- Discernment is understanding and discriminating between right and wrong.
- Yeshua is speaking about forgiving someone who has actually committed an offense against you. The reference is to personal insults and injuries and expresses the same principle of not standing on one's own rights, but rather showing love to other people, even at the cost of one's own pride and position.
- It does not mean abolishing the law and sanctions in society. That would not be an imitation of the character of God Who upholds the moral law and judges transgressors.
- God is a God of justice and mercy.
- Freely giving: the sheer generosity we should show toward others in return for the immense goodness of God.
- God's two measures:
  - One of goodness and generosity
  - One of justice
- A person is judged by whichever measure they choose to use.
- Human generosity is rewarded with divine generosity (Marshall, 1978).

6:39) Furthermore, He told them a parable, "Is it possible for the blind to lead the blind? Will not both of them fall into the ditch? 6:40) A disciple is not greater than his master, but a disciple who has learned fully is able to become like his master. 6:41) Why do you see the speck in your friend's eye but fail to see the log in your own eye? 6:42) How can you say to your friend, 'Friend, let me take the speck out of your eye' when you yourself have a log in your own eye? You pretender! First take the log out of your own eye, and then you will see clearly to take the speck out of your friend's eye.

6:43) "No good tree bears bad fruit, nor does a bad tree bear good fruit. 6:44) Each tree is known by its fruit. Figs are not harvested from thorn bushes, neither are grapes picked from briars. 6:45) The good person out of the treasure in his heart produces good. The evil person produces evil out of the evil of his heart. For out of the overflow of the heart a person's mouth speaks.

> "As a high school student, I never really thought about the Bible, but when I started learning and reading, it opened my eyes to the bigger picture. High school is hard, and we students face a lot of adversity through these four years, and sometimes we just don't know what to do. The Bible has impacted my life greatly because I wasn't sure what to do with my life, but the Bible has made me grow and given me a better way of life than I would've ever thought."
> Dyson Auschwitz II – Class of 2020

6:46) "Why do you call Me, Lord, Lord, but do not follow what I teach? 6:47) I will show you what everyone who comes to Me, hears My words, and obeys them is like: 6:48) That person is like a man building a house, who dug deep and laid a foundation upon bedrock. When the flood water rose, the torrent streamed down against the house but had no power to shake it, because it was well built. 6:49) The person who hears but does not obey is like a man building his house upon the ground without a foundation. The moment the torrent of water streamed against that house, it collapsed. Its ruin was total."

- Disciples are blind until they are enlightened by their teacher.
- In Judaism, the best pupil did not go beyond their teacher, but repeated their teaching. If Yeshua did not judge, neither should His disciples.
- Bad character cannot produce good deeds. What the heart is full of will produce good or evil deeds.
- Likewise, a person's words are determined by what is in their heart.
- What makes the heart good is a person's relationship with God.
- Wisdom, diligence, and obedience are advocated in building.
- The person who obeys will safely survive the crisis of divine judgement.
- The importance of keeping the Torah that is emphasized here is similar to Ezekiel 13:10-16 (Marshall, 1978).

Fun Fact

Rabbi Hillel the Elder was one of the most important teachers in Jewish history. He was known for his kindness, gentleness, and concern for humanity. It is said that he lived in such poverty that he could not pay the admission fee to study Torah, and because of him the fee was abolished (Buxbaum, 2004).

The Hillel Organization, a modern network of Jewish college student associations, is named for him. Hillel and his descendants established academies of learning and were the leaders of the Jewish community for centuries (Archaeological Study Bible, 2005).

About 60 BC, as a young man, Hillel went to Jerusalem – the heart of the Jewish people – to continue his Torah studies with "two of the greatest teachers of the generation." Every day Hillel attended their lectures at their Beit Midrash, their house of Torah Study. He endured hardship and poverty for the sake of the Torah. Hillel was a day-laborer and would gather every day with all the other men on a certain street corner and wait for an employer to come by to hire them.

Fun Fact Continued

He probably worked in the early hours and studied later in the day. He used half of the money that he earned every day to pay the entrance fee to the house of Torah Study and the other half to support himself and his family.

One day he was not able to find work, and he had no money to enter the house of Torah Study. So, he climbed up on the roof and "swung himself over the skylight to listen to the words of the living God" from the mouths of the two great teachers. This happened in the winter on a Friday afternoon before Shabbat.

"Snow started to fall, but Hillel was so absorbed in what he was hearing that he did not even notice. Before long, though, he was covered over with a blanket of snow and lost consciousness. He lay there through the night.

On Sabbath morning, when learning resumed in the House of Study," the teachers noticed that the hall where they were teaching was darker than usual. They looked up and saw Hillel on the skylight. They went to the roof and found him covered with snow. They removed the snow, brought him inside, and warmed him by the fire. When they realized what had happened, they said, "Someone like this is truly worthy that the Sabbath be violated for his sake" (Yoma 35b).

"Jewish law places saving life above all else, and the Sabbath prohibitions against work – such as what the two teachers did to revive Hillel – are disregarded if there is even the slightest doubt of a risk to life. The rabbis would have done the same for anyone. Their comment meant that Hillel was most worthy because of his self-sacrificing devotion and holiness" (Buxbaum, 2004, pp. 16-17).

Questions for review and discussion

What are Yeshua's disciples doing on Shabbat that made the spiritual leaders question Yeshua?

Why was this a concern to them?

What was Yeshua doing on another Shabbat day?

What made the spiritual leaders question Yeshua?

What does Yeshua teach about Shabbat?

What is the Oral Torah?

What does the Oral Torah say about "preservation of life?"

In verses 27-38, what is Yeshua teaching His followers?

Who was Hillel, and what is important about his story?

What do you think is a major theme of this chapter?

Summarize the study notes from this chapter and discuss:

Summarize the study notes from this chapter and discuss continued:

___

Re-read Luke Chapter 6 from the *Hebrew Heritage Bible* translation used in this book. Discuss. Summarize Luke Chapter 6 in one paragraph and discuss:

___

Choose one verse from Luke Chapter 6 that you think is the most important and write it here. Discuss why you think it is the most important verse:

___

Summarize in one or two sentences the most important or the most interesting things you learned in this chapter from your study:

___

What makes it important or interesting to you?

___

How did your understanding of Luke Chapter 6 change after you studied it and read it again? Discuss.

___

How can you apply what you learned from Luke Chapter 6 to your life? Discuss.

___

What question or questions do you still have about Luke Chapter 6 that you don't understand or want to know more about? Discuss

___

THE GOSPEL OF LUKE CHAPTER SEVEN

Lesson 9

Before you begin your study, read Luke Chapter 7 out loud (as a group) from your Bible.

In your own words, summarize Luke Chapter 7 in one paragraph and write at least two questions that you had about the chapter as you read the biblical text: (Discuss)

_____
_____
_____
_____
_____
_____
_____
_____
_____
_____
_____
_____
_____
_____
_____

Luke Chapter Seven begins with Yeshua returning to Kefar Nachum (Capernaum) and encountering a Roman centurion whose slave is very ill. Yeshua heals the slave. He then travels to the village of Nain where He is filled with compassion for the widow He sees there. Her only son had died, and Yeshua raises him from the dead. The news about Yeshua spreads throughout Yehudah (Judea) and the surrounding countryside. Yochanan's (John the Baptist's) disciples hear about the miracles of Yeshua and report to Yochanan. Yochanan sends two of his disciples to Yeshua to question Him. Yeshua is anointed by a sinful woman.

Take a trip online to the village of Nain in Yisrael. Today it is a small Arab village in northern Yisrael. What did you discover about this small village? How far is it from Natzeret? Write and discuss:

_____
_____
_____
_____
_____
_____
_____
_____
_____
_____
_____
_____
_____

Chapter 7

7:1) After He had completed these teachings in the hearing of all the people, He entered Kefar Nachum. 7:2) There, a Roman centurion's slave who was highly regarded had become very sick and was near to death. 7:3) The Roman centurion had heard of Yeshua. Through the elders of the Jewish community, he sent a message to Yeshua asking Him to come and heal his slave. 7:4) When they came to Yeshua, they implored Him earnestly saying, "This man is worthy of Your help. 7:5) He loves our nation and has built our synagogue." 7:6) Yeshua went with them. He was not far from the house when the Roman centurion sent friends to say to Him, "Lord, do not trouble Yourself because I do not deserve to have You come under my roof. 7:7) I do not consider myself worthy to come to

You. But speak the word, and my slave shall be healed. 7:8) For I myself am a man also submitted under authority, with soldiers under me. To this one I say, 'Go,' and he goes. To another I say, 'Come,' and he comes. I may say to my slave, 'Do this,' and he does it." 7:9) When Yeshua heard this, He marveled at him and turned to the crowd of people following Him. He said to them, "I tell you, nowhere, not even in Yisrael, have I found such great faith." 7:10) When those who had been sent returned to the house, they found that the slave had been healed.

- Kefar Nachum (Capernaum) had a population of about 2,000 people.
- Many villages and towns in antiquity had walls that surrounded them for protection. Kefar Nachum did not have a wall.
- It was a fishing village with agricultural crops such as wheat, olives, grapes, and figs that were grown near-by. This area in the Galil still produces and exports these crops.
- The people of Kefar Nachum traded with the Phoenician coastal cities of Tzur (Tyre) and Tzidon (Sidon).
- The road leading to Damascus passed just a couple of hundred yards north of the synagogue of Capernaum. This road provided a commercial link and tax station between the districts of Herod Antipas and Herod Philip.
- The centurion was probably a **God-fearer**. God-fearers were Gentiles who were associated with the synagogue, prayed the Jewish prayers, gave to the poor, and showed deep interest in Judaism. They had not fully converted to Judaism because they were neither circumcised nor baptized.
- Matthew and Luke infer that his house was not in Kefar Nachum but was in its immediate neighborhood, probably on the road to Tiberias (Edersheim, 1993).
- This Roman centurion loved the Jewish people and was a supporter of the local synagogue in Kefar Nachum. Many God-fearers supported local synagogues.
- The members of the Roman military forces worked their way up the ranks. This centurion was a member of Herod Antipas' forces and had authority over 80-100 men (Cultural Backgrounds Study Bible, 2016).
- Slaves could be viewed as members of a household, and in this case, the slave might have been the only member of his household or a significant member.
- During their 20 years of service, soldiers in the Roman army were not allowed to marry officially although they sometimes took concubines.
- Most soldiers could not easily afford servants (the average price of a slave was about 1/3 of the best paid legionary's annual wages). However, the average centurion made 15x the wages of the lowest soldiers (Cultural Backgrounds Study Bible, 2016).
- This slave was "seemingly dying," and the centurion, in the fullest sense, believes in the power of Jesus to heal (Edersheim, 1993).

> "Studying the Bible makes it real to me. There's now a difference between the characters of stories and the people who lived in history. We live so far removed from the time and culture of the Bible, that it's almost necessary to learn more or we run the risk of misunderstanding everything we read." Allie Grace Cook – Class of 2020

- The normal relationship between Jew and Gentile was not one of love and trust.
- However, this centurion demonstrated love for the Jewish people that moved the Jewish leaders to plead on his behalf to Yeshua.
- In Kefar Nachum, the centurion had learned to love Israel and serve Israel's God. He built a synagogue – the most splendid in Galilee – which had been consecrated by the presence and teaching of Yeshua (Edersheim, 1993).
- Elders of the Jews were highly respected in their community, but they were not necessarily the rulers of the synagogue (*Archaeological Study Bible*, 2005).
- Jewish people were not supposed to enter the homes of Gentiles because the Jews would become defiled. Jews considered the homes of Gentiles unclean. One source of uncleanness was idolatry.
- The higher the centurion placed Yeshua on the pinnacle of Judaism, the more natural it was for him to communicate through the Jewish elders, and he did not to expect Him to enter his home. He exhibited great humility and trust (Edersheim, 1993).
- The centurion understood authority. His soldiers obeyed him because he was backed by the authority of the Roman Empire. The Roman military was extremely well organized with a clear chain of command. The centurion knew that Yeshua was backed by God's authority.
- In verse 7, "speak the word"... People in antiquity sought healing at hot springs, special shrines, sometimes through magic and occasionally through contact with holy persons. Long-distance miracles, however, were considered extraordinary; this centurion expressed special faith (*Cultural Backgrounds Study Bible*, 2016).

7:11) Soon afterward, accompanied by His disciples and a large crowd of people, He went to a village called Nain. 7:12) As He arrived at the city gate, a dead person was being carried out—the only son of his mother. She was a widow. A large crowd of people from the village was with her. 7:13) When the Lord saw her, He was moved with compassion. He said, "Do not cry." 7:14) He came and touched the bier. Those carrying it stood still. He said, "Young man, I tell you to arise." 7:15) The dead man sat up and began to talk. Yeshua gave him to his mother. 7:16) Awe overwhelmed everyone. They glorified God, saying, "A great prophet has arisen among us!" and "God has visited His people!" 7:17) This news about Him kept spreading in all of Yehudah and throughout the surrounding countryside.

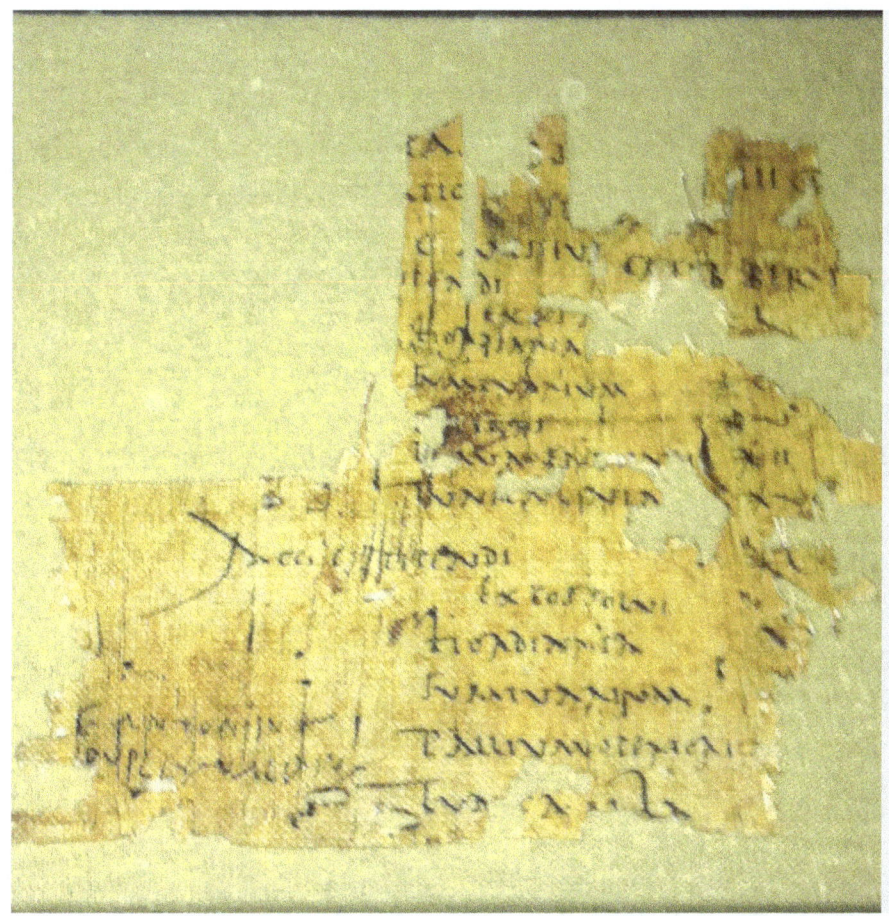

Pay slip of a Roman Cavalryman of the Tenth Legion. Like all cavalrymen, he received his salary three times a year. His pay slip included his gross pay minus expenses – such as the cost of his uniform.

This torn pay slip was written in Latin in 72 CE.

This papyrus was excavated at Masada, Israel, and is an extremely rare document.

(Photo: Masada museum, Israel, 2015)

The synagogue from the time of Yeshua was built using black basalt rocks and is directly below this limestone synagogue that was built in the 4th century.

Photo: The ancient synagogue at Kefar Nachum, Yisrael (2018)

GOSPEL OF LUKE   137

- Nain was a small village located about 6 miles southeast of Nazareth. (It is an Arab village today) (*Archaeological Study Bible*, 2005).

- Yeshua raises the son of the widow from the dead, thereby manifesting the kind of powers similar to those of Elijah and Elisha (1 Kings 17:17-24; 2 Kings 4:18-37). This led people to conclude that He was a prophet and that through His activity God was visiting His people.

- The helplessness of the widow, deprived of both the support of her husband and her son, draws attention to the gracious compassion of Yeshua. Because women ordinarily could not earn an adequate income, this widow would depend on her son's support in her old age (Edersheim, 1993).

- The story demonstrates how the mighty action of God in Yeshua leads to the believing acceptance of what has happened in praise and acknowledgement of His power.

- The story therefore provides evidence for the statement in 7:22 that the era of fulfilment, in which the dead are raised, has arrived (Marshall, 1978).

- The dead son was probably being carried in an open coffin, and by touching the coffin, Yeshua risked uncleanness (Numbers 19:16) (*Archaeological Study Bible*, 2005).

- Because bodies had to be buried outside the community, the procession was exiting the town (Edersheim, 1993).

- By custom, the widow or mother of the deceased would lead the procession.

- Members of the village would normally join the procession from behind.

- Because Jesus addresses the widow, it is clear that he approaches from the front.

- He was not planning to simply join in the mourning (*Cultural Backgrounds Study Bible*, 2016).

7:18) The disciples of Yochanan reported to him all these miracles. Yochanan called two from among his disciples and 7:19) sent them to the Lord to ask Him, "Are You the coming one, or should we look for another?" 7:20) When they came to Him, the men said to Him, "Yochanan the Immerser has sent us to You in order to ask, 'Are You the coming one or should we look for another?'" 7:21) At that time, Yeshua healed many with various sicknesses, diseases, and evil spirits. He gave sight to many who were blind. 7:22) He answered and said unto them, "Go tell Yochanan what you see and hear: the blind receive their sight, the lame walk, the lepers are cured, the deaf are healed, the dead are brought to life, and the poor hear the message of the good news proclaimed to them. 7:23) So then, blessed is the one who does not stumble over Me!"

- In verse 22, "Go tell Yochanan what you see and hear," may be translated more literally, "Go tell Yochanan what you have seen and heard...." In the Hebrew meaning, the stress of the words is a present tense. The past tense in Greek connected the message to what the two disciples of John the Baptist had witnessed in their observation of Yeshua's miracle ministry.

- In verse 23, the phrase, "one who does not stumble over Me," the Greek word is literally translated, "to stumble." The word was much stronger for the original listeners than is indicated by some of the recent translations, "to take offense." The force of the text means to stumble so as to fall. It means a complete failure (Young, 2019).

- Where was Yochanan (John the Baptist) when he sent his disciples to Yeshua? Apparently Yochanan had been imprisoned. According to Josephus, Herod Antipas imprisoned and executed John the Baptist at Machaerus on the east side of the Dead Sea.

- "Are you the coming one?" Yeshua's answer refers to prophecies in the book of Isaiah concerning the six signs that the Messiah will give when He appears.

- Six signs of the Messiah from Isaiah:

  1. He will make the blind see
  2. He will make the lame walk
  3. He will cleanse the lepers
  4. He will make the deaf hear
  5. He will raise the dead
  6. He will evangelize the poor

- The message should be clear...Yeshua is the Messiah; Yochanan should not look for another (Stern, 1992, p. 42).

- Here one can see this beautiful progression of miracles and the revelation of Who He is...healing the leper, the paralytic, the man with the shriveled hand, the Centurion's servant, and raising the widow's son at Nain.

- A great prophet has appeared among us...prophets like Elijah and Elisha had raised the dead ...The news spread throughout Yehudah (Judea) and the surrounding country (Marshall, 1993).

7:24) After the messengers of Yochanan the Immerser had left, Yeshua began to explain to the crowds about Yochanan: "What did you go out into the wilderness to see? A reed shaken by the wind? 7:25) No, what did you go out to see? A man dressed in fine apparel? Look, those who parade themselves around in expensive clothes and indulge in luxury are living in the kings' courts. 7:26) What did you go out to see? Nothing less than a prophet! Yes, and I tell you he is so much more than a prophet. 7:27) This is the one of whom it is written, 'Look! I send my messenger ahead of you, who shall prepare your way before your coming' (Mal 3:1). 7:28) I tell you that among those born of women there is none greater than Yochanan, but even the least person in the kingdom of heaven is greater than he." 7:29) When they heard this, all the common people and the tax collectors recognized God's mercy, for they had immersed themselves by the immersion in water under Yochanan. 7:30) But some of the spiritual leaders and Bible scholars had not acknowledged God's purpose for themselves because they had not immersed themselves under him.

- In verse 24, Yeshua recalls The Oak and the Reed story:
  "Which is more powerful the reed or the oak? The first response is a majestic oak. But in a storm with violent gusts, the oak is broken, but the reed is merely shaken. In such a storm, the flexible reed proves stronger than the mighty oak. John the Baptist was broken because of his prophetic call. He was unwilling to compromise his message. Those who occupy kings' palaces, however, are finely attired politicians who blow with the wind, this direction and that, according to the expediency of the moment. The satire of the fable has political implications. But Jesus applies the imagery to John, who is a prophet. He is no reed shaken by the wind" (Young, 1998, p. 20).

- John is the last of the "Old Testament" prophets (Young, 1998) and will not participate in the kingdom movement of Yeshua's followers (Lindsey, 2017).

7:31) "To what, then, may I compare the people of this generation? What are they like? 7:32) They are like children sitting in the open market calling out to each other saying, 'We played the flute to you but you refused to dance, and we sang a sad song to you but you did not cry.' 7:33) Yochanan the Immerser came to you, neither eating bread nor drinking wine, and you said, 'He has a demon!' 7:34) The Son of Man has come to you eating and drinking, and you say, 'Look at a glutton and a drunk! He is a friend of tax collectors and sinners!' 7:35) Wisdom is proven by all her children."

7:36) One of the spiritual leaders invited Him to eat with him. He went to the home of the spiritual leader and reclined at the table. 7:37) Consider this, a woman, known in the village as living a sinful life, found out that Yeshua was reclining at the table in the home of the spiritual leader. She brought an alabaster container of myrrh oil. 7:38) When standing behind Him at His feet, weeping, she began to wash His feet with her tears. She wiped them with the hair of her head, kissed His feet, and anointed them with the myrrh oil. 7:39) Now when the spiritual leader who had invited Him saw it, he said to himself, "If this man were [[the]] prophet, He would have realized who is touching Him and what kind of woman she is, namely, that she is a sinner!"

In verse 39, the definite article in the words, "[[the]] prophet," is supported by some manuscript readings and the external evidence. With the definite article, the question may well make reference to the prophet like Moses (Deut. 18:15) who would be a leader for the future redemption. Following a similar paradigm related to Moses leading the people of Israel out of slavery into freedom, the coming prophet would fulfill Jewish messianic expectations (Young, 2019).

7:40) Yeshua answered and said to him, "Shimon, I have something to say to you." Shimon replied, "Tell me, Rabbi." 7:41) "Two men owed some money to a certain money lender. One of them owed five hundred denarii and the other only fifty. 7:42) When they were unable to pay, he forgave them both. Now which of the two of them will love him more?" 7:43) Shimon answered, "I suppose the one who had the larger debt canceled." Yeshua said to him, "You have judged correctly." 7:44) Then turning to the woman, He told Shimon, "Do you see this woman? I came into your home, yet you did not give Me water to wash My feet. She has washed My feet with her tears and dried them with her hair.

> In verse 44, in all probability, Shimon assigned a servant to perform the custom of washing the feet of a guest with traditional hospitality. The woman, however, made herself a servant which demonstrated her strong and persistent [chutzpah style] faith (Young, 2019).

- In verse 36, maybe Yeshua is still in the Galilee or Nain after Shabbat. It's time for the Saturday evening meal after the synagogue service (Marshall, 1978).
- Inviting a traveling rabbi was considered virtuous, and because Yeshua was reclined at the table indicates that this banquet is given in His honor (Cultural Backgrounds Study Bible, 2016).
- The Babylonian Talmud states that "If one partakes of a meal at which a scholar is present, it is as if he feasted on the radiance/brightness of the Divine presence" (Bailey, p. 243).
- The fact that Yeshua was especially interested in despised people did not mean that He wasn't interested in the more respected members of society, like the spiritual leader who had invited Yeshua to his home
- As He was reclined with His feet behind Him (feet pointed away from the table), to approach His feet would be to walk up from behind Him (Cultural Backgrounds Study Bible, 2016).
- The woman who had lived a sinful life – the term refers to prostitutes, thieves, and others of low reputation whose sins were blatant and obvious – not the kind the establishment winked at (Stern, 1992).
- All the scholars agree that this event is only a fragment, a part of what had happened that day.
- The story assumes that before the drama opens, the woman had heard Yeshua proclaiming the Good News of God's mercy and love.
- Yeshua had taught in the community about the love of God for sinners (Bailey, 2008).

7:45) You did not give Me a kiss. Since I entered, she has not stopped kissing My feet. 7:46) You did not anoint My head with oil. She has anointed My feet with myrrh oil. 7:47) Therefore, I tell you, her sins, which are many, have been forgiven, for she has loved much. But the one who has been forgiven little loves little." 7:48) Yeshua said to her, "Your sins are forgiven." 7:49) Then those who were reclining at the table began to say among themselves, "Who is this who even forgives sins?" 7:50) He said to the woman, "Your [chutzpah style] faith has saved you. Go in shalom."

- The woman had heard Him and believed His liberating message, and she realized that the grace of God was available even to her!
- Anxious to show her gratitude, she found out where Yeshua was going to be, and she showed up (Bailey, 2008).
- She brought an alabaster flask of perfume.
  - Perfumes were much sought after.
  - They were used often and were common among Jewish women.
  - True balsam was literally worth its weight in gold.
  - These flasks were worn around the neck hanging down to the chest.
- Her intention might well have been to anoint Jesus' head with perfume (purchased with her immoral earnings).
- But it would seem that her emotions got the better of her.
- It would have been natural for her to stand behind Yeshua because He was reclining. Her tears fell on His feet, and in her anxiety, she forgot proper social behavior and wiped His feet with her hair.
- By kissing His feet, she was showing deep respect for and gratitude toward Him as a rabbi.
- Finally, she anointed His feet with perfume – unparalleled because the honor was normally bestowed on the head (Edersheim, 1993).
- This entire event makes sense when it is assumed that the woman's original intention was interrupted by her overwhelming emotions (Edersheim, 1993).
- It is the forgiven sinner who knows the true sorrow for sin (Marshall, 1978).
- If Yeshua were a prophet...THE prophet, He would know who this woman is. The prophet would not allow himself to be touched by a sinful, unclean woman.
- The mark of a prophet was clairvoyance (supernatural knowledge). Yeshua knows who she is and suggests that what she does is more welcoming to Him than the actions of the host (Young, 1998).
- Shimon, Yeshua's, host is polite to Yeshua: he calls Him "Rabbi."
- The three actions in the event contrasted their hospitality – Shimon was not discourteous – he had been correct enough as a host – but he had not done anything special either. He had done only the bare minimum. Shimon wasn't expected to wash Yeshua's feet. That was the duty of a slave. He didn't have to greet Him with a kiss, but it would have been nice. Shimon didn't anoint Yeshua, and she used expensive perfume. The woman's humble action receives Yeshua's attention (Edersheim, 1993).

- The woman's love was the result of her already having been forgiven – not the cause. Yeshua speaks to her as a confirmation of what has already taken place (Marshall, 1978).

- She had received forgiveness before the story even began (Edersheim, 1993; Marshall, 1978).

- She was "saved" by her faith – she had heard and believed.

- Go in peace is a common farewell in Judaism "May God's peace be yours" (Marshall, 1978).

- Both the woman and Shimon had needs, and Yeshua reached out to both.

- She had been forgiven grave wrongdoings and loved much.

- He had been forgiven little and didn't have the same concept (Marshall, 1978).

- Shalom means more than peace. It is a concept of peace, tranquility, safety, well-being, welfare, health, contentment, success, comfort, wholeness, and integrity (Stern, 1992).

Machaerus in modern-day Jordan was a palace fortress built by Herod the Great. According to the first century historian Josephus, Herod Antipas beheaded Yochanan (John the Baptist) at Machaerus.

Take a trip online to Machaerus, Jordan. Where is it located? What is the climate like there? What was important about its location? What did it look like? Write and discuss:

_____
_____
_____
_____
_____
_____
_____
_____
_____
_____
_____
_____
_____

Questions for review and discussion

Define God-fearer in your own words:

How did the centurion in this story feel about the Jewish people?

How do you know?

What did he ask Yeshua to do?

What did Yeshua do in Nain?

Why was it so important?

What were the signs of the Messiah as prophesized by Isaiah?

At this point in Luke, which of these has Yeshua done?

What happened that was so important with the sinful woman who anointed Yeshua's feet?

Who was Shimon in this story?

Was Yeshua an honored guest at his house? _____ How do you know?

Summarize the study notes from this chapter and discuss continued:

___

Do you see a theme in Luke Chapter 7? _____ What do you see?

___

Re-read Luke Chapter 7 from the *Hebrew Heritage Bible* translation used in this book. Discuss. Summarize Luke Chapter 7 in one paragraph and discuss:

___

Choose one verse from Luke Chapter 7 that you think is the most important and write it here. Discuss why you think it is the most important verse:

___

Summarize in one or two sentences the most important or the most interesting things you learned in this chapter from your study:

_____
_____
_____
_____
_____
_____
_____
_____
_____
_____

What makes it important or interesting to you?

_____
_____
_____

How did your understanding of Luke Chapter 7 change after you studied it and read it again? Discuss.

_____
_____
_____
_____

How can you apply what you learned from Luke Chapter 7 to your life? Discuss.

_____
_____
_____
_____

What question or questions do you still have about Luke Chapter 7 that you don't understand or want to know more about? Discuss

_____
_____
_____
_____
_____

THE GOSPEL OF LUKE CHAPTER EIGHT

Lesson 10

Before you begin your study, read Luke Chapter 8 out loud (as a group) from your Bible.

In your own words, summarize Luke Chapter 8 in one paragraph and write at least two questions that you had about the chapter as you read the biblical text: (Discuss)

_____
_____
_____
_____
_____
_____
_____
_____
_____
_____
_____
_____
_____
_____

In Luke Chapter 8, Yeshua continues His ministry as He travels from village to village teaching about the Kingdom of God. His mother and brothers come to see Him. His followers, both women and men, are with Him as he continues to heal the sick, cast out demons, and raise the dead. Yeshua's power over nature is shown as he calms the storm.

One of Yeshua's close followers was Miryam, called the one from Migdal (Mary Magdalene). Miryam was from the fishing village of Migdal (Magdala). Migdal is located on the shore of the Lake of Kinneret near Kefar Nachum. Its history is fascinating with recent excavations of the ancient village and synagogue. Take a trip online. Write and discuss what you discovered about this site:

___
___
___
___
___
___
___
___
___
___
___
___

The menorah is the most ancient symbol of Judaism. It is a seven-branched candelabra. During the time of Yeshua, the menorah did not burn candles, instead it used olive oil and wicks. The ancient synagogue that was excavated at Migdal had an image of a menorah carved in stone. This discovery dates to the Second Temple.

GOSPEL OF LUKE   148

Chapter 8

8:1) After this, along with His twelve disciples, Yeshua traveled through towns and villages proclaiming the kingdom of God and delivering the message of good news. 8:2) Some women who had been healed of evil spirits and sicknesses: Miryam, called the one from Migdal from whom seven demons had been removed; 8:3) Yochanah, the wife of Chuza, Herod's administrator; Shoshana; and many others helped to provide for them out of their means.

The Women Who Followed Yeshua

The women who followed Yeshua included women who had been healed like Miryam from the fishing village of Migdal not far from Kefar Nachum. This Miryam was not the woman in chapter 7, nor the Mary from Bethany. Yochanah (Joanna) was the wife of Chuza (who was the manager of Herod Antipas' household). Shoshana (Susanna) and many others followed Yeshua. These women even helped financially support His ministry. However, there were almost no women who were disciples among Jewish schools for the study of the Torah (Cultural Backgrounds Study Bible, 2016). What was the place of women in Jewish society during the time of Yeshua? What was the place of women in Yeshua's ministry? To answer these questions, one must explore the role of women in the Hebrew Bible (Old Testament) (Bailey, 2008), and how it had changed.

The Hebrew Bible offers excellent examples of the roles of women. Women served in the Tabernacle (Exodus 38:8; 1 Samuel 2:22), and in Micah 6:4, Miryam (Moses' sister) is listed as one of the "three leaders of the people" (Kaiser, 2015, p. 144). The books of Ruth and Esther and the stories of Deborah and Huldah the prophetess show the importance of women, their heroism, and their significant contributions to the Jewish people and their faith (Bailey, 2008). However, in the time between the "Old Testament" and the "New Testament" a theology immerged that was detrimental to women. "It was not the 'Old Testament' that placed women in an inferior position, but a set of rabbinic traditions that were later infused with more pagan ideas that introduced these deviant views of women" (Kaiser, 2015, p. 145). Most notably, it was the writings of Ben Sirach the aristocratic scholar of Yerushalayim in the second century BC, that diminished women and their role in society (Bailey, 2008). Women were considered inferior and devalued during the time of Yeshua's ministry.

However, when one studies the story of the Gospel of Luke, a picture immerges of a relevant and powerful role that Yeshua gives to women. He restores their value and heals their brokenness. He calls them to follow Him and participate in the kingdom movement that He is leading.

8:4) When a large crowd had gathered together with people from the surrounding towns, He told them a parable. 8:5) "A sower went out to sow his seed. As he spread the seed, some of it fell along the path and was trampled upon, and the birds of the air ate it. 8:6) Some of the seed fell on the rocky soil. As soon as the plants grew up, they began to wither away because they lacked moisture. 8:7) Other seeds fell among thorns. As the plants grew, the thorns grew up around them and choked them. 8:8) But some of the seed was planted into good soil. It grew up and produced a hundredfold return!"

What is a Parable?

A parable is "Jewish storytelling." The Jewish rabbis of Jesus' day commonly used parables to communicate biblical truths to the people. They are mini docudramas, or simple stories, about things that would be familiar to the audience. They were very common during the time of Yeshua's ministry. "The reality of God is revealed in the word-picture of a parable. Jesus and the rabbis of old taught about God" (p. 3) by using these short stories. Parables were not difficult for the original audience to understand, but they did demand that the listener makes a decision (Young, 1998).

8:9) When His disciples asked Him about the parable, 8:10) He said to them, "To you has been given to know the mysteries of [[the kingdom of]] God, but to the others they are only parables so that seeing they may not see, and hearing they may not understand. 8:11) The parable is this, the seed is the word of God. 8:12) The ones which fell along the path are those who after having heard allow the devil to come and take the word out of their hearts, so that they do not believe and are not saved. 8:13) The ones which fell upon rocky ground are those who when they hear the word receive it with joy, but they lack roots. They believe for awhile, but when a time of trial comes they fall away. 8:14) The ones who fell among the thorns are those who hear but allow the cares, riches, and pleasures of this life to come and choke them as they go on their way. Their fruit never matures. 8:15) As for the ones who were planted in the good soil, they are those who hear the word with a good heart. They produce fruit with perseverance.

- The condition of the soil determines the growth of the seed and the success or failure of the of the harvest.
- The relationship between the good soil and the good heart is critical for correct understanding. One is to receive the word with a good heart.
- Yeshua is saying to hear the teachings of the Torah and obey them with the proper attitude.
- The word of God is received into good soil and produces a hundredfold harvest (Young, 1998).

8:16) "No one lights a lamp and covers it with a pot or places it under a bed, but instead puts it on a lamp stand so that all who enter may see the light. 8:17) For nothing is hidden that shall not be disclosed, nor anything secret which shall not be made known and brought to light. 8:18) Take heed how you hear. For to the one who has more will be given. To the one who has not, even what that person thinks he has will be taken away."

Oil lamps and flasks from the time of Yeshua. These lamps would fit into the palm of the hand. Olive oil was used as fuel for the lamp and was poured into the opening in the middle. The wick protruded from the spout. Houses usually had several oil lamps.

Photo: Davidson Center, Jerusalem Archaeological Park (2015)

8:19) Then His mother and brothers approached Him but could not reach Him because of the crowd. 8:20) Then He was told, "Your mother and brothers are standing outside and want to see You." 8:21) But He said unto them, "My mother and My brothers are those who hear the word of God and put it into practice."

- Lamps are not meant to be hidden, but to give light to the entire house. It was foolish to put it under a bowl, and even more foolish to put it under a bed.
- The lamp gives light to those who enter the house, but it gives no light until it is lit.
- Whatever is hidden or secret will be made known.
- The disciples will make known publicly what Jesus has been teaching them – future manifestation of the Kingdom.
- A person who responds to the message by hearing it and obeying it is regarded as a member of the family of Yeshua.
- Hearing and doing corresponds to faith in other parts of the New Testament (Marshall, 1978).

GOSPEL OF LUKE   151

- Yeshua's brothers did not believe in him at this time. "Up till then, not even His brothers were believing in Him." (John 7:5, *HHB*)
- Who were Yeshua's "brothers"? How is the word "brother" understood? According to different interpreters:
  - They were sons of Yosef by a previous marriage (according to Epiphanius).
  - They were Yeshua's cousins (according to Jerome).
  - The most natural conclusion (suggested by Helvidius) is that they were the sons of Yosef and Myriam. So, they were younger half-brothers of Yeshua.
  - They are named in Mark 6:3, "Is this not the carpenter, the son of Miryam, brother of Yaakov, Yose, Yuda, and Shimon? Are not His sisters here with us?" (*HHB*)
  - Since Yosef is not mentioned here, it is probable that he has already died (Archaeological Study Bible, 2005).
- What happens to Yeshua's family after His death, burial, and resurrection?
  - Miryam (Yeshua's mother) joins the apostles in Yerushalayim (Acts 1:14) (Flusser, 2001).
  - Yaakov (James) becomes a believer after Jesus' resurrection. "Then He appeared to Yaakov (James), and then to the twelve." (1 Corinthians 15:7, *HHB*)
  - Yeshua's brother Yaakov (James) was the author of "James" and his other brother Yuda was the author of "Jude."

8:22) One day He and His disciples climbed on board a boat. He said to them, "Cross over to the other side of the lake." They set out 8:23) and as they sailed, He fell asleep. A gale of wind descended upon the lake. Their boat was filling with water and their lives were in peril. 8:24) They went to Him saying, "Master! Master! We are going to die!" He got up and rebuked the wind and the raging waves of water. They stopped and everything became calm. 8:25) He said to them, "Where is your faith?" They were afraid and marveled saying one to the other, "Who then is this? He even commands the wind and the water and they obey Him!"

- Beginning in verse 22, Luke presents a sequence of events that demonstrate Yeshua's divine power over:
  - The elements (Yeshua calms the storm). Yeshua is Lord of the elements exhibiting the power possessed by God in the Hebrew Bible.
  - Demons and physical evil (the healing of the demon possessed man).
  - Death (a dead girl and a sick woman) (Marshall, 1978).

- The sequence of events prepares the way for the confession of Yeshua as Messiah.
- The emphasis is not simply on the power of Yeshua. His compassion and willingness to save in situations of human need are revealed.
- The cries of the disciples are a forgetful faith rather than a complete lack of faith. The disciples are characterized by faith, even if it can become weak or fleeting sometimes (Marshall, 1978).
- Maybe they had a vague, undefined belief that was uncertain and unclear, but it was being revealed and made clearer.
- This is a belief which also accounts for the co-existing (not of disbelief, nor even unbelief), but of inability to grasp or understand. They were waiting for the Holy Spirit to reveal the mystery of who He is (Edersheim, 1993).

8:26) They arrived in the region of [[Girgashim]] which is on the opposite side of the Lake of Galil. 8:27) As He stepped out on land, a man from the city who had demons met Him. For some time, this man had not worn clothes; he did not reside in a house, but lived in the tombs. 8:28) When he saw Yeshua, he fell down before Him and yelled out in a loud voice, "What are You going to do to me, Yeshua, Son of the Most High God? I beg You, do not torture me!" 8:29) He commanded the unclean spirit to come out of the man. Many times it had seized him. He was kept under guard and was chained hand and foot. He broke the chains and was driven by the demon into the desert. 8:30) Yeshua asked him his name. He told him, "Legion," for many demons had entered him. 8:31) They begged him not to throw them into the bottomless pit. 8:32) On the hillside, there was a large herd of swine grazing. They pleaded with Him to allow them to enter these. He gave them permission. 8:33) The demons went out of the man and entered the swine. The herd stampeded down the steep bank into the lake and were drowned. 8:34) When the herdsman saw what had happened, they ran away and spread the news throughout the city and the countryside. 8:35) Then the people came out to see what had happened. They went to Yeshua and found the man from whom the demons had been forced out. He was sitting at the feet of Yeshua, clothed and in his right mind. They were filled with awe. 8:36) Those who had witnessed what had happened told them how the man tormented with demons had been healed. 8:37) Then all the people from the surrounding region of [[Girgashim]] asked Yeshua to leave them because they were overcome with great fear. So He climbed into the boat and returned. 8:38) The man from whom the demons had left begged Yeshua to allow him to go with Him. Yeshua sent him away saying, 8:39) "Return to your home, and tell how much God has done for you." So the man went back, telling everyone all over the city how much Yeshua had done for him.

The traditional location of this story in the region of Girgashim is identified as Kursi. Archaeological remains and a Byzantine church suggest Kursi is on the northeast shore of the lake which some authorities have identified as Gergesa. This location fits the Gospel description and is supported by textual witnesses (Young, 2019). Kursi is the only spot on the shore with a steep bank overlooking the sea. "There were Jewish communities in the cities of the Decapolis which were predominantly gentile." The Gentiles were raising pigs (Aharoni, Y., 2002, p. 171).

Take a trip online to Kursi, Yisrael and discover the archaeological ruins that have excavated there. What is the story of Kursi? Write and discuss:

___

- The main point of this passage is the demonstration of the power of Yeshua to deal with an especially severe case of demon possession. Through Yeshua, God did great things for an unhappy victim.

- He had been violent for a long time. The only thing people knew to do with someone who was so violent was to restrain him. He was bound with hand-chains and shackles on his ankles. However, he had continued to break loose and would be driven into the desert (Marshall, 1978).

- The Jews regarded anything associated with tombs or the dead as impure. Many associated spirits with such sites (Cultural Backgrounds Study Bible, 2016).

- Bottomless pit (Abyss) – The Hebrew understanding of the watery deep below the earth to which the seas are connected and the spirits are confined (Marshall, 1978), and Jewish sources portrayed spirits being imprisoned there (Cultural Backgrounds Study Bible, 2016). According to the Torah swine are unclean, so for a Jewish audience it would be appropriate for demons to inhabit swine.

- This result made it clear that the man was freed from the demons (Marshall, 1978).

- The Gentiles may have thought of Jesus as a dangerous magician, whose power had destroyed their herds (Cultural Backgrounds Study Bible, 2016).

Yeshua and his disciples land on the other side of the lake late in the night before dawn, when perhaps the silvery moon is shedding its pale light on the weird scene and casting shadows upon the sea by the steep cliff where the herd of swine would fall. The area is burrowed with limestone caverns and rock-chambers for the dead. These were the dwellings of the demonized. From these tombs the demonized came forth to meet Yeshua. According to the common Jewish superstition, the evil spirits dwelt especially in the lonely, desolate places. They would dwell in the tombs. The demonized man comes out of the tombs as soon as Yeshua touches the shore. His violence, the impossibility of control by others, absence of self-control, homicidal, almost suicidal frenzy are all depicted. The power of evil, a legion of hurtful spirits, stand out in sharp contrast, challenging the overwhelming manifestation of the divine.

When Yeshua casts the demons out of the man and gives them permission to enter the swine, panic seized the herd. The scene is of a terrified herd running down the cliff unable to recover its foothold and hurling itself into the lake below.

Now it is morning; the weird scene over which the moon had shed its light was past. The unearthly utterances of the demonized and the wild panic of the herd – the splashing of the water – vivid and terrible was over. Now there was only silence. From above, the keepers of the herd had seen it all.

He who had been possessed by foul and evil spirits and deprived of his human individuality is now "sitting at the feet of Yeshua," learning from Yeshua, and clothed in his right mind. He has been brought to God – restored to self and society (Edersheim, 1993, p. 420).

8:40) When Yeshua returned, the crowd welcomed Him because they all had been anxiously waiting on Him. 8:41) Consider this, a man named Yair who was the presiding rabbi of the Jewish learning center came to Him. He fell at Yeshua's feet and begged Him to come to his house. 8:42) His only daughter, who was about twelve years old, was dying. As He went, the crowd pressed in around Him. 8:43) But a woman who had a flow of blood for twelve years, [[who had spent her life savings on physicians]] but could not be cured by anyone, 8:44) came up behind Him and touched the [prayer shawl] fringe of His garment. Immediately her flow of blood was stopped. 8:45) Yeshua said, "Who was it that touched Me?" When all denied it, Kefa said, "Master, the crowds press in all around You!" 8:46) But Yeshua said, "Somebody touched Me because I felt power flow forth from Me." 8:47) When the woman saw

> "Through studying the Scriptures, I have learned more than I ever thought possible about God and myself. Quite possibly my favorite part of the Bible is that it shows real, genuine people with real, genuine struggles being made new through the redemptive power of God's grace. By reading stories throughout the books, I am reminded again and again that the same grace is offered every day in my own life, cleansing me of my past and making me a new creation in Him."
> Emma Goins – Class of 2021

that she had been found out, she came trembling and fell down before Him. She explained in the presence of all why she had touched Him and how that she had been immediately healed. 8:48) He said to her, "Daughter, your [chutzpah style] faith has healed you. Go in shalom!" 8:49) While He was yet speaking, a man came from the presiding rabbi of the Jewish learning center's home saying, "Your daughter is dead. Do not trouble the Rabbi any longer." 8:50) But when Yeshua heard it, He replied, "Do not be afraid. Only believe and she shall be healed." 8:51) When He came to the house, He did not permit anyone to enter with Him, except Kefa, Yochanan, and Yaakov, along with the father and mother of the child. 8:52) Everyone was crying and pounding their chests in lament for her. Yeshua said, "Do not cry. She is not dead but asleep." 8:53) They laughed at Him, knowing full well that she was dead. 8:54) But He took the child's hand, calling out to her, "Rise up, my child." 8:55) Her spirit returned and, at once, she arose. He asked them to give her something to eat. 8:56) Her parents were astonished. He asked them not to tell anyone what had happened.

- The crowd was anxiously waiting for Yeshua and looking forward to the healing He would bring.
- There is a multitude pressing in on Yeshua making it difficult for Him to pass through.
- The rabbi was responsible for conducting services, selecting participants and maintaining order. His responsibilities were also administrative and included such duties as looking after the building and supervising worship (Archaeological Study Bible, 2005).
- The rabbi's only daughter was near death.
- She was twelve years old – the age where marriage might take place (Marshall, 1978).
- The crowds are so dense that they crush Yeshua, thus delaying the journey to Yair's (Jairus') house and also forming the scene in which the woman with the hemorrhage could secretly approach Yeshua for healing.
- A uterine hemorrhage would have made the woman religiously unclean for twelve years, and she had gotten worse despite spending all of her money on medical care (Marshall, 1978).
- On one leaf of the Talmud, at least eleven different remedies are proposed; five of them are merely superstition.
- Picture her, mingling with those who thronged and pressed upon the Lord; she put her hand out and touched the border of His garment, the long tzitzit of the corners of His tallit. She believed that would bring perfect healing.
- It is a strong faith to expect that contact with the touch of His garment would carry such divine power (Edersheim, 1993).
- True faith in its proper context can be linked to chutzpa.
- Prayer with expectant faith in the nature of God may be expressed with bold persistence or brazen tenacity (chutzpa).
- Knowing who God is and recognizing one's own place in the divine scheme of creation will build a solid life of prayer with perseverance even in the greatest of hardships.

- This radical concept of faith preserved in the Gospel texts is deeply rooted in early Jewish thought (Young,1995), and chutzpa was considered a positive characteristic (Young, 1998).
- The forthgoing of the power that is out of Him was neither unconscious nor unwilled on His part (Edersheim, 1993).
- Her healing was caused by her faith, not by her touch.
- Yeshua knew who had touched his tzitzit and wished through her confession to bring her to clearness in her exercise of faith.
- She learned that it was not from His garment, but from the Savior, that the power had proceeded (Edersheim, 1993).
- All of this had caused considerable delay on the journey to Yair's (Jairus') house.
- Not only had his daughter died but the house of mourning was already filled with relatives, hired mourners, wailing women, and musicians in preparation for the funeral.
- It was in the interval of this delay that the messengers came and informed Yair (Jairus) of the death of his child.
- It is unknown how Yeshua dismisses the crowd. Only the inner circle of Kefa (Peter), Yaakov (James), and Yochanan (John) go inside with the child's father and mother.
- "She is not dead but asleep" (the rabbis frequently used the expression "sleep" instead of "die.") They understood Him, but they didn't understand Him at all.
- The Gospel writers regarded the raising of the dead as not only beyond the normal range of Messianic activity but also beyond even the miracles of Yeshua (Edersheim, 1993).

"Studying the Bible has confirmed that my trust in God is not in vain. It has shown me how real and impactful Christ is. It has given me peace on my darkest days and hope for the future." Brayden Armentrout – Class of 2020

In verse 44, the Hebrew word tzitzit refers to the tassels or knotted fringe of a Jewish individual's clothes or prayer shawl (tallit). A prayer shawl refers to the traditional clothes worn by devout Jewish individuals who were faithful to remember the commandments of the LORD (Numbers 15:38-40; Deuteronomy 22:12.) Tzitzit refers to the stringed knots on the four corners of the prayer shawl. Sometimes this word is translated as "hem" or "edge" which obscures the reference. The prayer shawl was the cloak worn as daily clothing (Young, 2019). Photo: Modern prayer shawl (tallit) with tzitzit.

Questions for review and discussion

At the beginning of this chapter it says, "After this..." After what? Look back at the previous chapters of Luke and list 10 things that are about Yeshua's ministry beginning with His baptism:

_____
_____
_____
_____

What did you learn from "The Women Who Followed Yeshua"?
_____

Why is this important?
_____

What is a parable?
_____

Were parables common in the Jewish culture?
_____

What is Yeshua talking about in the parable of the seed and the soil?
_____
_____
_____

What sequence of events begins in verse 22?
_____
_____
_____

What is chutzpa?
_____
_____

What makes it important?
_____
_____

What happens in the story of the man with demons?

_____
_____

What was so tragic about the woman with the issue of blood?

_____
_____

What did Yeshua do for her?

_____
_____

What happened to the little girl because Yeshua was delayed?

_____
_____

What did He do for her?

_____
_____

What is a tzitzit?

_____
_____

Summarize the study notes from this chapter and discuss:

_____
_____
_____
_____
_____
_____
_____
_____
_____

Do you see a theme in chapter 8? _____ What is the theme?

_____
_____

Re-read Luke Chapter 8 from the *Hebrew Heritage Bible* translation used in this book. Discuss. Summarize Luke Chapter 8 in one paragraph and discuss:

_____
_____
_____
_____
_____
_____

Choose one verse from Luke Chapter 8 that you think is the most important and write it here. Discuss why you think it is the most important verse:

_____
_____

Summarize in one or two sentences the most important or the most interesting things you learned in this chapter from your study:

_____
_____

What makes it important or interesting to you?

_____
_____

How did your understanding of Luke Chapter 8 change after you studied it and read it again? Discuss.

_____
_____

How can you apply what you learned from Luke Chapter 8 to your life? Discuss.

_____
_____
_____

What question or questions do you still have about Luke Chapter 8 that you don't understand or want to know more about? Discuss

_____
_____
_____

THE GOSPEL OF LUKE CHAPTER NINE

Lesson 11

Before you begin your study, read Luke Chapter 9 out loud (as a group) from your Bible.

In your own words, summarize Luke Chapter 9 in one paragraph and write at least two questions that you had about the chapter as you read the biblical text: (Discuss)

Luke Chapter 9 begins with Yeshua calling the twelve together and anointing them with power and authority before He sends them out to proclaim the kingdom of God. Herod the Tetrarch tries to see Yeshua. Yeshua and His emissaries travel to Beit Tzaidah to get away from the crowds. The crowds follow them. Yeshua feeds the multitude. Yeshua questions His disciples. Kefa confesses that Yeshua is "The Anointed One of God." Yeshua and His disciples withdraw again, and He is transfigured on the mountain in front of Kefa, Yaakov, and Yochanan. Yeshua heals the boy with the unclean spirit. Yeshua continues to teach His followers even when they are not welcomed by the Samaritans.

Yeshua and His disciples travel to Beit Tzaidah (Bethsaida), an ancient fishing village on the northern shore of the Lake of Kinneret. Exciting archaeological discoveries were made in 2016 at Beit Tzaidah by Dr. Steven Notley (Dr. Notley received his undergraduate degree in Tulsa at Oral Roberts University). Take a trip online and find out more about the fascinating discoveries at Beit Tzaidah, Yisrael. Write and discuss:

_____
_____
_____
_____
_____
_____
_____
_____
_____
_____
_____
_____
_____
_____

Chapter 9

9:1) He called the twelve together. He gave them power and authority over all the demons and to heal diseases.

- In Luke Chapter 8, the emphasis was on the ministry of Yeshua among the people, His teaching and mighty works demonstrating His divine power and compassion.
- The Twelve have been accompanying Him – observing.
- From now on the emphasis is on the relationship of Yeshua with His disciples and the teaching that He is giving them. It's time to participate – moving from observing to doing (Marshall, 1978).

9:2) He sent them to proclaim the kingdom of God and to heal sicknesses. 9:3) He said to them, "Do not take anything for your journey, neither staff, nor bag, nor bread, nor money. Do not pack an extra tunic. 9:4) When you are received into a home, stay there, and do not take leave from that place. 9:5) Where they do not accept you, shake the dust from your feet as a warning against them as you leave that town." 9:6) They went forth through the villages, in every place, proclaiming the good news and healing the sick.

- Do not take the usual provisions for travel:
  - Staff – protection from robbers and snakes and for balance.
  - Bag – wandering philosophers living on the streets carried a bag for begging.
  - Bread/money – provisions
  - Extra shirt – The poorest had only one shirt. The prophets lived simply.
- Avoid the appearance of other missionaries in the Hellenistic world who made a "good thing out of their preaching."
- They should be wholly absorbed in the service of the Lord.
- Jews shook impure dust from their feet when entering a more holy place or when they left a pagan or Gentile area and entered into the Holy Land (Edersheim, 1993).

9:7) Now Herod the Tetrarch heard about all that was happening. He was bewildered because some people were saying that Yochanan had risen from the dead, 9:8) some that Eliyahu had appeared, and still others that one of the old prophets had risen. 9:9) Herod said, "I myself beheaded Yochanan, but who is this about whom I hear such amazing things?" So Herod earnestly wanted to see him.

- Yochanan (John the Baptist) has been beheaded.
- Eliyahu is Elijah the prophet from the Old Testament.
- Herod the Tetrarch (Herod Antipas) is afraid. Has Yochanan been raised from the dead? Who is this person? This sets the stage for Peter's confession in verse 18 (Marshall, 1978).

9:10) When they came back, the emissaries told Yeshua what they had done. He took them and withdrew privately to a town called Beit Tzaidah. 9:11) The crowds found out and followed Him. He welcomed them and told them about the kingdom of God, healing all those who were ill.

- In verse 10, The word for "emissaries" in Greek is apostolos and in Hebrew, it comes from sheliach. As emissaries, they receive delegated authority from their master. As authoritative delegates they represent their master. Their word is the word of the one who sent them (Young, 2019).

9:12) Late in the day, the twelve came and said to Him, "Send away the crowd to go into the surrounding villages and countryside to find food and lodging, because we are in a remote area." 9:13) He said to them, "You give them something to eat." They said, "We only have five loaves of bread and two fishes. How do you expect us to go and buy food for so many people?" 9:14) There were around five thousand people. He said to His disciples, "Make them sit down in groups of about fifty each." 9:15) They did this, asking all the people to sit down. 9:16) Taking the five loaves and two fishes, He lifted His eyes to heaven and pronounced the blessing over them. He broke them and gave them to His disciples to serve the crowd. 9:17) They all ate their fill! Moreover, they picked up twelve baskets full of broken pieces which were left over.

Hebrew Names

Beit Tzaidah – "Beit" means "house" and "Tzaidah" means "hunting" or "fishing."

- In verse 10, Yeshua takes the disciples and leaves Herod Antipas' territory and goes to a friendlier district (Beit Tzaidah) ruled by Herod Philip (a more accommodating ruler) (Marshall, 1978).
- The crowds discover where they are and follow them to this unnamed remote place. It is now late in the day, before sunset, the usual time for the evening meal in Jewish culture.
- The people here were not local people. They were looking for lodging maybe even further into Gentile territory where they would not be welcomed (Edersheim, 1993).
- The element of Yeshua's concern, His compassion for the crowds, stands out by contrast with the unwillingness of the disciples, springing from their inability to act.
- What God did through Moshe (Moses) and Eliyahu (Elisha) – manna in the desert/barley loaves and grain, He now does again with plenty through Yeshua.
- The five loaves were barley loaves, the poor person's bread. The two fishes were small dried or pickled fish that were eaten like sardines. Salting and pickling fish was a special industry among the fishermen of the Lake of Kinneret (Edersheim, 1993, pp. 467-468).
- The question is building. Is this a prophet like Moses or one who is greater? (Marshall, 1978)

The Jewish prayer over bread recited in Hebrew has been the same prayer for centuries, and is probably the same prayer offered by Yeshua over the bread in this story and all others in the Gospels: "Baruch atah Adonai, Eloheinu Melech ha'olam, hamotzi lechem min ha'aretz. Blessed are You, Lord our God, King of the universe, who bringeth forth bread from the earth."

9:18) While He was alone praying, His disciples gathered around Him. He asked them, "Who do the crowds of people say that I am?" 9:19) They answered, "Yochanan the Immerser in water—some say that You are Eliyahu and others that one of the old prophets has arisen." 9:20) He asked them, "But who do you say that I am?" Kefa declared, "The Anointed One of God."

9:21) He charged and commanded them not to tell anyone that, 9:22) "The Son of Man must undergo much suffering and be rejected by the elders, chief priests and scribes. He will be killed, but on the third day, He will rise."

The location for verse 18 is named in Markos (Mark) 8:27 and Mattityahu (Matthew) 16:13, "Now when Yeshua arrived at the district of Caesarea Philippi..."(Mat. 16:13). First known as Paneas for the pagan god Pan, Caesarea Philippi was made an administrative center for the Romans by Herod Philip.

Take a trip online to Caesarea Philippi, Yisrael. Discover its beauty and rich history. Write and discuss what you learn:

_____
_____
_____
_____
_____
_____
_____
_____

Hebrew Names

Kefa – Means "rock" in Aramaic. The Greek Petros is a translation of the Aramaic name (Young, 2019).

Archaeological site of Caesarea Philippi and the Hermon River Springs. This site is located at the base of Mount Hermon (the highest mountain in Yisrael at 9230 feet). The Hermon Springs form the headwaters of the Yarden (Jordan) River.
Photo credit: David Anderson, 2018

- In contrast to those who were shutting people out of the kingdom of God, those who confess Yeshua as Messiah can usher people in.
- Yeshua told His disciples not to tell anyone. Perhaps He did not want to risk being viewed as a threat and hunted down by the Romans prematurely or because He knows that it is beyond the people's ability to understand.
- Yeshua is predicting His upcoming death, burial, and resurrection.
- The disciples have seen resurrection with the raising of the widow's son and Jairus' daughter. What was difficult was that it was going to happen to Yeshua (Marshall, 1978).

9:23) He said to all, "If anyone desires to come after Me, let him deny himself, take up his cross and follow Me. 9:24) The one who desires to save his life will lose it, and the one who loses his life for My sake will save it. 9:25) How will it profit a man if he wins the whole world and yet loses or forfeits his soul? 9:26) For whoever is ashamed of Me and of My words, of him will the Son of Man be ashamed when He comes in His glory with His Father accompanied by the holy angels. 9:27) For truly I say unto you that there are some standing here who will not taste of death before they see the kingdom of God."

- Yeshua issues the summons to His followers to be willing to say "no" to themselves and their own ambitions and to follow Him, even to the point of daily readiness for martyrdom.
- The use of the basic imagery appears to have been known in Judaism: "Abraham took the wood and laid it on his son Isaac, like a man who carries a cross on his shoulder" (Marshall, 1978).
- Those condemned to execution would often carry the horizontal beam of their cross to the site of their execution, through an often hostile and mocking crowd.
- Jewish apocalyptic writers agree that eternal life was well worth losing one's life in this age (e.g., 1 Enoch 108:10) (*Cultural Backgrounds Study Bible*, 2016).
- In verse 26 Yeshua is saying that it is about one's attitude toward Him that ultimate salvation depends.
- The text refers to the rejection of the message of Yeshua.
- He will be ashamed of him, i.e. will refuse to own him. (Daniel 7:13 in the TANAK) This is an allusion indicating the idea of coming for judgment.
- The saying contrasts the present lowly condition of Yeshua – one of whom men might be tempted to be ashamed – with his future glory as the Son of Man – the one in whose hands is human destiny (Marshall, 1978).

9:28) About eight days after these events, He took Kefa, Yochanan, and Yaakov with him up a mountain to pray. 9:29) As He was praying, the appearance of His face was changed, and His clothes became dazzling white. 9:30) Look, two men talked with Him, Moshe and Eliyahu; 9:31) they appeared in divine glory. They spoke with Him concerning His death, which was to be fulfilled in Yerushalayim. 9:32) Now Kefa and his companions were heavy with sleep. They woke up and saw His divine glory and the two men standing with Him. 9:33) As the men were leaving them, Kefa said to Yeshua, "Master, it is good for us to be here. Let us build three temporary shelters, one for you, one for Moshe, and one for Eliyahu," not really realizing what he was saying. 9:34) While he was talking, a cloud overshadowed them. They were gripped with fear as they entered the cloud. 9:35) A voice came from the cloud saying, "This is My Son, My chosen; obey Him!" (Isa. 42:1). 9:36) After the voice had spoken, Yeshua was found alone. At that time, they kept silence and did not tell anyone about what they had seen.

Where is this mountain? The early tradition placed Yeshua's transfiguration on Mount Tabor, a rounded peak (elevation 1,929 feet) at the northeast corner of the Jezreel Valley. The other view, which is gaining scholarly momentum, places the transfiguration on Mount Hermon. Eusebius first suggested this location in the fourth century (*ESV Archaeology Study Bible*, 2017).

 Take a trip online to Mount Tabor and Mount Hermon. What did you discover about each? Write and discuss:

_____

_____

- In verse 29, His "face was changed" is literally translated "his countenance became different" which is a good phrase in Hebrew.
- In verse 31, the word "death" is translated from the Greek euphemism exodus which literally means "departure." The word "exodus" may well have alluded to the event of the redemption of the people of Israel from Egypt in the mind of the Greek editor of the text (Young, 2019).
- Locations for this event could have been Mount Tabor or Mount Hermon. Both had sacred associations among the pagans who lived in the region in antiquity. In the Bible, high mountains and prophetic revelation went hand-in-hand, lending appropriateness to either setting (ESV Archaeology Study Bible, 2017).
- Verse 29 is like the scene with Moshe (Moses), when he talked with God on a mountain and his face reflected God's glory (Ex. 34:29-35). The cloud of God's glory overshadowed Mount Sinai, from which God spoke from heaven (Cultural Backgrounds Study Bible, 2017).
- Here is the Heavenly Voice again. This is the same Voice that was heard at Yeshua's baptism. Now the Voice is speaking to the three (Marshall, 1978).
- Moshe (Moses) and Eliyahu (Elijah) appear. Eliyahu had been taken to heaven alive (2 Kings 2:11). God had buried Moshe (Dt. 34:6) although some Jewish traditions said that he was preserved alive.
- The presence of Moshe and Eliyahu could also reflect that the Torah (written by Moshe) and the Prophets (of whom Eliyahu is maybe the greatest) testify about who Yeshua is (Stern, 1992).
- The Jewish people expected the return of Eliyahu (Mal. 4:5-6) and the coming of a prophet like Moshe (Dt. 18:15-18) (Cultural Backgrounds Study Bible, 2016).
- Kefa (Peter) knew how to construct the shelters; Jewish men build them annually for Sukkot.
- The cloud that covers the mountain is the glory of God (Ex. 24:15-18).
- God's own dwelling place comes to earth and accommodates His people.
- The glorious scene here had not come to stay (Marshall, 1978).
- Three had gone up with Jesus. The rest stayed on the plain (Edersheim, 1993).

Sukkot is also known as the Feast of Booths or the Feast of Tabernacles or the Feast of Ingathering or the festival for rejoicing It is a pilgrimage feast that is described in the Torah in Leviticus 23:40. It is celebrated in the fall. "Sukkot" is the Hebrew word for "booths." It commemorates the temporary dwellings God made to shelter the Israelites on their way out of Egypt. Some say that it refers to the miraculous clouds of glory that shielded the Israelites from the desert sun (Chabad.org).

Take a trip online and explore the history of this great Jewish festival. Discover the different ways the Jews celebrate the holiday now in Yisrael and around the world. What did you discover? Write and discuss:

_____
_____
_____
_____

9:37) On the next day, when they had come down from the mountain, a great crowd of people gathered together to see Him. 9:38) All at once, a man in the crowd called out, "Rabbi, I beg you to examine my son. After all, he is my only child. 9:39) Look, all of a sudden a spirit seizes him, and he screams out. It throws him into convulsions, accompanied by foaming at the mouth. Bruising him badly, it will scarcely leave him alone. 9:40) I begged Your disciples to drive it out, but they were not able." 9:41) Yeshua answered and said unto them, "O generation without faith and so perverse, how long can I put up with you? Bring your son here!" 9:42) Even while he was coming, the demon threw the boy down in a convulsion. But Yeshua rebuked the unclean spirit. He healed the boy and gave him back to his father. 9:43) They were all astonished at the mighty power of God. While they were marveling at all the miracles He performed, He said to His disciples, 9:44) "Let these words sink into your ears, for the Son of Man is to be delivered into the hands of heathen men." 9:45) They could not comprehend this saying. It had been hidden from them and was beyond their grasp. They were afraid to ask Him about this saying. 9:46) An argument arose among them as to who should be leader. 9:47) But when Yeshua realized what they were pondering in their hearts, He took a child by the hand and had him stand by His side. 9:48) He said to them, "Whoever honors this child in My name, honors Me. Whoever honors Me, honors Him who sent Me. The one who is least among you all is the one who should be considered great."

9:49) Yochanan answered, "Master, we saw someone driving out demons in Your name. We tried to stop him because he did not follow along with us." 9:50) But Yeshua said to him, "Do not hinder him! The one who is not against you is for you."

- In verse 43, the Greek text does not contain the word, "miracles"; this term would have been implied to the original reader especially in the Hebrew source of the Greek canonical Gospel. The mention of what Yeshua had done would refer to the miracles of healing.

- In verse 44, the idiom, "Let these words sink into your ears," forms a clear Hebraic expression. Hebrew is fond of using references to the physical body such as "place these words in your ears."

- In verse 46, the Greek word for "leader" (meizon from megas) is usually translated "greatest." The word "greatest" in Hebrew, rav, or even, hagadol, most probably referred to a position of leadership. Compare Gen 25:23b, "the elder [Hebrew, rav, literally "greater"] will serve the younger" (Young, 2019).

- In verse 37, they had come down from the mountain of transfiguration. The transfiguration happened at night. This is the next morning when Yeshua, Kefa, Yaakov, and Yochanan come down from the mountain (Marshall, 1978).

- Here is a terrible contrast between transfiguration and glory and the scene of chaos below. This is reminiscent of Israel's temptation in the wilderness.

- Why had the disciples failed to drive out the demon? The same reason that they weren't taken with the three – they were faithless and unbelieving (Edersheim, 1993, p. 547).

- Who is the unbelieving generation? the people present, the father, and the disciples.

- This reflects the scene in Deuteronomy 32:5 when Moshe was confronted by the faithless and disobedient generation in the wilderness.

- Here is the compassion and powerful saving presence of God. What was visible only to the chosen three on the mountain is now visible to all (Marshall, 1978).

- Who is the greatest? It is the one who is least in importance who is really the greatest. Children in the ancient world were regarded as of no importance.

- Whoever receives a "child" – welcoming and caring for a person – the needy and afflicted. This is a connection of Yahweh's close link with the needy in the TANAK (Matthew 25:35-40).

- Receiving Yeshua means receiving the Father.

- The person who is willing to take the lowest place is really the greatest. There can be no question of greatness among the disciples – since the person who is prepared to act as a servant has abandoned all desire for greatness (Marshall, 1978).

9:51) As the time came for Him to make His ascent, resolutely Yeshua set His face to go up to Yerushalayim. 9:52) He sent messengers on ahead of Him. They entered into a village of the Samaritans to prepare a place for Him, 9:53) but the people there would not welcome Him because He was going toward Yerushalayim. 9:54) When His disciples Yaakov and Yochanan saw this, they asked,

"Lord, do You want us to command fire to fall from heaven and burn them up like Eliyahu?" (2 Kgs 1:10). 9:55) At that He turned and sternly corrected them saying, "You do not know what spirit you are coming from! The Son of Man did not come to destroy people but to save them." 9:56) Then they went on to another village.

- Having already faced the question of their attitude toward other people, they are now confronted by the hostility of a Samaritan village, which is an object lesson to them as Yeshua indicates how such a situation is to be met.
- The story forbids returning hostility with hostility.
- The attitude is not opposition to the Gospel, but it is inherent racial prejudice between the Jews and Samaritans (Marshall, 1978).
- The tensions between the Samaritans and the Jews were sometimes violent. It could be particularly dangerous for Jews to pass through the territory of the Samaritans especially if the Jews were headed to Yerushalayim to worship (Cultural Backgrounds Study Bible, 2016).

9:57) As they were traveling along the way, a man came to Him and said, "I will follow you wherever you lead." 9:58) Yeshua said to him, "Foxes have holes, birds of the air have nests, but the Son of Man has nowhere to lay down His head." 9:59) He said to another person, "Follow Me." But he replied, "Lord, first let me go and bury my father." 9:60) With this He said to him, "Let the dead bury their own dead. As for you, go and proclaim the kingdom of God." 9:61) Still another said, "I will follow You, Lord. But first allow me to go and say good bye to everyone back home." 9:62) Furthermore Yeshua said to him, "No one who puts his hand to the plow and then looks back is worthy for the kingdom of God."

- Burial of the dead was a religious duty that took precedence over all other duties – even priests could touch dead bodies in the case of their relatives (Lev. 21:1-3) (Marshall, 1978).
- To assist in the burial of a person (not a relative) was a work of love which carried a great reward from God.
- To bury a father was a very important duty. To leave it undone was scandalous, but maybe the father was just old and not dead yet.
- The urgency of preaching the Gospel could not be clearer (Marshall, 1978).
- Yeshua challenges those whose commitment is weak, and to those who reject him altogether, he withdraws his offer.
- Any type of excuse offered seems foolish.
- A strong argument can be made that the father is not dead yet, because if he were dead, his son would have been at home sitting Shiva (seven days of mourning) (Stern, 1992).

- Perhaps the son wants to go home, live in comfort with his father until his death (maybe for years), collect his inheritance, and then at his leisure, become a disciple.
- Let the spiritually dead (those who are concerned with the benefits of the world including inheritances) remain with each other in life and eventually bury their own physically dead.
- A true disciple must get their priorities right (Stern, 1992).
- There is a higher duty, absolute self-denial and homeless in the world as well as immediate and complete self-surrender to Yeshua and his work – undivided.
- To postpone the immediate call is to reject it (Edersheim, 1993).

Questions for review and discussion:

Find the following locations on the map and discuss events that happened at each place:

Beit Tzaidah	Machaerus
Kefar Nachum	Lake of Kinneret
Mount Hermon	Yarden River
Caesarea Philippi	Mount Tabor
Kursi	Migdal

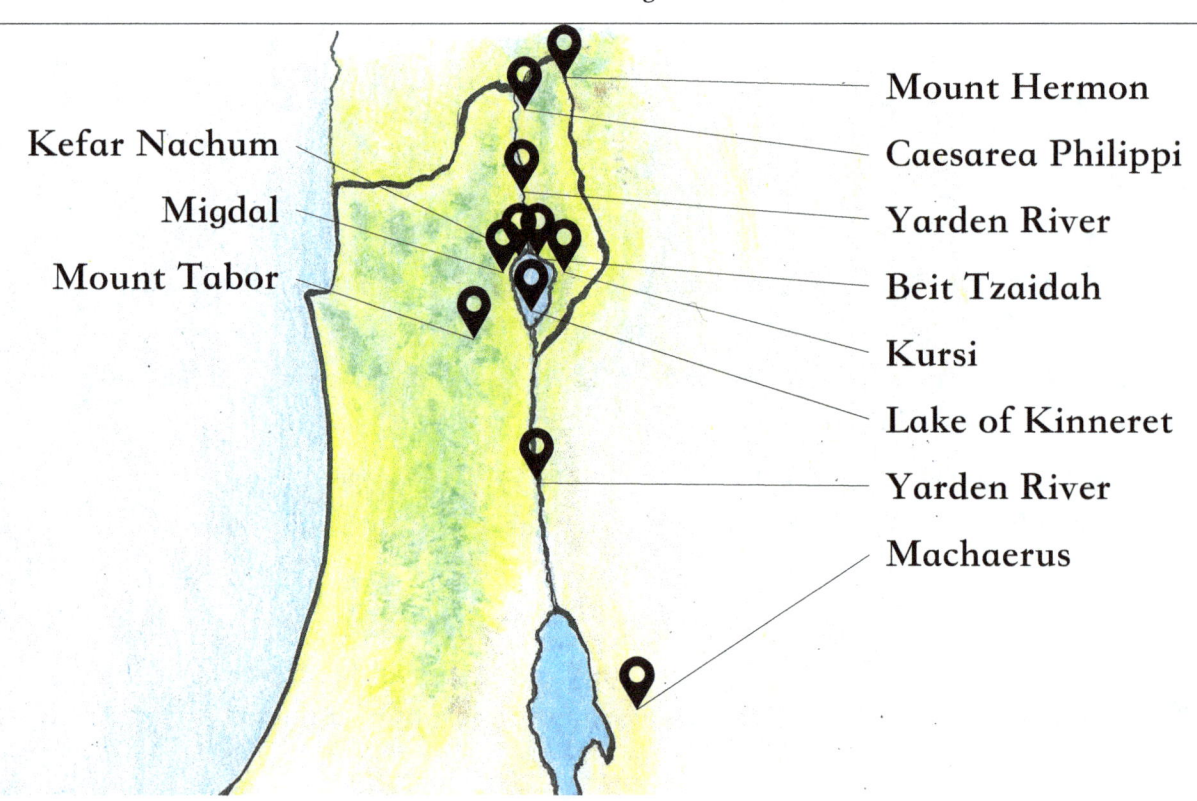

How does the role of the disciples change from Luke Chapter 8 to Luke Chapter 9?

What is Yeshua teaching them?

What is Yeshua's expectations for them?

Why do you think Yeshua tells His disciples not to take the normal provisions for their journey?

What new thing did you learn about the "loaves and fishes" story?

What makes this story important?

What happened on the mountain with Yeshua?

How did that relate to Moshe and the Exodus?

Why is that event important?

From what you learned about Sukkot, why do you think Kefa (Peter) wanted to build three temporary shelters?

Who are the Samaritans? (If you need to, refer back to Lesson 2)

What lesson was Yeshua teaching His disciples here?

What do verses 57-62 mean?

What do you think is the theme of chapter 9?

Summarize the study notes from this chapter and discuss:

Re-read Luke Chapter 9 from the *Hebrew Heritage Bible* translation used in this book. Discuss. Summarize Luke Chapter 9 in one paragraph and discuss:

Choose one verse from Luke Chapter 9 that you think is the most important and write it here. Discuss why you think it is the most important verse:

Summarize in one or two sentences the most important or the most interesting things you learned in this chapter from your study:

What makes it important or interesting to you?

How did your understanding of Luke Chapter 9 change after you studied it and read it again? Discuss.

How can you apply what you learned from Luke Chapter 9 to your life? Discuss.

What question or questions do you still have about Luke Chapter 9 that you don't understand or want to know more about? Discuss

THE GOSPEL OF LUKE CHAPTER TEN

Lesson 12

Before you begin your study, read Luke Chapter 10 out loud (as a group) from your Bible.

In your own words, summarize Luke Chapter 10 in one paragraph and write at least two questions that you had about the chapter as you read the biblical text: (Discuss)

_____
_____
_____
_____
_____
_____
_____
_____
_____
_____
_____
_____
_____
_____
_____
_____
_____

Yeshua appoints seventy, gives them instructions, and sends them out to proclaim the Kingdom of God. Yeshua teaches about loving one's enemies as He tells the parable about the Good Samaritan. Yeshua visits the home of Marta and Miryam.

This chapter is packed full of Yeshua's teachings. He also pronounces judgement on the community of Korazim. The archaeological excavations of Korazim in Yisrael just three miles north of Kefar Nachum include a synagogue. A remarkable find in the synagogue was "Moses' Seat" – a chair of honor used for visiting rabbis (Matthew 23:2). Korazim was a major producer of wheat during the first century. The main road to Damascus passed nearby. Take a trip online to Korazin, Yisrael. Discover its history. Did you see the "Moses' Seat"? Look up Matthew 23:2. Write and discuss what you discovered about Korazim:

___

Chapter 10

10:1) After this the Lord appointed seventy others. He sent them out two by two before Him into every town and place where He Himself was about to come. 10:2) He told them, "The harvest is plentiful, but the workers are few. Pray to the Lord of the harvest, therefore, to send out workers for His harvest. 10:3) Go! Consider this, I am sending you as lambs among the wolves. 10:4) Carry neither a purse nor a pack. 10:5) First speak, 'May shalom bless this household!' 10:6) If a child of shalom is there, your shalom will rest upon him. If not, it shall return to you. 10:7) Remain in the same house, eating and drinking whatever they provide for you. A worker is worthy of his pay. Do not go from house to house. 10:8) Whenever you enter a town and they welcome you, eat what has been served to you. 10:9) Heal the sick in it and explain to them, 'The kingdom of God has come upon you.' 10:10) But whenever you enter a town and they do not welcome you, go out into its streets and say, 10:11) 'We wipe off even the dust of your town which sticks to our feet. Nonetheless, you must recognize this: The kingdom of God has come!' 10:12) I tell you, on that day, it will be more tolerable for Sedom than for that town.

Hebrew Names and their English Equivalents

Hebrew	**English**
Sedom	Sodom
Shalom	Peace
Korazin/Korazim	Chorazin
Yericho	Jericho

10:13) "Retribution threatens you, Korazin! Retribution threatens you, Beit Tzaidah! For if the mighty miracles which have been performed in you had been done in Tzur and Tzidon, they would have repented at once, wearing sackcloth and sitting in ashes! 10:14) Surely it will be more tolerable for Tzur and Tzidon at the judgment than it will be for you. 10:15) As for you, Kefar Nachum, will you be lifted up to the heaven? No, but you shall be brought low to hell. 10:16) The one who listens to you, listens to Me. The one who rejects you, rejects Me. The person who rejects Me, furthermore, rejects the One who sent Me."

Photo: Moses' Seat at Korazim. During the first century, itinerant rabbis would visit various synagogues to teach. They would sit in Moses' Seat as a place of honor. The original seat is on exhibit at the Israel Museum, Jerusalem.

10:17) The seventy returned with joy exclaiming, "Lord! Even the demons are subject to us when we speak your name." 10:18) He said to them, "I am watching Satan fall like a flash of lightning from heaven. 10:19) Now listen, I have given you authority to walk all over snakes and scorpions, and over all the power of the enemy. Nothing will harm you. 10:20) Stop rejoicing in this, nevertheless, that the demons are subject to you. Rejoice rather that your names are recorded in heaven."

- Yeshua sends seventy of His followers to proclaim the Kingdom of God. These seventy were reminiscent of the seventy elders Moshe appointed in the Exodus who received the Spirit and prophesied (Numbers 11:16, 24-25) (Stern, 1992, p. 121).
- Similar to the instructions given to His followers in chapter 9, the disciples are to avoid the appearance of Hellenistic missionaries and be completely absorbed in the service of the Lord (Edersheim, 1993).
- The disciples are to be happy with the accommodations of the house that welcomes them. They should not look for a better place to stay when they are visiting a village.
- In whatever village they are to enter they must find a "son of peace" (Hebrew for goodhearted person) and stay with him, letting their "peace rest upon him."
- This was a kind of "field practice" that Yeshua sent these shelichim (emissaries) out to perform. You learn by doing (Lindsey, 2017, p. 161).
- The idea of "kingdom" is one of the most important spiritual concepts in the New Testament. In Hebrew "kingdom" is active; it is action. It is God ruling in the lives of people. Those who are ruled by God are part of the Kingdom of God.
- One sees God's Kingdom when one sees God in action (in healings and miracles for example). In the same way, people saw the Kingdom when they saw Yeshua in action.
- Yeshua also used "kingdom" to refer to those who followed Him as the members of His movement by demonstrating His presence and power in their lives (Bivin & Blizzard, 2004).
- The cause for true joy is in the fact that their names are recorded in heaven (Book of Life). The personal relationship of a believer with God should be the cause of great joy (Walvoord and Zuck, 1983).

10:21) In that same hour, He rejoiced in the Holy Spirit and exclaimed, "I thank You, [My] Father, Lord of heaven and earth, that You have concealed these matters from the wise and learned but have revealed them to the simple. Yes! [My] Father, for this was pleasing in Your sight. 10:22) Everything has been given to Me by My Father. No one knows who the Son is, except the Father, and no one knows who the Father is without the Son, and anyone to whom the Son wills to reveal [Him]."

10:23) He turned to His disciples and said, "Blessed are the eyes which witness what you see!

- In verse 23, some translations read, "He turned to His disciples [[in private]]." The words, "in private," are missing in Codex Beza which sometimes preserves Semitisms better than some other manuscripts. The idea that this is private communication to the disciples may well be a later scribal idea (Young, 2019).

10:24) Surely I tell you that many prophets have yearned to see what you see, but did not see it, and to hear what you hear, but could not hear it."

10:25) Consider this, a certain Torah theologian stood up to learn from Him saying, "Rabbi, what shall I do to inherit eternal life?"

- In verse 25, the Greek verb ekpeirazō is often translated, "to put him to the test" (NRSV). Careful linguistic analysis and the cultural context suggest "to learn from Him" as a better translation. Jewish learners examined and tested teachers to learn from them (Young, 2019).

10:26) But He asked him, "What is written in the Torah? How do you read?" 10:27) He answered Him, saying, "Love the LORD your God with all your heart, and with all your soul, and with all your strength, and with all your understanding," as well as, "Love your neighbor as yourself." (Deut. 6:5; Lev 19:18) 10:28) He answered him, "You have answered correctly. Do this and you shall live." 10:29) He then desired to justify his [question] by asking Yeshua, "But who is my neighbor?" 10:30) Yeshua responded, "A man was traveling down from Yerushalayim to Yericho. Robbers jumped him. They stripped him, beat him up, and ran off leaving him in the convulsions of death.

10:31) Now it just so happened by chance that a priest was going down that road. But when he saw the man, he passed by on the other side. 10:32) In the same way, a Levite came to the place, looked [the man] over, and then passed by on the other side. 10:33) But then a certain man who was a Samaritan was traveling along the way. He came up to him. When he saw [the dying man], he was filled with compassion. 10:34) He went over to him and dressed his wounds, pouring on oil and wine. He mounted [the man] on his own donkey and brought him to an inn. He took care of him. 10:35) The next day, he took out two denarii and paid the innkeeper saying, 'Take care of him, and whatever more you spend, I will pay you when I come back.' 10:36) Which of these three, in your opinion, proved to be a neighbor to the man who was jumped by robbers?" 10:37) He said, "The one who demonstrated compassion for him." Yeshua said to him, "Go and do the same to others."

- Yeshua tells this parable as an answer to the Torah scholar's question.
- The Torah scholar's question is genuine because the term for neighbor in Hebrew has a variety of meanings, and at the time of Yeshua's ministry the Hebrew language was changing.
- How is the term for neighbor, "rea" in Hebrew, to be understood? Did it mean "anyone" or "coworker" or "colleague" or "close friend" or "enemy?"
- The holiness code of the book of Leviticus commands the people of Israel to "love your neighbor as yourself." It is very important to this Torah scholar to know the definition of neighbor so that he can follow the commandment of God.
- Questions about the Torah and the proper approach to others were not uncommon (Young,1998, p. 102).
- The emphasis of early Jewish thought during this period is expressed in the well-known biblical passage "Hear O Israel, the LORD our God, is one LORD," which precedes the commandment "you shall love the LORD your God" in the Torah passage (Deut. 6:4-5).
- This discussion between Yeshua and the scholar was not hostile or confrontational.
- Understanding the characters of the story is vital to making the correct interpretation of the parable.
- The priest and Levite were Sadducees who did not believe in the "preservation of life" theology of the Pharisees. The priest and the Levite probably lived in Yericho (many priests and Levites lived in Yericho) and served in the Temple in Yerushalayim. Ritual purity was very important to them. They could not risk becoming unclean by touching a dead body.
- The Samaritan's beliefs were similar to the priest and Levite. Like the priest and the Levite, he only believed in the first five books of the Bible – the Torah. He did not follow the belief of the "preservation of life" like the Pharisees.
- The Samaritans and the Jews were bitter enemies. Because of this location, on the road from Yerushalayim to Yericho, the Samaritan is probably in a location that could be dangerous for him. The Samaritan risked his life to save this unidentified man from certain death. He showed him compassion.
- When Jesus asked the Torah scholar, "Who was the neighbor to the man in need?" The Torah scholar answered correctly: "the one who demonstrated compassion for him" (Young, 1998).

10:38) Now as they went their way, He came to a certain village where a woman named Marta welcomed Him as her guest. 10:39) She had a sister named Miryam, who sat at the feet of Yeshua [as a disciple] listening to His teachings. 10:40) But Marta was very stressed about serving [her guests]. She said to the Master, "Lord, do You not care that my sister has left me all by myself to serve? Tell her to help." 10:41) Answering her, the Lord said, "Marta, Marta, you are stressed out and troubled over many things. 10:42) Only one is needful and Miryam has chosen the good portion which shall not be taken away from her."

The Samaritans live by a literal version of Torah law. They believe only in the first five books of Moses and observe only holidays found in the Pentateuch (first five books), such as Passover and Sukkot. Their practices mirror those of antiquity. On Passover, for example, their high priest sacrifices a sheep in a community-wide ritual. Today there are only about 800 Samaritans. (Lieber, Chavie. "The Other Torah," Tablet, May 13, 2013. Tabletmag.com)

Take a trip online and discover more about the Samaritan people and their Torah. Where in Yisrael do they live today? Write and discuss:

_____
_____
_____
_____
_____
_____

Take a trip online on the road from Jericho to Jerusalem. What is the road like? How far is it? What is the climate? What did you learn? Write and discuss:

_____
_____
_____
_____

Photo: Traveling along Highway 1, from Yericho to Yerushalayim. Some of the modern highway follows the ancient route that was the setting of the Parable of the Good Samaritan.

GOSPEL OF LUKE

> "Studying the Bible has caused me to actually think about our faith and what truly happened. I've been able to process what actually went down instead of thinking of them as children's stories in some picture book."
> Alex Cook – Class of 2020

Hebrew Names

Marta – means "The lady" or "The mistress" and is the feminine form of master (Marshall, 1978).

- Hospitality was and continues to be a very important part of the culture of the Middle East and Judaism.
- In verse 39, Miryam sat at the feet [as a disciple] listening.
- In Acts 22:3 Paul uses the same term to describe his relationship with his teacher the Rabbi Gamaliel… "a disciple at the feet of Gamaliel."
- To sit at the feet of the Rabbi meant that you were his disciple.
- It was very significant to Yeshua's audience that He was giving a place for women to listen and that He encouraged them to learn from Him.
- To hear the word is of utmost importance. Yeshua praises Miryam for choosing to listen, and He will not allow Marta (nor anyone else) to deprive Miryam of the opportunity to do so.
- Yeshua is teaching not about practical hospitality but about spiritual goals.
- Miryam should not be deprived of the spiritual good portion that she desired by helping Marta, and Marta should cut back her domestic cares so that she can have the one thing that matters (Marshall, 1978).

Rabbi Regina Jonas

Born August 3, 1902 in Germany, Regina Jonas became the first woman to be confirmed as a rabbi. She was ordained in 1935. Her thesis was titled, "May a woman hold rabbinic office?" On the last page of her thesis she wrote, "Almost nothing halakhically (laws in the written and Oral Torah) but prejudice and lack of familiarity stand against women holding rabbinic office."

She also wrote this, "If I confess what motivated me, a woman, to become a rabbi, two things come to mind. My belief in God's calling and my love of humans. God planted in our heart skills and a vocation without asking about gender" (Regina Jonas, June 23, 1938).

She was murdered at Auschwitz in October 1944 (Jewish Women's Archive).

Questions for review and discussion

What is meant by the Kingdom of God?

What should be the cause of great joy?

What does the Torah theologian/scholar ask Yeshua?

Why does he want to know?

Why is it important that the Torah scholar understand?

Explain the parable in your own words:

___

Is the same thing that Yeshua taught the Torah Scholar important for you to understand? Why?

___

How does it apply to your life?

___

What did you learn from the story of Marta and Miryam?

___

How is this story important to you?

___

Summarize the study notes from this chapter and discuss:

___

Summarize in one or two sentences the most important or the most interesting thing you learned in this chapter from your study:

___

What makes it important or interesting to you?

___

Re-read Luke Chapter 10 from the *Hebrew Heritage Bible* translation used in this book. Discuss. Summarize Luke Chapter 10 in one paragraph and discuss:

_____
_____
_____
_____

Choose one verse from Luke Chapter 10 that you think is the most important and write it here. Discuss why you think it is the most important verse:

_____
_____

How did your understanding of Luke Chapter 10 change after you studied it and read it again? Discuss:

_____
_____
_____

Who was Regina Jonas and what is important about her story?

_____
_____
_____

Looking back on Lesson 10, and adding it to what you read in Lesson 12 about women and Yeshua, what did you learn?

_____
_____
_____

How can you apply what you learned from Luke Chapter 10 to your life? Discuss.

_____
_____
_____
_____

What question or questions do you still have about Luke Chapter 10 that you don't understand or want to know more about? Discuss:

_____
_____
_____
_____

Additional Notes

THE GOSPEL OF LUKE CHAPTER ELEVEN

Lesson 13

Before you begin your study, read Luke Chapter 11 out loud (as a group) from your Bible.

In your own words, summarize Luke Chapter 11 in one paragraph and write at least two questions that you had about the chapter as you read the biblical text: (Discuss)

_____
_____
_____
_____
_____
_____
_____
_____
_____
_____
_____
_____
_____

Luke Chapter 11 begins with Yeshua teaching His disciples how to pray. He tells them a parable about the goodness and dependability of God. As Yeshua delivers a man from demons, He is falsely accused of sorcery. The chapter continues and concludes with Yeshua teaching about the Kingdom of God.

📍 Prayer is very important to Yeshua. He teaches His disciples to pray as He reminds them about the loving character of God. Reflect on prayer for a few minutes. Can you find other Scriptures that talk about prayer? What Scriptures did you find? What did you learn about prayer from these Scriptures?

_____
_____
_____
_____
_____

📍 Prayer is important in the Jewish faith. Find out more about Jewish prayers. What are the prayers like? Are there different prayers for different life events? What about praying at meals? Are there set times during the day for prayer? What are tefillin (phylacteries)? (A couple of sites to utilize might be Chabad.org or Aish.com) What did you learn? Write and discuss:

_____
_____
_____
_____
_____
_____
_____
_____

Chapter 11

11:1) It came to pass one day as He was praying alone in a certain place that His disciples came to Him and asked, "Lord, teach us to pray as Yochanan also taught his disciples." 11:2) With that, He taught them, "This is the way you should pray. Say, 'Father, may Your name be celebrated as holy. Continue establishing Your kingdom. 11:3) Give us every day our daily bread. 11:4) Forgive us our sins because we ourselves also forgive all who wronged us. Lead us not into temptation [[but deliver us from evil]].'"

- This prayer sums up the teachings of Yeshua and expresses the desire that the disciples should feel for the action of God in establishing His kingdom, their dependence on Him as Father for their daily needs, their relationship of reconciliation with Him and with other humans, and their need for Him to preserve and protect them (Marshall, 1978).

- Luke's version of the prayer is shorter than in Mattityahu's (Matthew's) Gospel, but they contain the same topics (Stern, 1992).

- This prayer is very similar to other Jewish prayers that Yeshua's disciples would have already been very familiar (Cultural Backgrounds Study Bible, 2016).

- To address God as Father emphasizes that humanity is His creation, and people are His children. The Jewish concept of a father was one of love and provision.

- May the name of the Lord be sanctified – made holy. The name of the Lord can be made holy or profane by how His followers live. One sanctifies God by living a holy life (Young, 2001, p.8).

- May God continue to establish His kingdom- submitting to His will in one's life. Doing the will of God is participating in His kingdom (Young, 2001, pp. 18-19).

- Daily bread reminds the disciples of manna in the desert during the Exodus. Bread represents every need being met.

- One of the most important aspects of Yeshua's teachings is forgiveness. Here He emphasizes the absolute importance of people forgiving one another.

- The plea is to be led away from temptation which can result from a person's evil impulses (Young, 2001, p. 34).

Forgiveness

Stories from the book of Genesis and throughout the Hebrew Bible (Henrich, 2007) reveal the forgiving character of God. God's plans for His followers include that they have knowledge of and exercise forgiveness toward all people (Hart, 2005).

- The Jews understood that God is a God of justice and mercy (Flusser, 2001).

- "In early Jewish thought, the concept of B'tzelem Elohim (humanity is made in God's image) demanded that genuine mercy be granted each person to another in the same way that God himself gives grace to the sinner" (Young, 1998, p. 124). Every individual must seek to understand and imitate God's ways (Young, 1998, p. 125).

Forgiveness Continued

- God's followers are "to behave with compassion toward the wicked as well as the good, and they are not to distinguish between people. Out of this Jewish view emerged an idea of love and forgiveness toward those who have caused your personal injury" (Flusser, 2009, p. 158).

- God's mercy is an overflow of His love. And, because God is a God of justice, He demands that people forgive one another.

- "Mercy from above depended upon showing mercy to those below" (Young, 1998, p. 124).

- Forgiveness means letting go of negative thoughts, behaviors, and emotions toward the transgressor (Henrich, 2007, p. 34).

- Forgiveness begins with a decision to forgive. It is a process and involves a change in behavior. However, one must see forgiveness "within the context of justice" (Worthington, 2006, p. 40).

- Forgiveness does NOT mean pardoning, condoning (justifying the transgression), or excusing (McCullough, 2001, p. 194).

- Seeking justice is important.

- Forgiveness does NOT always mean reconciliation in relationships. Sometimes reconciliation is not possible, advisable, or safe for people (Worthington, 2006).

- Forgiveness always remembers the importance of the preservation of life.

- Yeshua teaches His disciples what to pray, and then He teaches them how to pray – or the attitude of prayer – by telling them a parable.

- One of the biggest obstacles that a person faces when they pray is their concept of the character of God.

- Yeshua tells this parable to illustrate the divine character of a good God as compared to a bad friend (Young, 1998).

11:5) He said to them, "Who among you who has a friend who comes to him at midnight and says to him, 'Friend, lend me three loaves. 11:6) I need your help, because my friend on a journey has dropped by to visit me and I have nothing to set before him to eat.' 11:7) Then from within, he will answer his request saying, 'Do not bother me! The door is already shut. My children are with me in bed. I will not get up to give you anything.' 11:8) I tell you, although he will not get up and give him anything because he is his friend, yet, because of his shameless chutzpah, he will get out of bed and give him anything he needs!

11:9) "I say unto you, ask and [God] will give to you. Seek and [God] will cause you to find. Knock and [God] will open doors for you. 11:10) Everyone who asks receives. The one who seeks finds. The one who knocks will have [God] open doors.

11:11) Who among you who is a father, when his son asks him for a fish, will instead of a fish give him a snake? 11:12) If he asks for an egg, will give to him a scorpion? 11:13) In spite of being evil, you know how to give good gifts to your children—how much more will your heavenly Father give the Holy Spirit to those who ask Him.

- Yeshua begins His parable in verse 5, getting the attention of His audience by asking them a question. The setting is one with which His listeners would be completely familiar – that of village life.
- In the small villages all around Galil, houses were packed closely together. Big families lived in small houses, and everybody knew each other. If the village were large enough, it had a synagogue in the middle of town.
- Hospitality was extremely important in first century Judaism. An entire village would help provide for an unexpected guest (Young, 1998).
- At midnight, the entire village would be deathly quiet. Parents and children would be sleeping together in their small homes. Everyone would be able to hear the slightest commotion.
- As Yeshua tells His story, His audience would be anticipating a turn of events.
- For the man in the house to refuse his friend's call for help would be unheard-of. "What true friend could refuse in such a contemptible way to help his neighbor?" (p. 45)
- The beginning of the story seems quite plausible. The opening question grabs the attention of the audience. The neighbors are friends. The need is urgent. The visitor is the guest of a friend, and because of the importance of hospitality in the culture, the friend is really the guest of the entire village. However, the man in the home refuses to help.
- Yeshua's audience is surprised by the man's response. Everyone listening to the story knows that the children would be awake after all this commotion. The entire village would be awake at this point. When the man in the house refuses to help, he breaks "every rule of accepted etiquette." Yeshua's listeners would be outraged (p. 48).
- The man outside will respond by banging on the door and shouting until his contemptible friend opens up. In the end, he will get everything he needs. The reason the homeowner opens the door, however, is not friendship but persistence – chutzpah. The story is very humorous to Yeshua's listeners (Young, 1998, p. 48).
- In verse 8, the term, "chutzpah," means "raw nerve, strong-willed determination, unrelenting resolve, or persistence." The Greek term behind this text literally means "shamelessness" (Young, 2019).

- In the same way, it is impossible to imagine a father who would give his son a snake when he asked for some fish to eat (p. 45).

- True faith is related to chutzpah.

- Yeshua is teaching His disciples to pray with expectant and persistent faith, understanding the character of a loving Father.

- God is a good friend who is full of compassion and mercy who is righteous and conscientious. He is absolutely opposite of the friend in verse 7, and the father in verse 11 (Young, 1998, p. 42).

The houses and synagogue in Kefar Nachum from the time Yeshua were built using black basalt rock. This type of rock is plentiful in the area around Galil. Basalt rock is formed by volcanic activity, and the kind found around Kefar Nachum is the most common volcanic rock on earth.

Illustration: Kefar Nachum by Debbie Willey

11:14) On one occasion He was forcing out a demon who prevented a man from being able to talk. When the demon was forced out, the man could speak. 11:15) But some of them claimed, "He is able to force out demons because He is in league with Baal Zevul, the leader of demons." 11:16) Others examined Him by asking for a sign from heaven. 11:17) But He, aware of their thoughts, said to them, "Every kingdom which fights against itself goes to ruin, and a home which is divided will break apart. 11:18) If Satan is divided against himself, how will his kingdom stand? But you claim that I force out demons because I am in league with Baal Zevul. 11:19) If I force out demons by Baal Zevul, then by whose help do your disciples expel demons? So let them be your judges! 11:20) But if I myself force out demons by the finger of God, then the kingdom of God has already overtaken you. 11:21) When an armed strong man guards over his own place, his belongings are safe. 11:22) But when someone even stronger than he attacks and overpowers him, he will take his weapons in which he had trusted and divide his spoil (Isa 53:12). 11:23) Whoever is not with Me is against Me, and whoever does not gather with Me scatters.

11:24) "When an unclean spirit leaves a person, he travels through dry lands seeking a place of rest. After finding no [relief], he says, 'I will return to my house from where I left.' 11:25) When he comes, he finds it swept and put in order. 11:26) So then he goes and takes seven other spirits more evil than himself. They enter and live there. It shall be that the final state of that person is far worse than before."

- In verse 20, the understanding is that "the Kingdom of God has taken charge of this situation. God has broken through from the infinite to the here and now." He is ruling. His power is at work (Lindsey, 2017, p. 149-50).
- Disease is of the devil, and the kingdom of God comes when Satan is conquered and rendered powerless (Flusser, 2001, p. 49).
- According to Luke 10:18, Yeshua once said, "I saw Satan fall like lightning from heaven." According to a book, The Assumption of Moses, which was written when Yeshua was a child, "Then will his kingdom over all creation appear, Satan will be destroyed and grief will depart with him." The coming of the kingdom is thus bound up with the overthrow of Satan and his spirits. When Yeshua heals the sick and casts out unclean spirits, He is the victorious conqueror who makes real the kingdom of God (Flusser, 2001, p. 50).
- A person must first bind a strong man before his goods can be plundered. This means that Yeshua is "plundering" Satan by releasing the man from the control of demons. The goods of the strong man are safe until someone stronger comes along. The stronger man represents God.
- In verse 23, Yeshua is saying that it is impossible to be neutral. One must pick a side. A person who does not help to gather the flock together is helping to scatter the flock (Marshall, 1978).

11:27) As He said these things, a woman in the crowd raised her voice and said to Him, "Blessed is the womb that carried You and the breasts that nursed You." 11:28) But He replied, "Blessed rather are those who hear the word of God and practice it."

11:29) As the crowds of people were increasing, He began to say, "This generation is an evil generation. It seeks a sign, but no sign will be given to it except the sign of Yonah. 11:30) Certainly, just as Yonah became a sign for the people of Nineveh, so will the Son of Man be a sign to this generation. 11:31) The queen of the south will rise up in judgment against the people of this generation and condemn them. After all, she came from the ends of the earth to hear the wisdom of Shelomo. Take notice! One greater than Shelomo is here. 11:32) The people of Nineveh will arise in judgment against the people of this generation and condemn them. After all, they repented when they heard the preaching of Yonah. Take notice! One greater than Yonah is here.

11:33) "No one lights a lamp and places it in storage or under a bushel basket, but rather on a lamp stand, so that everyone who enters will see by the light. 11:34) Your eye is the light of your body. If your eye is good [showing generosity], then your whole body will be full of light. When your eye is bad [uncovering a stingy temperament], your body is full of darkness. 11:35) Make certain that the light in you does not become darkness. 11:36) So if your whole body is full of light, without any part of darkness, it will be wholly bright, as when a lamp illuminates you with rays of light."

- In verse 34, the good eye was a Hebrew expression of the time which referred to generosity (compare Proverbs 22:9). The bad or evil eye described an individual with a stingy temperament (Deut. 15:7-9; Prov. 23:6; Matt. 20:15) (Young, 2019).

11:37) When He finished speaking, a spiritual leader invited Him over for dinner. 11:38) The spiritual leader noticed with surprise that He did not ceremonially wash before the meal. 11:39) But the Lord said to him, "You spiritual leaders purify the outside of the cup and the plate, but the inside of you is full of greed and wickedness. 11:40) Fools! Did not the One who made the outside also make the inside? 11:41) Give benevolence from what is yours, then see how pure everything will be for you. 11:42) Severe retribution looms over you, you spiritual leaders! You pay tithes on mint and rue and every garden herb, but neglect justice and the love of God. These you ought to have done without neglecting the other matters. 11:43) Severe retribution looms over you, you spiritual leaders! You love the front seats in the learning centers and greetings of honor in the open markets. 11:44) Pay the strictest attention for yourselves! You are like graves which are not seen. People walk over them without knowing it." 11:45) One of the disciples of Torah replied to him, "Rabbi, when You say this, You insult us too." 11:46) But He said, "Severe retribution looms over you, you disciples of Torah, because you weight down people with heavy burdens difficult to carry while you yourselves will not touch the loads with one of your fingers. 11:47) Pay the strictest attention for yourselves! You build tomb monuments to honor the prophets whom your ancestors murdered.

11:48) "Consequently, you testify that you support the actions of your ancestors. They murdered them and you build [their tomb monuments.] 11:49) For this reason, moreover, the wisdom of God teaches, 'I will send to them prophets and emissaries. Some of them they will murder and others they will persecute, 11:50) in order that this generation will be held responsible for the blood of all the prophets which has been spilled since the beginning of the world. 11:51) From the blood of Hevel to the blood of Zecharyah, who was murdered between the altar and the Temple—yes, I tell you this generation will be held responsible. 11:52) Pay the strictest attention for yourselves, you disciples of Torah! For you have taken away the key of knowledge. You did not enter in yourselves and you hindered those who were entering."

11:53) As He started to leave, the scribes and spiritual leaders began to hold on closely [to His teachings] and to question Him precisely on many subjects, 11:54) earnestly desiring to find out what He would say.

- Yeshua is attacking the kind of religiousness that is concerned with outward purity, but ignores inward greed and covetousness. If the spiritual leaders would only learn to free themselves from inward greed and covetousness by practicing charity (giving money or food to the poor), the outward purity would take care of itself.
- The spiritual leaders were concerned with unimportant man-made rules and were ignoring the justice and love of God (Marshall, 1978).
- The spiritual leaders had interpreted the written Torah and added their own rules (Stern, 1992).
- They were filled with pride and self-importance (inward sins) as religious teachers. They were misleading the people who were not aware of their inner unfitness (Marshall, 1978).
- In verse 43, the front seats may be referring to the seat of honor in the synagogue. See Moses' Seat in Lesson 12.
- If a person had visited the marketplace and touched an item that was ceremonially impure, the only way to remove the impurity was to wash. In this context, hand washing before a meal has nothing to do with hygiene. It has everything to do with ceremonial purity.
- Yeshua does not condemn the tradition, He only objects to their practices that put human tradition above God's command.
- Purity is not ritual, it is spiritual (Stern, 1992).
- The ritual of only washing the outside of a man is as foolish as only washing the outside of a dirty cup. The vessel might be full of unclean things – clean on the outside, but inside full of covetousness and greed. The inside is as important as the outside.
- Yeshua is saying to give alms (charities) from the heart.
- The Old Testament law required the payment of tithes from garden produce. Tithes on mint and rue were not required. Such meticulous legalism stands in contrast to their neglect of justice and righteousness. They did all of that but were indifferent to the rights of the poor and to the love demanded by God (Marshall, 1978).

- Contact with tombs produced uncleanness, but people would walk over them without realizing it. Tombs would be whitewashed so people would know not to walk over them and be defiled. However, Yeshua stresses the incidental beautifying effect of the whitewash.
- What looks alright on the outside is evil (unclean) on the inside. Inside they were corrupt (Marshall, 1978).
- Your fathers killed the prophets, and you make sure they stay dead. They are boasting that they honor the prophets, and they are better than their fathers, but they are not really repenting and honoring the words of the prophets. Hevel (Abel) was the first martyr and Zecharyah was the last Old Testament prophet (Marshall, 1978).

Questions for review and discussion

What did you learn about the prayer that Yeshua taught His disciples?

Why is this prayer important?

What does the Torah theologian/scholar ask Yeshua?

What did you learn about forgiveness?

Why is forgiveness important?

What did you learn about the character of God in the parable of the friend at midnight?

What did you learn about prayer in this parable and why is this important?

How do you apply this to your life?

How do you apply this to the way you pray?

What is chutzpah?

What is Yeshua talking about when He visits the spiritual leader's house?

Summarize the study notes from this chapter and discuss:

Summarize in one or two sentences the most important or the most interesting thing you learned in this chapter from your study:

What makes it important or interesting to you

Choni the Circle Drawer

The first century historian Josephus mentions Choni the Circle Drawer as a man with a strong personality who left a lasting legacy in Jewish history. Choni was a humble and deeply devout man of God who lived a holy life of obedience. He had a radical approach to prayer and exhibited a lot of chutzpah when he prayed his famous prayer for rain. "God hears the prayers of this righteous man. In many ways, it is his life that is answered rather than his prayer" (Young, 1998, p. 62).

Discover more about Choni. Who was he? When did he live? What did he pray? How was it answered? Research online. Write and discuss what you discovered about Choni and his life:

___

Yom Kippur

Yom Kippur is the "Day of Atonement." It is observed in the fall at the end of the "Ten Days of Awe." It is considered the holiest day of the year. The day is spent in the synagogue fasting and praying in repentance of sins. At the end of the day, God seals the Books of Life and Death for the year. Research more about Yom Kippur and the Ten Days of Awe. (Use sources like Chabad.org or myjewishlearning.com) Write and discuss what you learned:

___

Re-read Luke Chapter 11 from the *Hebrew Heritage Bible* translation used in this book. Discuss. Summarize Luke Chapter 11 in one paragraph and discuss:

_____
_____
_____
_____
_____
_____
_____
_____
_____
_____

Choose one verse from Luke Chapter 11 that you think is the most important and write it here. Discuss why you think it is the most important verse:

_____
_____

How did your understanding of Luke Chapter 11 change after you studied it and read it again? Discuss.

_____
_____
_____
_____
_____

How can you apply what you learned from Luke Chapter 11 to your life? Discuss.

_____
_____
_____
_____

What question or questions do you still have about Luke Chapter 11 that you don't understand or want to know more about? Discuss

_____
_____
_____
_____

For more thought and discussion

How often do you pray? When do you pray?

What do you usually pray about?

What is prayer like in the church you attend? (Do you recite prayers led by the pastor or elders? Are the prayers part of a liturgy? Does your church have a "prayer team" or take prayer requests?) Discuss these aspects of prayer as you experience them where you attend church.

How do you feel when you pray at church or at school?

How has your understanding about prayer changed after studying this chapter?

THE GOSPEL OF LUKE CHAPTER TWELVE

Lesson 14

Before you begin your study, read Luke Chapter 12 out loud (as a group) from your Bible.

In your own words, summarize Luke Chapter 12 in one paragraph and write at least two questions that you had about the chapter as you read the biblical text: (Discuss)

_____
_____
_____
_____
_____
_____
_____
_____
_____
_____
_____
_____
_____
_____

In Luke Chapter 12, Yeshua is continuing to teach. At the beginning of the chapter He is addressing His disciples while they are surrounded by a crowd of thousands of people. The number of people who have heard about Yeshua has increased dramatically. He is encouraging His disciples to remain faithful and not to be hypocrites. They are to confess fearlessly the good news of the Kingdom of God. Yeshua continues to teach on the theme of inward purity and wholehearted commitment to God.

📍 Yeshua encourages His followers to continue to follow faithfully and proclaim the Kingdom of God even when they are persecuted. Tradition and history tell the rest of the stories of many of Yeshua's Twelve disciples. Research online and discover more about their stories. What happened to them? Write and discuss. Whom did you research and what did you discover?

_____
_____
_____
_____

📍 What about another martyr who died for their faith? Tell his or her story:

_____
_____
_____
_____

Chapter 12

12:1) Meanwhile, as many groups of people gathered together, making crowds so that they were stepping all over one another, Yeshua began to teach His disciples first, "Be cautious of the leaven of the spiritual leaders, which is hypocrisy. 12:2) There is nothing unknown which will not be revealed and hidden which will not be made known. 12:3) What you have spoken in the night will be heard in the daylight, and what you have whispered in the private rooms will be proclaimed from the housetops. 12:4) I say to you, my friends, do not fear the ones who kill the body, but after that, can do nothing more to you. 12:5) I will show you the One whom you should fear; fear Him who possesses the authority to cast [you] into hell after He has killed [you]. Yes, I tell you this is the One whom you must fear! 12:6) Do not sparrows sell five for two cents? Yet not one of them is forgotten in the presence of God. 12:7) Even the hairs of your head have been counted [by God]. Indeed, you are of inestimable value, exceeding beyond all the sparrows! 12:8) I tell you that everyone who owns Me before others, the Son of Man will claim before the angels of God. 12:9) But whoever disowns Me before others, I will deny before the angels of God. 12:10) Everyone who speaks a word against another person will be forgiven, but everyone who blasphemes the Holy Spirit will not be forgiven. 12:11) When they bring you into the meeting places, before rulers and those in authority, do not be stressed out over how to defend yourselves or what you should say, 12:12) because the Holy Spirit will teach you in that very moment how you must respond."

- In verse 10, the words, "another person," represent the Semitism, "son of man," which in this context is best understood as a reference to every human being. In other contexts in the Gospels, it is a reference to the messianic title, "Son of Man," which developed in part from Daniel 7:13 (Young, 2019).
- The crowd size is identified as many thousands, but Yeshua is speaking to His disciples first – His closest followers – not everybody (Marshall, 1978).
- He is warning His disciples against the "leaven" (here it means "sin" – Hebrew *chametz*) or hypocrisy of the spiritual leaders (Stern, 1992). Hypocrisy is defined as being outwardly correct but inwardly corrupt. It is the opposite of honesty and sincerity.
- These statements summarize the previous section (in Chapter 11) that are directed against the spiritual leaders' greed and covetousness.
- Hypocrisy is ultimately futile, for the secret thoughts of a person will eventually be revealed (Marshall, 1978).
- The disciples might be tempted to conceal their real allegiance to Yeshua before people, but they should not fear what people might do to them. They should fear God.
- They can depend on God to take care of them when they are persecuted.
- When the disciples face persecution and are tempted to give up their commitment, they should not be afraid because the Holy Spirit will direct them and help them.
- Yeshua told His opponents that speaking against Him is forgivable, but He warned them that denial of the work of the Holy Spirit was unforgivable (Marshall, 1978).
- Blaspheme means slander, defamation, reviling judgment, or irreverent speech (Stern, 1992, p. 124).
- Only when a person understands the Gospel in their mind and heart and spirit, yet still rejects it, are they blaspheming the Holy Spirit and risking eternal punishment (Stern, 1992, p. 125).

12:13) One of the people in the crowds said to Him, "Rabbi, tell my brother to divide the inheritance with me." 12:14) But He said to him, "Dear man, who appointed Me to be a judge or arbiter for you?" 12:15) He said to them, "Take caution and guard against all greed, because an individual's life is not found in the abundance of possessions." 12:16) He told them a parable saying, "It should be compared to the wealthy man whose land brought forth an abundant harvest. 12:17) He began to reason with himself saying, 'What shall I do? I do not have room to store my crops.' 12:18) He said, 'This is what I shall do. I will tear down my barns and build larger ones. There I will store the abundance of all my grain and my goods. 12:19) Then I will say to my soul, "Soul, you have an abundance of goods laid up for yourself for many years. Take life easy, eat, drink, and enjoy yourself."

12:20) But God said to him, 'You fool! This very night your soul will be taken from you. What then will happen to the goods you have stored up?' 12:21) This is what happens to the one who stores up treasures for himself but is not rich in God."

- Yeshua was initially speaking to His disciples, but now the crowd is involved in the discussion.
- Yeshua has just come from the religious leader's house and has been speaking against covetousness (the desire for someone else's possessions) and greed (Marshall, 1978).
- In verse 13, the man is interrupting Yeshua's teaching with his question.
- The man calls on Yeshua as a Rabbi to intervene in a dispute, but Yeshua refuses to intervene because He is opposed to the underlying covetousness of the question.
- A disciple has a true sense of values and recognizes that real life is not measured by possessions.
- Attachment to wealth can make a person unfit for the day of judgement. By hoarding earthly wealth, people can become poor in things that ultimately matter.
- The man who is not rich in regard to God is indeed poor – no matter how big his bank account.
- He is a fool – a Godless and senseless man.
- He has prepared for his own comfort but has not prepared for his ultimate destiny (Marshall, 1978).

12:22) He said unto His disciples, "Therefore I tell you, do not have anxiety about your life, what you shall eat or about your body, what you shall wear. 12:23) Life is more than food and the body more than clothes. 12:24) Learn from the ravens, for they neither sow nor reap. They do not possess a storeroom or a barn, but God feeds them. How much more value are you than birds! 12:25) Who among you is able to add a cubit of height to his stature by worry? 12:26) Since you are not able to change the least little thing [with worry], why do you have anxiety about so much? 12:27) Contemplate the lilies how they grow. They do not work or spin, but even so, I tell you, Shelomo in all his grandeur was not so finely clothed as one of these. 12:28) But if God so clothes the grass in the field which is alive today and thrown into the furnace tomorrow, how much more will God clothe you! O people of little faith! 12:29) Do not seek what you shall eat or what you shall drink. Do not keep worrying! 12:30) These things the nations of the world eagerly seek after, but your Father knows what you need. 12:31) But seek first His kingdom and all these things will be given to you. 12:32) Do not fear, little flock, for it is your Father's good pleasure to give unto you the kingdom. 12:33) Sell your possessions and give charity. Make for yourselves wallets which do not wear out, with an inexhaustible treasure in heaven, which a thief cannot steal and a moth does not destroy. 12:34) Where your treasure is, there will your heart be as well.

- Yeshua warns the listeners that at any time a crisis might come. They are to live their lives in an appropriate fashion and be ready. They are not to be taken by surprise.

- Yeshua addresses the man's question and returns to His previous theme in verse 22, about God's provision for His followers.

- Yeshua uses the crowd's greed (for wealth and material gain) to introduce more teachings for His disciples about:
  - Trusting in God
  - Freedom from greed for material possessions (Marshall, 1978)

- Judaism taught that money should be used to alleviate human need.

- Genuine religious piety must be characterized by contributions to those less fortunate (Young, 1998).

Tzedakah

In Judaism, tzedakah is charitable giving, justice or righteousness. All are related to each another. A person of faith should be characterized by charity and good deeds. Tzedakah must be performed regardless of your financial standing. "Acquire for yourselves this world and the world to come by your mammon [that is, give to the needy and you will acquire both this world and the world to come]" (Young, 1998).

Do more research online about tzedakah and how it is such an important part of the Jewish faith. What is a tzedakah box? A good place to start is Chabad.org or Aish.com. What did you discover? Write and discuss:

_____
_____
_____
_____
_____

(For a cool art project – make your own tzedakah box.)

12:35) "Let your belts be fastened [ready for action] and your lamps be burning; 12:36) be like people who are waiting for their master to come home from the marriage feast so that when he comes and knocks, they will be ready to open up for him immediately. 12:37) Blessed are those servants whom when the Lord comes, He will find them anticipating [His return]. Truly I say unto you, He will fasten his belt and have them recline at the table. He will serve them. 12:38) Whether He returns in the second watch, or should come in the third watch, but should still find them on alert, blessed are those servants! 12:39) Know this, that if the householder had known at what time the thief would break in, he would not leave his house unguarded. 12:40) You yourselves must be on alert, therefore, so that the Son of Man will not come at a time when you are not expecting Him."

12:41) Kefa said, "Lord, are you telling this parable for us or for everybody?" 12:42) At that, the Lord said, "Who then is the faithful and wise steward, whom his master will give authority over his household, to give them their ration of food at the proper time? 12:43) Blessed is that servant whom the Lord will find doing this when He comes. 12:44) Truly I tell you, He will give him authority over all his possessions. 12:45) But if that servant will say in his heart, 'My master is delayed in coming,' and begins to beat the male and female servants; to eat and to drink; and to get drunk: 12:46) the master of that servant will come on a day when he does not expect him, and at an hour he does not know, and will cut him in pieces, and assign him a place with the unbelievers. 12:47) That servant, moreover, who knew the will of his master but did not prepare and do his will, shall be beaten with many lashes. 12:48) Furthermore the one who did not know [his master's will] but did what deserves a beating will receive only a few lashes. The one who has been given much, from this one much will be required in return. To the one who has been entrusted with plenty, from this person all the more will be expected.

- Here Yeshua's theme switches from telling His disciples not to be anxious about worldly possessions to that of being spiritually prepared for the coming of the Son of Man.
- Let your belts "be fastened" means that Yeshua's disciples are to be ready always. When someone was at home relaxing, he or she would wear garments loosely around their waist. To tie them up was a sign of readiness. Their lamps were to "be burning" means that the disciples are to be ready for activity during a period of darkness. They must remain awake and aware (Marshall, 1978).
- The Son of Man will come suddenly (Lindsey, 2017), and this will have serious effects for those who are not ready (Marshall, 1978).
- For the leaders, there will be more reward and authority if they are faithful, but they risk greater judgment if they are not.
- They are to anticipate His return by remaining alert and awake – ready for action – not weary, lazy, or participating in self-indulgence.
- The imagery is of the present world being a place of darkness in which one is tempted to sleep.
- The master will fasten his belt and serve them at the Messianic banquet (Marshall, 1978).

- The Jewish understanding is that the three watches represent the interval before His Second Coming.
- The tone transitions from encouragement, to faithful service, to promise of reward, to a warning for those who are not ready. Those who are not ready will be separated from the faithful and punished most severely (Marshall, 1978).

12:49) "I have come to hurl fire upon the earth; yet how I do not wish to see it already start to burn! 12:50) But I have an immersion of judgment to administer, and how distressed I am until it is finished! 12:51) Do you suppose that I came to give shalom [to everyone] upon the earth? I tell you no, but rather division. 12:52) From now on five members in one household will be divided, three against two, and two against three. 12:53) They will be divided, father against son, and son against father; mother against daughter, and daughter against mother; mother-in-law against daughter-in-law, and daughter-in-law against mother-in-law" (Mic 7:6).

12:54) He said to the multitudes, "When you see a cloud rise in the west, you are quick to say, 'Rain is coming!' And come it does. 12:55) When the south wind blows, you say, 'It will be scorching hot!' And so it is. 12:56) You pretenders! You know how to read the face of the earth and the sky, but why do you not know how to discern the present time?

12:57) "Why not judge for yourselves what is just? 12:58) While you are going with your adversary to appear before the magistrate, there make every effort to settle with him on the way, before he has the chance to take you before the judge who will hand you over to the officer, and the officer will throw you into prison. 12:59) I tell you that you will not get out of there until you have paid the last penny."

- These events do not lead to peace, but they lead to division.
- To the crowds, this is a warning to join the ranks of the faithful before it is too late.
- The crowds are being reprimanded because of their unwillingness to discern (understand) the meaning of the present time.
- God demands a decision.
- The time of salvation is now. If one is smart enough to discern the signs of the weather, they should be smart enough to discern the signs of God.
- Be ready (Marshall, 1978).

Questions for review and discussion

Describe the size of the crowd at the beginning of this lesson:

Where had Yeshua been in the previous chapter?

What was He teaching at the end of the previous chapter?

How did it connect to the beginning of this chapter?

At the beginning of this chapter was Yeshua teaching His disciples or the entire crowd?

What did the man want to know?

How did Yeshua answer him?

What would you say is the theme of this chapter?

Summarize the study notes from this chapter and discuss:

Summarize in one or two sentences the most important or the most interesting thing you learned in this chapter from your study:

_____
_____
_____
_____

Re-read Luke Chapter 12 from the *Hebrew Heritage Bible* translation used in this book. Discuss. Summarize Luke Chapter 12 in one paragraph and discuss:

_____
_____
_____
_____
_____
_____
_____
_____
_____
_____
_____

Choose one verse from Luke Chapter 12 that you think is the most important and write it here. Discuss why you think it is the most important verse:

_____
_____
_____
_____

How did your understanding of Luke Chapter 12 change after you studied it and read it again? Discuss.

_____
_____
_____
_____
_____

How can you apply what you learned from Luke Chapter 12 to your life? Discuss.

What question or questions do you still have about Luke Chapter 12 that you don't understand or want to know more about? Discuss

THE GOSPEL OF LUKE CHAPTER THIRTEEN

Lesson 15

Before you begin your study, read Luke Chapter 13 out loud (as a group) from your Bible.

In your own words, summarize Luke Chapter 13 in one paragraph and write at least two questions that you had about the chapter as you read the biblical text: (Discuss)

_____
_____
_____
_____
_____
_____
_____
_____
_____
_____
_____
_____
_____

Luke Chapter 13 begins with Yeshua in Galil. He receives a report of a tragedy in Yerushalayim. Some people from Galil have been murdered by Pontius Pilate. Another eighteen people died when the Tower of Siloam fell on them. Yeshua addresses the concerns of His audience and warns them to repent. He tells them a parable about God's mercy. He heals a woman on the Sabbath and continues to teach about the Kingdom of God as He travels. Yeshua grieves over Yerushalayim.

The tragic events reported to Yeshua at the beginning of this chapter happened in Yerushalayim. The catalyst for the first event was related to construction of an aqueduct. Research online about the ancient aqueducts in Israel (especially in Caesarea and Jerusalem). What did you learn? Write and discuss.

_____
_____
_____
_____
_____
_____

An exciting excavation is happening right now at the Pool of Shiloach (Siloam) in Yerushalayim (Jerusalem). Research online about the history of the Pool of Siloam and what archaeologists have discovered there. Write and discuss:

_____
_____
_____
_____
_____
_____
_____

Hebrew Names and their English Equivalents

Hebrew	English
Shiloach	Siloam
Avraham	Abraham
seah	unit of measurement *(three seah measures = 60 pounds*

Chapter 13

13:1) On that same occasion, there were some [people] present who reported to Him about the people of Galil, whose blood Pilate had mixed together with their sacrifices. 13:2) He answered and said to them, "Do you suppose that these people of Galil were greater sinners than all others from the Galil because they died like that? 13:3) I tell you, no! Unless you repent, all of you may die in a similar way. 13:4) Or what about those eighteen people upon whom the Tower of Shiloach fell and killed them—do you suppose that they were worse wrongdoers than everyone else who lives in Yerushalayim? 13:5) I tell you, no! Unless you repent, all of you may die in a similar way." 13:6) He told them this parable saying, "[The matter may be compared] to a fig tree which a certain man planted in his vineyard. He came seeking fruit from it but did not find any. 13:7) He said to the keeper of the vineyard, 'Look, for three years I have come seeking fruit from this fig tree but I do not find any; cut it down already! Why should it use up ground space?' 13:8) But he answered and said to him, 'Lord, let it go for this year as well so that I may dig around it and fertilize it with manure. 13:9) If it produces fruit next year fine, but if not, then you cut it down.'"

- In verse 2, the word "died" is taken from the Greek word "suffered." In Hebrew, the verb suffer usually refers to death. Pilate killed these men of Galilee by mixing their blood with their sacrifices in the holy Temple of God, during the time that they were making their pilgrimage to Jerusalem (Young, 2019).

- This event is not mentioned anywhere else in the Scriptures. It is probably referring to the occasion when Pontius Pilate massacred a crowd of people in Yerushalayim because they protested against his use of Temple funds to build an aqueduct.

- Nothing from the Tower of Shiloach has been excavated, but it would have been located near the Pool of Shiloach (Siloam) (*ESV Archaeology Study Bible*, 2017).

The Pool of Shiloach is located south of the Temple Mount in Yerushalayim. Water still flows into this pool from the Gihon Spring. Spring fed water is considered "living water" and is ritually pure in Judaism (*ESV Archaeology Bible*, 2017).

GOSPEL OF LUKE

- Having people killed when they were offering sacrifices in the Temple fits Pilate's reputation (*Archaeological Study Bible*, 2005).
- This event may have happened during Passover, and there probably was no literal mixing of blood, but the events occurred at the same time.
- The people from Galil were notorious rebels.
- Pilate built an aqueduct to improve the water supply, and the collapse of the tower was related to that project.
- The point is that people who suffer like those mentioned here are not worse sinners than anybody else. They are not being punished for their sins by these events (Marshall, 1978).
- In ancient times, it was often assumed that something bad happened only to people who were extremely sinful (*Archaeological Study Bible*, 2005).
- What is important is the fact that all sinners face the judgement of God unless they repent (Marshall, 1978).
- Fig, palm and olive trees were extremely valuable (Edersheim, 1993) and were often planted in vineyards (Marshall, 1978).
- It typically took 4-5 years before a fig tree would produce fruit. If a tree did not bear fruit, it would be uprooted or cut down to make room for other plants to grow (*Cultural Backgrounds Study Bible*, 2016).
- Fig trees produce a lot of fruit: They are harvested three times a year. Fig trees produce so much fruit that they are excluded from the commandment to leave the corners of the fields for the poor (Edersheim, 1993).
- To dig around the tree and fertilize was an effort to help the plant as much as possible to produce.
- "Between the tree and the axe nothing intervenes but the intercession of the gardener, who would make one last effort" (Edersheim, 1993).
- Yeshua tells this parable to illustrate that the day of grace will come to an end despite the intercession of the vinedresser (gardener), which could only offer a limited postponement of judgement (Marshall, 1978).

13:10) Now He was teaching in one of the learning centers on Shabbat. 13:11) Look, there was a woman suffering with sickness caused by a spirit for eighteen years. She was bent over and could not straighten herself up. 13:12) So when Yeshua saw her, He called her over and said to her, "Woman you are free from your sickness." 13:13) He laid His hands upon her, and immediately she stood up straight. She glorified God. 13:14) But the presiding rabbi of the learning center spoke up with his concerns because Yeshua healed on Shabbat. He said to the congregation, "Are there not six days in which you may work? You should come to be healed on one of them but not on the day of Shabbat." 13:15) But the Lord answered him and said, "Pretenders! On the day of Shabbat, each one of you will untie your ox or donkey from the stall and lead him to water. 13:16) This woman is a daughter of Avraham whom Satan has bound for eighteen years. Is it not proper that she should be set free from this bond on the day of Shabbat?" 13:17) His words put to shame all who disagreed with Him. But everyone else in the crowd of people was rejoicing over all the wondrous deeds being done by Him.

People have been growing and harvesting figs in Yisrael for thousands of years.

Take a trip online to Yisrael and find out more about fig trees. What kind of fig trees grow in Israel? What do they look like? When do they produce their first fruit of the year? What does the fruit look like? How difficult is it to grow a fig tree? Write and discuss:

_____
_____
_____
_____

- What is permitted on Shabbat?
  - Healing to save a life
  - Healing of the seriously ill
- What is not permitted on Shabbat?
  - Healing of minor ailments
  - Making medicine by grinding because grinding is work (Stern, 1992).
- This healing shows the power of God to deliver His people from the power of Satan. She is being released from literal bondage as a medically diagnosed fusion of the spinal bones or scoliosis. She had been unable to raise herself or her head for eighteen years.
- The action of Yeshua is spontaneous and arises from His compassion for her (Marshall, 1978).
- Yeshua argues that doing good deeds is more important than observing an interpretation of the Shabbat rules. He strengthens His case with a kal v'chomer (how much more) argument. If it is permitted to untie an ox or a donkey and lead them to water (untying a knot is considered work on Shabbat) to release them from bondage, then how much more they should allow healing a person! (Stern, 1992)

13:18) Then He told [them a parable], "To what may the kingdom of God be compared? What illustration may I use to show you what it is like? 13:19) It resembles a mustard seed which a man took and planted in his garden. It grew up and became a tree. Finally even the birds of heaven were able to make nests in its branches." 13:20) He told another [parable], "What illustration may I use to show you what the kingdom of God is like? 13:21) It is like leaven which a woman took and hid away in three seah measures of flour until it was all leavened!"

- Whenever the sick are healed of illnesses, whenever possessed persons are liberated from demonic influences, whenever debts are cancelled by divine patience, whenever peace is made – the kingdom increases.
- As the community increases in number, the kingdom grows (Jerusalemperspective.com).
- In verse 18, Yeshua is still in the Jewish learning center (the synagogue) and is commenting on what just happened when He tells this parable. The healing of the woman – the defeat of Satan – is a sign of the advancing Kingdom of God.
- The imagery of the parable suggests the growth of the Kingdom of God from a tiny beginning to a world-wide movement.
- The emphasis is not on the growth itself. The emphasis is that what appears tiny and insignificant will prove to have been the beginning of a mighty kingdom (Marshall, 1978).
- The mustard seed was very common in the area of Galil. The tiny seed would grow into a yellow-flowering plant that was over six feet tall. Its seed was used for oil and medicine (ESV Archaeology Study Bible, 1017).
- Leaven in this story represents good – not evil.
- Leaven is old fermented dough that is added to new bread to start the fermentation process (and make it rise).
- The work of the leaven cannot be seen, but a small amount will spread through the whole batch (here it is enough to feed 160 people). The process of leavening takes place overnight and by morning the entire amount of dough has been affected. This represents the powerful influence of the Kingdom of God (Marshall, 1978).

13:22) He was passing through towns and villages, teaching along the way, and making His ascent up to Yerushalayim. 13:23) Someone said to Him, "Lord, are there really only a few who are being saved?" Then He said to them, 13:24) "Fight with all your might to enter in by the narrow door, for many, I tell you, will seek to enter and will not have the strength. 13:25) Once the master of the house rises up and locks the door [it will be too late to go in]. You will stand outside and knock on the door pleading with him, 'Lord, open up for us!' But he will answer and say to you, 'I do not even know where you are from.' 13:26) Then you will begin to say, 'But you must remember that we ate and drank with you, and you taught in our streets.' 13:27) He will say, 'I tell you, I do not know where you are from; go away from me all you workers of wrongdoing.' 13:28) At that place, there shall be crying and grinding of teeth, especially when you see Avraham, Yitzchak, Yaakov, and all the prophets within the kingdom of God, while you are being thrown out. 13:29) They shall come from the east, west, north, and south and recline at the table enjoying the kingdom of God. 13:30) See this, the last shall be first, and the first shall be last."

- The rule of God has dawned and this divinely willed movement will spread among the people of the earth where God's unconditional love for all becomes visible. The barriers between sinner and righteous are shattered.
- For Yeshua and the rabbis, the Kingdom of God is both present and future. Yeshua taught that the Kingdom of God began breaking out on the earth with Yochanan (John the Baptist) and the new age of salvation had already begun (Flusser, 2001).
- In verse 22, the question is from the crowd, not from one of Yeshua's disciples.
- As narrow and as difficult as it is, enter the door and make the decision to turn from evil.
- The picture is of the master who closes the door of his house once he knows that all the guests are present. The late-comers stand outside and yell. The master says, "I do not acknowledge you." Their claim is hollow. They have not had real fellowship. They had not responded to Yeshua's teachings. The rejection leads to weeping, sorrow and rage about the loss. The grinding of teeth represents the rage and the hatred shown by the enemies of the kingdom.
- The participants of the kingdom will come from the whole world and recline at the table. Reclining indicates that this is the heavenly banquet (Marshall, 1978).
- The period of opportunity for entry is limited and depends not just on hearing the message of Yeshua and having fellowship with Him, but above all it depends upon repentance (Marshall, 1978).
- In the kingdom of God, human dignity becomes null and void. The last become first and the first become last. The poor, the hungry, the meek, the mourners, and the persecuted inherit the kingdom. His message is His promise for the sinners who repent. The tax collectors and the harlots enter before those who are self-righteous (Flusser, 2001, p. 112).

13:31) At that same time, some of the Pharisees came to him to warn him, "Go away and leave this place, because Herod wants to kill you." 13:32) But he said to them, "Go and tell that [sly] fox, 'Look, I force out demons and perform cures, today and tomorrow, but on the third day I will finish.' 13:33) Nonetheless, I must keep moving on, today, tomorrow, and the next day, for it is unthinkable that a prophet should die outside of Yerushalayim. 13:34) O Yerushalayim, Yerushalayim, the city that kills the prophets and stones those sent to her! How often I wanted to gather your children together, just as a hen gathers her young chicks under her wings, but you would not have it! 13:35) Take notice of this, God's presence has left your house! I say to you, moreover, that you shall not see Me again until the time comes when you say, 'Blessed is He who comes in the name of the LORD'" (Ps 118:26).

- The Pharisees are helping Yeshua by warning him about Herod.
- They are telling Him to get out of Herod's territory because he wants to murder Yeshua. Did Herod think that Yeshua was Yochanan (John the Baptist) returning from the dead?
- Yeshua regarded Herod Antipas (Herod the Tetrarch) and his court as a kind of "animal farm."
- That "sly fox" comment is an insult toward Herod. It is used to indicate that Yeshua thinks Herod is insignificant.
- Unlike the lion, bear, or wolf, the fox is a second-tier predator. This is a jab at Herod's second-rate status under Rome. Herod is a "small fry" (Flusser, 2001).
- Yeshua laments (mourns, weeps) over Yerushalayim. He is speaking like the ancient wisdom literature from the TANAK (Old Testament).
- The children are the those who live in the city.
- The mother hen is protecting her babies. Under the wings of the Shekinah (Glory or divine Presence of God) Yeshua longs to protect the people of Yerushalayim.
- The abandonment of God's presence results in the city becoming prey to its enemies (Ezekiel 10:15-19) (Marshall, 1978).

Yisrael is home to some fascinating animals. Many of these animals are mentioned in the biblical text. For example, the eagle that is mentioned in Proverbs 30:18-19; Deuteronomy 32:11; and Exodus 19:4 is the Griffon vulture. It is a powerful bird of prey that is now an endangered species. The Gamla Nature Reserve in northern Israel is currently studying and monitoring its population in an effort to save the species from extinction.

 Take a trip online and learn more about the Griffon vulture. What does it look like? Where does it live? What happened to make it almost extinct? Where is the Gamla Nature Reserve? What are they doing to help the Griffon vulture? Write and discuss what you learned:

_____

_____

Another animal that is mentioned in the biblical text is the badger or coney. It is the Syrian rock hyrax. Mentioned in Leviticus 11:4-5; Proverbs 30:26; and Psalms 104:18, this little animal is found all over Yisrael and makes its home in the rocks.

 Take a trip online and discover more about the Syrian rock hyrax. What does it look like? Where does it live? What does it eat? Write and discuss what you learned:

_____

_____

The Nubian ibex is beautiful animal that lives in the deserts of Yisrael. They have lived at Ein Gedi in the Judean Desert for thousands of years. Ein Gedi means "spring of the goat", and the "goat" is a Nubian ibex. Ein Gedi is mentioned in 1 Samuel 23:29; 24:1-2 and Song of Solomon 1:14. The Nubian ibex is mentioned in Deuteronomy 14:4-6. Today, this endangered species still lives in the Ein Gedi Nature Reserve. It is the symbol of the Israel Nature and Parks Authority (Darom).

Take a trip online and discover more about the Nubian ibex and Ein Gedi. Write and discuss what you learned:

_____
_____

Questions for review and discussion

What does Yeshua say about those who were killed in Yerushalayim?
_____

Why is that important for His listeners to understand?
_____

What is He teaching all of His listeners to do?
_____
_____

What is the gardener doing when he digs around the fig tree?
_____

What is the spiritual meaning of this?
_____
_____

What is the Kingdom of God compared to?
_____

What does that mean?
_____

Who is participating in the Kingdom of God?
_____

Who is not participating in the Kingdom of God?
_____

How do you participate in the Kingdom of God?
_____

Summarize the study notes from this chapter and discuss:

_____
_____
_____
_____
_____
_____

Summarize in one or two sentences the most important or the most interesting thing you learned in this chapter from your study:

_____
_____

What makes it important or interesting to you?

_____

Re-read Luke Chapter 13 from the *Hebrew Heritage Bible* translation used in this book. Discuss. Summarize Luke Chapter 13 in one paragraph and discuss:

_____
_____
_____
_____
_____

Choose one verse from Luke Chapter 13 that you think is the most important and write it here. Discuss why you think it is the most important verse:

_____
_____

How did your understanding of Luke Chapter 13 change after you studied it and read it again? Discuss.

_____
_____

How can you apply what you learned from Luke Chapter 13 to your life? Discuss.

_____
_____

What question or questions do you still have about Luke Chapter 13 that you don't understand or want to know more about? Discuss.

_____
_____

THE GOSPEL OF LUKE CHAPTER FOURTEEN

Lesson 16

Before you begin your study, read Luke Chapter 14 out loud (as a group) from your Bible.

In your own words, summarize Luke Chapter 14 in one paragraph and write at least two questions that you had about the chapter as you read the biblical text: (Discuss)

_____
_____
_____
_____
_____
_____
_____
_____
_____
_____
_____
_____
_____
_____
_____

In Chapter 14, Yeshua is invited to the home of a chief spiritual leader (some translations say a prominent Pharisee) for a meal on Shabbat. There He meets a man who is suffering from dropsy. This man has abnormal swelling in his body. Yeshua heals the man and teaches the spiritual leaders. Yeshua tells the Parable of the Great Banquet as a lesson about the Kingdom of God. On His journey after the Shabbat is over, Yeshua again teaches the crowds who are following Him.

The Hebrew Heritage Bible Translation says that Yeshua goes to the house of one of the chief spiritual leaders on Shabbat to eat bread. For many years, the traditional bread of Shabbat has been challah bread. Research and find out more about challah bread. What is it? What does it look like? Why is it braided? Why are two loaves served on Friday evening? Often times you can find challah bread at the grocery store on Friday. It is delicious. Or make some of your own. Recipes are online. Write and discuss what you learned:

_____
_____
_____
_____
_____
_____
_____
_____
_____
_____
_____

Chapter 14

14:1) So it happened when He went into the house of one of the chief spiritual leaders on Shabbat to eat bread, that they were observing Him, wanting to learn. 14:2) There before Him was a man suffering from dropsy. 14:3) Yeshua spoke to the Torah scholars and spiritual leaders explaining to them, "Is it permitted on Shabbat to heal or should it be forbidden?" 14:4) They were quiet. He took hold of him, healed him, and let him go. 14:5) With that, He gave answer and said to them, "Which one of you that would have a donkey or an ox fall into a pit would not haul him out right away even on the day of Shabbat?" 14:6) They agreed, not being able to respond to all this.

- In verse 6, "They agreed" is literally, "But they could not respond to these things." They became quiet (verse 4) and could not respond because they came into agreement. They listened to Yeshua's teachings and saw what happened. In this cultural context, they would voice an argument if they disagreed. "They agreed" is often simply translated, "they could not reply to this" (NRSV). The original audience understood that when the questions have been discussed and answered convincingly, the consensus is agreement. When He silenced inquisitive debate, the audience understood that agreement had been reached. They accepted the argument and the authority of the one who expressed it (Young, 2019).

- It is important to understand the cultural context of Jewish learning. Discussion, debate, and argument are part of Jewish history. "Ever since Abraham's famous argument with God, Judaism has been full of debate. Jews debate justice, authority, spirituality, and more. No wonder Judaism cherishes the expression machloket l'shem shamayim, 'an argument for the sake of heaven'" (Schwartz, 2012).

- Too often commentators assume that the spiritual leaders (the Pharisees) invited Yeshua to dinner in order to trap Him or insult Him. There is ample reason in the original language to believe that the Pharisees wanted to honor Yeshua and find out more about Him (Young, 1998; Flusser, 2001; and Marshall, 1978).

- It was an honor to host a famous teacher for a meal. Yeshua had probably just taught in the synagogue (Cultural Backgrounds Study Bible, 2016).

- The setting of this healing is a special Shabbat meal that was probably held after the synagogue service where Yeshua had taught.

- The man had dropsy – edema – swelling caused by excess fluid in the body's tissue. This serious condition could have been caused by underlying kidney or liver disease (Walvoord & Zuck, 1983).

- According to the rabbis, the disease was a result of the man's immorality (sin). Yeshua couldn't help but notice him (Marshall, 1978).

- Was this life-threatening? No one knows for sure. Life-saving procedures were acceptable, but other treatments were debatable. For example, Hillel the Elder (see Lesson 8) allowed prayer for the sick on Shabbat, his contemporary Rabbi Shammai did not.

- The Pharisees did allow people to help their animals out of pits on Shabbat, sometimes using a rope (otherwise they could not tie or untie a knot on Shabbat because it was considered work). Some others would allow an animal to pulled out of a pit as long as no tools were used. It was a matter of interpretation and debate among the Jews (Cultural Backgrounds Study Bible, 2016).

- Because there were so many interpretations about what was allowed and not allowed among the Jewish scholars and sects, this was a legitimate question being asked of Yeshua.

- Obviously, the man was healed and the question was answered.

14:7) So then He began to tell a parable to the invited guests when He noticed how they were seeking out the places of honor [at the banquet]. He explained to them, 14:8) "When you are invited by someone to a wedding banquet, do not take the place of honor because someone more highly esteemed by your host may have been invited. 14:9) Afterwards the one who invited both you and him will come, and say to you, 'Give place to this man!' Then in shame you will head for the least honorable place. 14:10) But when you are invited, go and recline at the least honorable place, so that when the one who has invited you comes, he may say to you, 'Friend, move up higher.' Then you will have honor in the sight of all who are at the table with you. 14:11) For every individual who exalts himself will be humbled [by God] but every person who humbles himself will be exalted [by God]." 14:12) But He said to the man who invited Him, "When you plan a dinner or a banquet, do not invite your friends or your brothers or your relatives or wealthy acquaintances, lest they also invite you in return, and you be repaid. 14:13) Instead, when you plan to give a reception, invite the poor, the crippled, the lame, the blind, 14:14) because they do not have the means to repay you, but you will be blessed and rewarded at the resurrection of the righteous!" 14:15) When one of those reclining at the table with him heard this, He said to him, "Blessed is the one who eats bread in the kingdom of God!"

- This is still "table talk" between Yeshua, the spiritual leaders and the Torah scholars at the Shabbat meal.
- Rabbis considered hospitality one of the most important functions of the home. "Great is hospitality; greater even than early attendance at the house of study or than receiving the Shekhinah (Glory of God)"(Babylonian Talmud, Shabbat 127a) (Wilson. 1989, p. 219).
- One is not to discriminate in the showing of hospitality. The rabbis taught that the home was to be open to all classes and kinds of people. "Let your house be open wide, and let the poor be members of your household" (Mishnah, Abot 1:5) (Wilson, 1989, p. 220).
- Yeshua is recommending that guests not automatically take the places of honor and run the risk of being humiliated. This is sound advice. However, the meaning is much deeper. It is about the Kingdom of God. A person's position depends on God and not on their own self-seeking. It is an expression of God's verdict on people (Marshall, 1978).
- Verse 11 may refer back to Luke 13:30, where the last will be first and the first will be last (Walvoord & Zuck, 1983).
- The future tense for people who are in last place indicated that, in the world to come, the places will be reversed. Those who regard themselves as oppressed and hopeless will gain entry into the kingdom. While those who think they alone are worthy, will be excluded (Marshall, 1978).

14:16) At that, He taught him, "A certain man was planning to give a great banquet, and he invited many guests. 14:17) When the banquet hour arrived, he sent his servant to call those who had accepted the invitation, 'Come now for everything is ready!' 14:18) But every one of them began to make up excuses. The first one said to him, 'I have bought a field. I need to go out and look at it. I ask you to excuse me.' 14:19) Another one said, 'I have bought a yoke of oxen. I must go try them. I ask you to excuse me.' 14:20) Another one said, 'I have married a wife, and so I cannot come!' 14:21) So the servant went back and reported this to his master. Then the master of the household became angry. He said to his servant, 'Go out, right now, into the streets and alleys of the city and bring in here the poor, crippled, blind, and lame.' 14:22) The servant said, 'Master, what you have commanded has been done, but there is still more room.' 14:23) Then the master said to the servant, 'Go out along the main thoroughfares as well as the out of the way hedges, and compel people to come in, so that my house may be filled. 14:24) For I tell you that none of those people who were invited shall taste of my banquet.'"

- This entire parable stresses the open invitation to the outcasts.
- The surprise in the plot of the story is the action of the invited guests, who come up with inadequate excuses to avoid going to the banquet.
- The urging of the hour of invitation is revealed when the ones who are called do not recognize the significance of the time.
- The message is about the Kingdom of God and the divine invitation that calls all people to come to His banquet table.
- This is a very large dinner party with a long invitation list. Invitations were sent to the "common" people too.
- The servants would have invited the guests many hours or even days before the actual event began.
- It was a lot of work to prepare for the dinner party. The best meats, vegetables, fruits, breads, and wines were carefully selected, purchased, and prepared. It took a lot of time and effort, perhaps days to make everything just right.
- The guests would have accepted the initial invitation with an obligation to attend. They would have been waiting eagerly for the party to start. Drums would have been used to alert the guests that it was time to begin. Musicians would been present at the feast. The entire village would have been filled with the delicious aroma of the fine foods being prepared (Young, 1998).
- When everything was ready, the host would send his servants to the guests telling them it was time to come.
- The excuses are ridiculous. Does anybody buy property without seeing it first? No, worthless excuse. Does anybody buy livestock without inspecting them first? No, lame excuse. The third excuse is absurd. Who would have time between the first invitation and the second to go through all of the engagement proceedings and already be preparing for the seven blessings of the wedding? No way (Young 1998).

- Rabbi Akiva said, "God's call will come. Will the people be ready?" The banquet refers to life in the world to come.
- The host is insulted. His honor has been shamed.
- In one charitable act, his honor can be reclaimed, and he can shame those who insulted him. He will invite those who are completely outside the respected community to come. This act is highly honored.
- The host compels these new invitees to come in. The man wants his house to be full.
- He sends his servants to the economically disadvantaged and disabled. Then he sends his servants out with an invitation that is completely unlimited and universal. Go anywhere that people can be found and invite them to come.
- The call is for everybody.
- The "house" means family. The meal is not complete if a family member is missing.
- No one is to be left outside the banquet except those who refuse to come. This invitation is a never-to-be-repeated opportunity (Young, 1998).

14:25) Now great crowds of people were going along with Him. So He turned and said to them, 14:26) "If anyone follows Me, and does not hate his own father and mother, and wife and children, and brothers and sisters, yes, and even his own life, he cannot be My disciple. 14:27) Whoever does not pick up his own cross and come after Me cannot be My disciple. 14:28) For which one of you, when he wants to build a tower, does not first sit down and calculate the cost, to see if he has enough to complete it? 14:29) Otherwise, after he has laid a foundation but is not able to finish, all who see it will begin to mock him 14:30) saying, 'This man began to build and was not able to finish.' 14:31) Or what king, going to battle against another king in war, will not first sit down and decide whether he is able with ten thousand to conquer him who comes against him with twenty thousand? 14:32) And if not, while the other is still a long way off, he sends a delegation to ask for terms of peace. 14:33) So it is with every one of you—whoever does not give up everything he possesses cannot be My disciple.

14:34) "Salt is good, but if salt has lost its flavor, how will you restore its salty taste? 14:35) It is not fit for the dirt heap or for the manure pile, but people will just throw it away. Everyone who has ears to hear, must listen!"

- It is after Shabbat and Yeshua is traveling again.
- He is on His way to Yerushalayim. The crowds are great and so is their enthusiasm. Their enthusiasm must be dampened by a sense of reality.

- If the guests in the preceding parable refused to face the cost of accepting the invitation, others may be tempted to underestimate the cost of discipleship and begin a journey that is beyond their abilities. This section takes up the theme that is begun in verse 18, and develops it further.
- Yeshua is telling them that total commitment is required to be a disciple.
- They need to evaluate the situation before they begin. The disciple should be sure they are able to pay the cost to finish the task and not leave it half complete and subject to ridicule.
- The Semitic understanding of the use of the word "hate" means to "love less." The thought is not of psychological "hate" but to dismiss – leave aside. This is a hyperbolic or exaggerated statement that is made to prove an important point. Yeshua is calling people to follow Him on a path of self-denial.
- The disciples must be ready for the ultimate in self-denial. Because anybody who takes on the task without being ready to pay the total cost involved will only make a fool of themselves (Marshall, 1978).
- The closing statement by Yeshua expresses the ultimate uselessness of the half-hearted disciple who can only expect judgement.
- Salt was considered an absolute necessity in antiquity. It was used for flavoring, as a preservative, and was part of the sacrifices given at the Temple.
- Salt was obtained from the Dead Sea. Dead Sea water is full of minerals. Evaporation produces a mixture of salt crystals and carnallite. Salt crystallizes first and can be collected. Bitter tasting carnallite could sometimes be collected by mistake (Marshall, 1978).
- Disciples who cannot stay-the-course are as useless as salt which has lost its flavor or has been contaminated. It is of no further use (Marshall, 1978).
- Yeshua is preparing His disciples for what is about to happen to them.

Photo: The Dead Sea at sunrise. Notice all of the mineral deposits.

At over 1300 feet below sea level, the Dead Sea is the lowest point on the surface of the earth. Called the "Salt Sea" in the "Old Testament," the Dead Sea is located in the basin of the northern section of the Great Rift Valley. Today, many industries are located along the Dead Sea. Numerous hotels are located at Ein Bokek, where tourists from all over the world come to float on the Dead Sea and receive spa treatments using Dead Sea mud.

📍 Take a trip online to the Dead Sea in Israel. Research the different industries that produce ingredients for all types of products from Ahava cosmetics to fertilizer (and even table salt). What did you discover about these industries? Write and discuss:

_____
_____
_____

📍 The level of the Dead Sea has been dropping dramatically every year for the last few years. What is the cause? Write and discuss:

_____
_____
_____

What are some possible solutions? Write and discuss:

_____
_____
_____

The covenant of salt is an interesting topic that can be explored further with research online. What are the covenants of salt? (Begin your research at Aish.com) What did you discover? Write and discuss:

_____
_____
_____
_____
_____

Questions for review and discussion

What happened on Shabbat at the spiritual leader's house?

_____
_____
_____

Why was Yeshua invited to leader's home?

Was Yeshua a guest of honor?

Yeshua told a parable while He was at the leader's house. What was it about?

What does the parable mean?

What does that mean to you?

What does Yeshua talk about after he leaves the Shabbat dinner and begins to travel again?

What does that mean you?

Summarize the study notes from this chapter and discuss:

Summarize in one or two sentences the most important or the most interesting thing you learned in this chapter from your study:

GOSPEL OF LUKE 229

What makes it important or interesting to you?

Re-read Luke Chapter 14 from the *Hebrew Heritage Bible* translation used in this book. Discuss. Summarize Luke Chapter 14 in one paragraph and discuss:

Choose one verse from Luke Chapter 14 that you think is the most important and write it here. Discuss why you think it is the most important verse:

How did your understanding of Luke Chapter 14 change after you studied it and read it again? Discuss.

How can you apply what you learned from Luke Chapter 14 to your life? Discuss.

What question or questions do you still have about Luke Chapter 14 that you don't understand or want to know more about? Discuss.

THE GOSPEL OF LUKE CHAPTER FIFTEEN

Lesson 17

Before you begin your study, read Luke Chapter 15 out loud (as a group) from your Bible.

In your own words, summarize Luke Chapter 15 in one paragraph and write at least two questions that you had about the chapter as you read the biblical text: (Discuss)

_____
_____
_____
_____
_____
_____
_____
_____
_____
_____
_____
_____
_____
_____
_____
_____

Yeshua is drawing those who are tax collectors and sinners to Himself. This chapter is dedicated to His teachings about the Kingdom of God and includes several parables.

The first parable in chapter 15 is about a shepherd and his lost sheep. The Bible is full of stories about shepherds and sheep. List some of the scriptural references here and discuss:

_____

_____

Where is the reference for the "Good Shepherd" found in the New Testament?

_____

Who is the Good Shepherd?

_____

In Ezekiel 34:11-16, who is Israel's shepherd?

_____

What does He do?

_____

_____

Who are the sheep?

_____

How is the Good Shepherd in the New Testament related to the Shepherd of Israel in the TANAK ("Old Testament")?

_____

_____

_____

_____

Chapter 15

15:1) Now many tax collectors and sinners were coming closer to hear Him. 15:2) But some of the spiritual leaders and the scribes complained saying, "This man welcomes sinners and eats with them." 15:3) But He said to them this parable saying, 15:4) "What man among you who owns a hundred sheep but loses one will not leave the ninety-nine in their desert pasture and go search for the one which is lost until he finds it? 15:5) When he has found it, he saddles it around his shoulders, absolutely delighted. 15:6) When he comes home, moreover, he calls his friends and his neighbors together, saying to them, 'Celebrate with me! I have found my sheep which was lost!' 15:7) In the same way, I tell you, there will be more celebration in heaven over one sinner who repents than over ninety-nine completely righteous persons who need no repentance. 15:8) Or what woman among you who owns ten silver coins, if she loses one will not light a lamp, sweep the house, and search relentlessly until she finds it? 15:9) Moreover, when she has found it, she calls her friends and neighbors together saying, 'Celebrate with me! I have found the coin which I had lost!' 15:10) In the same way, I tell you, there is celebration of joy before the angels of God over one sinner who repents."

- The publicans and sinners were constantly drawing near to Yeshua. He not only received them when they sought Him, He sought after them as well. He sought after them so that they would not remain sinners, but that they would be restored to the kingdom and that there would be joy in Heaven over them.

- Remember, Yeshua is speaking to the Jews, and the focus centers on the lost, the search, and the restoration (Edersheim, 1993).

- The "sinners" are those who lead an immoral life (adulterers, swindlers, etc.) and/or people who followed a dishonorable calling (an occupation that notoriously involved immorality or dishonesty). Because they followed an immoral lifestyle or engaged in a dishonest occupation, they were deprived of civil rights such as holding a public office or being a witness in a legal proceeding. Examples of such include: excise-men (excise tax), tax collectors, shepherds, donkey-drivers, peddlers, and tanners (Jeremias, 1972).

- In antiquity, to eat with someone, or to have table fellowship with them, created a covenant relationship of friendship with them.

- Urban people looked down on shepherds, and courts did not accept their testimonies nor the testimonies of women (Cultural Backgrounds Study Bible, 2016).

- There were two types of shepherds: those who lived in towns or villages as residents or those who lived as nomads (ESV Archaeology Study Bible, 2017).

- In Yeshua's parable, he is talking about a shepherd who has a herd that is about average in number. A herd size of 100 sheep was a medium-sized flock, and the shepherd probably did not have a watchman, but he shared the responsibility of his herd with other shepherds who had similar-sized flocks. A flock of 300 sheep would have been unusually large.

- A shepherd would count his flock in the evening before he would bed them down for the night to make sure that none was lost (Young, 1998).

- When the sheep is lost, it lies down helplessly and will not get up. The shepherd carries the lamb on his shoulders so that he can carry his staff in his hand.

- The folly and ignorance of the sheep to stray is only natural. Sheep are very vulnerable. The shepherd labors to find the sheep who is in solitude among the stony places (Young, 1998).

- The work of the Father through Yeshua to restore the lost is the very work of the Good Shepherd. (See John 10 and Ezekiel 34) (Jeremias, 1972; Young, 1998).
- Yeshua is telling two parables (twin parables) about the same subject. One involves a man of average wealth, and the other is about a very poor woman. He does this so that regardless of their background (urban or rural, male or female, average wealth or very poor), all of His listeners can relate and understand.
- The main character in the parable about the lost coin is a very poor woman (Young, 1998).
- Each silver coin represents one-day's wage for a day-laborer.
- The woman's headdress is decorated with the coins, and it is probably part of her dowry (money that is transferred when she gets married). This may not be laid aside even when sleeping at night. If the woman's ten silver coins were on her headdress, she was indeed very poor. Today, many of these headdresses will have hundreds of coins on them (Jeremias, 1972).
- The floors of most homes in the villages were composed of rocks or packed dirt. The common building material in the Galil was black basalt rock. The walls were thick and the windows were small. It would have been dark in the house even during the daylight. To find anything, she would need a lamp and a broom. Because she was so poor, finding this coin would be cause for great celebration (*ESV Archaeology Study Bible*, 2017).
- How many people do not need to repent? No one. "The righteous who need no repentance do not exist" (Young, 1998, p. 195).
- The emphasis in both parables is on the diligent search and the celebration (Edersheim, 1993; Young, 1998).

Even now shepherds can be found all over Yisrael. A particular group of people known as the Bedouins have lived as nomads in Yisrael and Jordan for thousands of years. Some continue to move from place to place following their herds.

Take a trip online and discover more about the Bedouin people of Israel and Jordan. Who are they? How do they live? What is their religion? Are they citizens? Write and discuss:

_____
_____
_____
_____

15:11) He taught, "There was a man who had two sons. 15:12) The younger of them said to his father,

'Father, give me the share of your estate that is coming to me.' He divided all he had from his life between them. 15:13) Not many days later, the younger son sold out everything and ran away to a far country. There he squandered everything he had in loose living. 15:14) When he had spent everything, a mighty famine arose in that country. He began to be in want. 15:15) So he tried to ingratiate himself to one of the citizens of that country, who sent him into his fields to feed the pigs. 15:16) He was longing to fill his stomach with the pods the pigs were eating. No one would give him anything. 15:17) But when he came to himself, he said, 'How many of my father's hired servants have more than enough bread, but I am dying here with hunger! 15:18) I will arise and go to my father, and will say to him, 'Father I have sinned against heaven, and before you. 15:19) I am not worthy to be called your son; treat me as one of your hired servants.' 15:20) He arose and returned to his father. But while he was still far away, his father saw him and felt compassion for him. He ran to meet him. He flung his arms around his neck and kissed him. 15:21) The son said to him, 'Father, I have sinned against heaven and before you; I am not worthy to be called your son.' 15:22) But the father said to his servants, 'Quickly, bring out the finest robe and clothe him. Place a ring on the finger of his hand and put sandals on his feet. 15:23) Bring out the calf we have fattened and slaughter it because we must feast and celebrate. 15:24) After all, this my son was dead and has come to life again. He was lost and has been found.' They began to celebrate. 15:25) At this time, his older son was in the field. As he came and got closer to the house, he heard music and dancing. 15:26) He summoned one of the servants and asked what was happening. 15:27) He explained to him, 'Your brother has come, and your father has slaughtered the fattened calf because he has received him back safe and sound.' 15:28) But he became angry and was not even willing to go in. His father came outside and pleaded with him. 15:29) But he answered his father, 'Look, these many years I have worked for you, and I never disobeyed your command; but you have never even given me a young goat so that I could throw a party with my friends. 15:30) Now when this son of yours turns up again, who has wasted your living on prostitutes, you slaughtered the fattened calf for him.' 15:31) He said to him, 'Child, you have always been with me, and everything I possess is yours. 15:32) But we had to celebrate and rejoice, because this is your brother. He was dead and is alive again, he was lost and has been found!'"

Before you read the study notes about this parable: What do you think Yeshua is saying here? Who are the main characters? What is the point of this story? How does it relate to what He has been teaching? Write and discuss:

_____
_____
_____
_____
_____
_____

- This parable focuses on the broken relationships between God and people. The father is loving and compassionate, but both of his sons are lost. The younger son is the person who is living without God – running away from Him. The older son is a lot like the religious person who misunderstands the character of God and does not have a meaningful relationship with Him. The older son does not show that he loves his father, and he has much difficulty forgiving his brother.
- This parable reaches out to both the biggest sinner and the outwardly religious person.
- The father figure represents God "and His great compassion both for those who pretend to serve Him (the elder son) and for those who flagrantly abandon Him (the younger son)" (Young, 1998, p. 134).
- The younger son approaches his father with an immediate demand for his inheritance. In other words, "he wants his father to die, and the elder [son] quietly receives his double portion of the inheritance, doing nothing to bring reconciliation. Neither of them tries to build a relationship with the other or their father" (Young, 1998, p. 137). These events were so contrary to typical family life that the audience was shocked into listening.
- In ancient Judaism, "a father could execute his will even before his death." However, the request of the younger son was extremely disrespectful and would have shocked Yeshua's audience. The elder son receives two-thirds of the estate, while the younger receives one-third (Young, 1998, p.138).
- Even though the father had already divided up his estate between his sons, he could still live on and use the property until his death.
- Yeshua's audience expects the elder son to be a mediator between the younger son and the father, but he does not. "Instead he acts out the part of a greedy hypocrite" (p. 140).
- The audience also expects the younger son to die, rather than to return in humility to his father.
- The father "loves his sons enough to allow them the freedom to make their own decisions" (p. 146).
- "To come home" means to repent. "The Creator of heaven and earth allows people to choose even when they make the wrong choices...and is eager to receive each one who comes to him" (p. 148).
- To put a ring on his finger was to restore him as a son, not as a hired servant.
- The parable stresses the importance of repentance, forgiveness, and the compassion of God.
- This parable demands a response and a call to action. "The outwardly righteous sinner is just as wrong as the blatantly wicked evildoer." One must return to God, accept His forgiveness, and forgive their brother. Relationships must be restored (Young, 1998).

The ring in this story was probably a signet ring. It would have contained a seal, signifying the son's right to conduct business in the father's name (*ESV Archaeology Study Bible*, 2017). In recent years, several seals from the First Temple Period have been discovered in the City of David excavations (Jerusalem). In 2019, a rare seal with the inscription "(belonging) to Nathan-Melech, Servant of the King" was discovered. Take a trip online and learn more about this exciting discovery. What is a seal? What is the significance of this seal? Write and discuss:

_____
_____
_____

Yeshua's audience would have been aware at how far the younger son had fallen when he was longing to eat the pigs' food. In Judaism pigs are "unclean" animals. What does it mean for something to be "clean" or "unclean" in Judaism? Where are the laws about "clean" and "unclean" found in the biblical text? What does "Kosher" mean? Write and discuss:

_____
_____
_____
_____
_____
_____
_____

Yeshua's listeners might have imagined that the younger son traveled to the Decapolis (ten cities). These sophisticated, pagan Gentile cities would have been quite a trap for this young man from a small Jewish village (*ESV Archaeology Study Bible*, 2017).

📍 Beit She'an (also known as Scythopolis) was one of the cities of the Decapolis. This city has a long and fascinating history. Take a trip online to Beit She'an, Israel and discover more about its history. What happened at Beit She'an that involved King Saul? What was the city like during the time of Yeshua's ministry? What does it look like today? Was it a wealthy city? Write and discuss: (See map in Lesson 18 for the location of Beit She'an)

_____
_____
_____
_____
_____
_____

Photo: The main street of the ancient Roman city of Beit She'an. In antiquity, this street was lined with markets and pagan temples. People would come from around the area to purchase all types of expensive items including rare perfumes and ointments.

"When you study the Bible, you gain more insight on what God meant for us to see. It's easy to just read a passage and call it good, but you gain so much more knowledge if you dive into it and really look at the significance of everything. Studying the Bible gives us insight on how people used to think, talk, and worship. We are able to see how God never left His people, and we can take comfort in that. It gives us a new way to look at life and the real reason that we are all here. For me personally, I was able to see the ways that people fell away from the Lord, or were confused with God's plan. But He came through and the person's eyes were opened to see how God has been working through their life. It gives me assurance that I am not alone, and God is not surprised by anything we do."
Katy Volinic – Class of 2021

Questions for review and discussion

Who is following Yeshua?

What is Yeshua talking about in the parables in this chapter?

Why does he tell "twin parables"?

What is the theme of this chapter?

Summarize the study notes from this chapter and discuss:

Summarize in one or two sentences the most important or the most interesting thing you learned in this chapter from your study:

What makes it important or interesting to you?

Re-read Luke Chapter 15 from the *Hebrew Heritage Bible* translation used in this book. Discuss. Summarize Luke Chapter 15 in one paragraph and discuss:

_____
_____
_____
_____
_____
_____
_____
_____
_____
_____
_____
_____
_____
_____

Choose one verse from Luke Chapter 15 that you think is the most important and write it here. Discuss why you think it is the most important verse:

_____
_____
_____

How did your understanding of Luke Chapter 15 change after you studied it and read it again? Discuss.

_____
_____
_____

How can you apply what you learned from Luke Chapter 15 to your life? Discuss.

_____
_____
_____

What question or questions do you still have about Luke Chapter 15 that you don't understand or want to know more about? Discuss

_____
_____
_____
_____

THE GOSPEL OF LUKE CHAPTER SIXTEEN

Lesson 18

Before you begin your study, read Luke Chapter 16 out loud (as a group) from your Bible.

In your own words, summarize Luke Chapter 16 in one paragraph and write at least two questions that you had about the chapter as you read the biblical text: (Discuss)

_____
_____
_____
_____
_____
_____
_____
_____
_____
_____
_____
_____
_____
_____
_____

Luke Chapter 16 begins with Yeshua telling His disciples a story. Few passages in the Scriptures have had so many different interpretations as the first parable in this chapter (Marshall, 1978). The setting for this chapter is unclear, but it is full of parables as Yeshua continues to teach powerfully about the Kingdom of God.

📍 To better understand the meaning of the first parable in chapter sixteen, one should become more familiar with the Dead Sea Community known as the Essenes. Refer to Lesson 2, History of the Jews, in this book as a reminder of what you have already learned about this Jewish sect who lived in isolation at Qumran. Visit jewishvirtuallibrary.org (Pharisees, Sadducees & Essenes – Jewish Virtual Library) and answer these questions: Who were the Essenes?

_____
_____
_____

How did they feel about the Pharisees and Sadducees?

_____
_____
_____

How did they live?

_____
_____
_____

The Dead Sea Scrolls were written and collected by the Essenes and are one of the most important and exciting archaeological findings in history. Discovered by accident in a cave near Qumran in 1947, the Dead Sea Scrolls have helped historians, theologians, scholars and archaeologists learn more about the biblical text and life in Judea 2,000 years ago.

📍 Take a trip online and learn more about this epic discovery. Who discovered the first scrolls? What happened to the scrolls after their discovery? Why are they so important? Why were they hidden in caves? Write and discuss:

_____
_____
_____
_____

GOSPEL OF LUKE

Photo: Cave 4 at Qumran, Israel (2015).

Some 15,000 scroll fragments were found in Cave 4 at Qumran.

Passages from all the books of the Hebrew Bible are represented among the scrolls from the Qumran caves with the exception of Nehemiah and Esther.

(Roitman, 2009, p. 43)

Photo: A replica of one of the jars and the "Isaiah Scroll" found at Qumran in Cave 1.

Besides the scrolls of the Bible, many other writings were found at Qumran. These included prayers, wisdom works, and manuals specific to the Essene community. The greatest discovery of all was the "Isaiah Scroll." It was written around 100 BC, and had survived for 2,000 thousand years in a jar in a cave at Qumran.

(Roitman, 2009, p. 43)

Chapter 16

16:1) He said to His disciples, "There was a certain wealthy man who had a manager for his estate. This manager was reported to him as squandering his goods. 16:2) So he called him in and said to him, 'What is this I hear about you? Give a record of your conduct as manager because you can no longer manage my estate.' 16:3) Then the manager said to himself, 'What shall I do? My master is taking my position away from me! I am not strong enough to dig. I am ashamed to beg. 16:4) I know what I shall do so that when I am removed from my position as manager of the estate, they will receive me into their homes.' 16:5) He summoned each one of his master's debtors. He asked the first, 'How much do you owe my master?' 16:6) He replied, 'One hundred vat jars of oil.' So he said to him, 'Sit right down, change your bill, and write fifty.' 16:7) Then he said to the next one, 'How much do you owe?' He answered, 'One hundred kor measures of wheat.' He said to him, 'Change your bill and write eighty.' 16:8) But the master praised the crooked manager because he had acted shrewdly, for the children of this age are more shrewd in dealing with their own kind than the children of light. 16:9) I tell you, make friends for yourselves by means of the mammon of unrighteousness, so that when it fails, they may receive you into the eternal homes. 16:10) The one who is faithful in the small matters will also be faithful in the greater. The one who is untrustworthy in the small matters will also be untrustworthy with greater responsibilities. 16:11) So if you have not proven trustworthy in the use of unrighteous mammon, who will entrust to you the true riches? 16:12) Moreover, if you have not been trustworthy with what belongs to someone else, who will give you what is your own? 16:13) No servant can be the slave of two masters, for either he will hate the one and love the other, or else he will be devoted to one and despise the other. You cannot serve both God and money."

- Shrewdness was a necessary survival skill in antiquity. In an environment with limited resources and harsh living conditions, the tendency among people was to develop a way to gain advantages over others.
- The wealthy man fired his dishonest manager but also praised him for shrewdly currying favor with his master's debtors by lowering the amount of money they owed.
- The manager had the power to change the contract, and instead of extorting more money from the debtors, he reduces the amount they owe at harvest (Cultural Backgrounds Study Bible, 2016).
- The manager saves himself and helps the debtors. He was very shrewd.
- The wealthy man (master) was charitable and big-hearted. He could have thrown the manager in jail, but he only fired him.
- The debtors were probably tenant farmers. Tenant farmers farm land that belongs to some one else, in this case the wealthy man. In exchange for using the land, the famers paid the wealthy man by giving him a portion of their harvest (Young, 1998, p. 234).

- The manager was the person who determined and collected the portion the farmers would pay to the wealthy man. The wealthy man probably had no idea how much the tenant farmers were paying. However, he had heard bad reports about his manager.
- The manager probably received a salary and a commission.
- He had exploited his master's wealth and profited greatly by overcharging the famers. "He probably took a cut at both ends" (p. 233).
- The manager was too proud to dig ditches, and he probably would not ever be able to get another job managing anyone's property.
- He had to act quickly before anybody discovered he had been fired.
- His best course of action was definitely unethical, but when he reduced the debts, he was actually helping the famers. "He was taking a percentage of the profits and returning it to those whom he had been overcharging" (Young, 1998, p. 233).
- "One hundred vat jars of oil" was about nine hundred gallons of olive oil – the product of about 150 olive trees.
- "One hundred kor measures of wheat" was about a thousand bushels of wheat or 30 tons – the harvest of about 100 acres (Cultural Backgrounds Study Bible, 2016).
- The reduction of debt totaled about 500 denarii, or about 20 months' wages (ESV Archaeology Study Bible, 2017) for each debtor (Cultural Backgrounds Study Bible, 2016).
- Careful study of the history and culture help modern readers better comprehend what would have been easily discerned by Yeshua's audience.
- In the end, the manager was helping somebody else by reducing the debt.
- The parable emphasizes the importance of faithfulness when it comes to money.
- Yeshua's references to "children of the light" and "mammon of unrighteousness" would have been clearly understood by those listening to Him.
- "Yeshua used these terms in reference to the Dead Sea community [the Essenes]" (Young, 1998, p. 233; Flusser, 2001).
- "The parable reveals Yeshua's opinion about the Essenes. The manager is like the "sons [or children] of light", the Essenes, who are taking unfair advantage of the people. The children of this age [people who are not Essenes] are wiser than the Essenes, who require total financial investment in the community, cutting each other off from the outside world" (Young, 1998, p. 233; Flusser, 2001).
- "Money of outsiders is 'unrighteous mammon,' whereas the money of the [Essene] community is viewed quite differently" (Young, 1998, p. 233; Flusser, 2001).

- The Essenes called themselves "sons of light" or "children of light," and absolutely everybody else, both Jew and Gentile, were "children of darkness" or "sons of darkness." The leader of the community referred to himself as the "teacher of righteousness." Because they believed that everybody else was corrupt, the Essenes completely isolated themselves in the desert. They also had no financial contact with the "outside world." When a person joined the community, they were required to give all of their property and money to the community and were obligated to live by a strict code of ethics. They did not help others. They only helped themselves. They devoted themselves to worship and to the study of and interpretation of Scripture (Roitman, 2009).

- The manager had been wasteful because he had hoarded the profits for himself. But, when he breaks away from that type of behavior and gives away his master's wealth to his clients, he is to be praised.

- Hoarding money is viewed as wasting God's resources. This was characteristic of the "children of light" (the Essenes) and the way they were frustrating the divine purpose (Flusser, 2001).

- The main focus of the parable is money or stewardship. In the pursuit of God's kingdom, people must come before money. When one makes God their master, money becomes a tool for assisting those in need. The Essene community did just the opposite of that. They hoarded their money and hated other people. In the parable, the manager had been keeping all the money for himself instead of helping others. "The 'children of this age' are more faithful stewards because they interact with each other." Faithful stewardship can only happen when people engage with each other and help each other with their needs. "Money must be used to help people. Financial resources should be put to work for social reform that benefits all" (Young, 1998, p. 234).

- God's abundant grace is accessible to everyone. One must reach beyond their group affiliation and self-righteous prejudice to help others (Young, 1998).

16:14) Now some of the spiritual leaders who were lovers of money heard these teachings and made fun of him. 16:15) He responded, "You are those who justify yourselves in the sight of the people, but God knows what is really in your hearts. What may be highly valued by people will be detested by God. 16:16) The Torah and the prophets prophesied until Yochanan; since then the message of the kingdom is proclaimed, and everyone is forcing his way into it. 16:17) So it is easier for heaven and earth to pass away than for one stroke of a letter from the Torah to be canceled. 16:18) Everyone who divorces his wife in order to marry another woman commits adultery; and he who marries that woman who is so divorced from her husband commits adultery.

- Most spiritual leaders (Pharisees) valued caring for the poor. The spiritual leaders were not members of the elite, but they were also not poor (*Cultural Backgrounds Study Bible*, 2016).

- Yeshua may be referring to 1 Samuel 16:7. The prophets often warned that God cares more about justice than He does outward religious practices.
- In verse 16, the "Torah and the prophets" refer to the TANAK ("Old Testament"). **TANAK** is an acronym for "**T**orah, **N**evi'im (Prophets), and **K**etuvim (Writings)."
- In verse 16, Yochanan is John the Baptist. Yeshua is referring to the Kingdom of God which began with Yochanan preparing the way for Yeshua. This is a powerful and forceful movement of God led by Yeshua. Everyone must make an effort to enter into it (force his way in).
- The Torah remains valid to the smallest detail! Yeshua is bringing a revelation and a fresh understanding of the Torah by His teaching (Young, 1998; Marshall, 1978).
- The period of time marked by the Torah and the Prophets lasted until Yochanan (John the Baptist). The validity of the Torah and the Prophets has not ended; it is the activity which produced them that has ended (Marshall, 1978).
- The Torah has lost none of its validity despite the coming of the Kingdom. The Torah is validated by the coming of the Kingdom. While the coming of Yeshua signaled the arrival of a new movement, the Torah and Prophets (TANAK) still remains in force. Indeed, it is sharpened by the teachings of Yeshua (Marshall, 1978).
- In verse 18, the more accurate translation of "'in order to marry another' is discussed by D. Bivin, 'And' or 'In order to' Remarry,' (*Jerusalem Perspective* Jan-March, 1996, pp. 10-16). See also B. Young, *Jesus the Jewish Theologian*, pp. 113-117. Jesus did not cancel Deut. 24:1-2 which allowed someone to remarry after divorce but rather protected the family and the sacredness of marriage by upholding Jewish teachings prohibiting divorce in order to marry someone new (m. Sotah 5:1). See Mark 10:11 and the note on Matt 19:9" (Young, 2019).
- Yeshua's teachings about divorce have been debated for centuries. What is He saying here?
- In Judaism during the time of Yeshua, marriage and family were of utmost importance. The home was foundational for the study of Scriptures, prayers, and blessings.
- However, the Torah taught that divorce, although not ideal, was permitted (Young, 1995).
- There was a dispute between Hillel the Elder and his contemporary, Shammai over the interpretation of Deuteronomy 24:1. Shammai said that "something indecent" meant marital unfaithfulness. Hillel said that in the context "who becomes displeasing to him" meant a man could divorce his wife for anything she did that displeased him – even if she burnt the food while she was cooking it [See "Fiddler on the Roof" scene in the synagogue discussing Hillel]. Yeshua clearly agreed with Shammai's interpretation (*Archaeological Study Bible*, 2005).
- Yeshua is saying that "when a man breaks the marriage bond through infidelity and divorces his wife to marry someone else, he has abused the laws of the Hebrew Scripture concerning divorce and remarriage. It is the same as adultery." In essence, Yeshua says that when one divorces someone in order to marry someone else, it is wrong" (Young, 1995, p. 116).

16:19) "Now there was a certain rich man who loved to dress up in purple and fine linen, and to relish a life of luxury every day. 16:20) A certain poor beggar named Lazar, covered with sores, was laid in front of his gate. 16:21) He longed to be fed with scraps which fell down from the rich man's table. Even the dogs would come and lick his sores. 16:22) Now it just happened that the poor man died. He was carried away by the angels to Avraham's open arms. The rich man also died and was buried. 16:23) In hell, where he was being tortured, he lifted up his eyes and saw Avraham far away. There was Lazar resting in his arms. 16:24) He called out and said, 'Father Avraham, have mercy on me! Send Lazar to dip the tip of his finger in water and cool off my tongue. Look at how I am being tortured in this fire!' 16:25) But Avraham said, 'Child, remember that during your lifetime you experienced your prosperity, but Lazar suffered misfortune. Now he is being comforted here, and you are in agony. 16:26) Besides all that, between us and you there is a deep drop-off which has been put into place so that anyone who wants to go from our side to yours cannot cross over, and also anyone who wishes to cross over from your side to us cannot.' 16:27) So he replied, 'Then I plead with you, Father, send him to my father's house 16:28) because I have five brothers. Let him strongly warn them, so that they will not also come to this place of torment.' 16:29) But Avraham said, 'They have Moshe and the prophets—let them listen and obey them.' 16:30) But he answered, 'They will not, Father Avraham, unless someone goes to them from the dead. Then they will repent!' 16:31) But he said to him, 'If they do not listen to Moshe and the prophets, neither will they be persuaded, even if one should rise from the dead.'"

- Yeshua continues to teach about how to live and the importance of the TANAK (Torah and Prophets – "Old Testament").
- The meaning of the name "Lazar" in Greek or "Eleazar" in Hebrew is "God helps." The rich man is unnamed. Was Lazar a sinner who was being punished by God?
- Hoping to get a gift from those passing by, the crippled Lazar had been placed in front of the rich man's mansion.
- Those who sat at the rich man's table would use pieces of bread dipped in liquid to wipe their hands.
- The dogs in the story are wild dogs roaming on the streets.
- Lazar is in a place of highest honor in the Heavenly banquet with Avraham (Abraham).
- The rich man appeals to his kinship with Avraham, and it is acknowledged, but that is not enough. The rich man is without repentance.
- The gulf is the irreversibility of God' judgement (Jeremias, 1972).
- To those who are slaves to luxurious living and ignore the needs of the poor, Yeshua has nothing further to say. Not even a message of the resurrection with its threat of judgement to come can move those who have not responded positively to the revelation of God's will in the TANAK (Torah and Prophets) (Remember Moshe [Moses] wrote the Torah).
- The wealthy will be brought low, and the poor will be exalted (Marshall, 1978).

Although imitation purple dye existed, the biggest source of the real dye came from crushing murex marine snails. These animals were found in the Mediterranean Sea close to Tzur (Tyre). See Lesson 8. The process of making the dye was extremely expensive. One source estimates it took 10,000 shellfish to produce a single gram (0.035 ounces) of dye. Clothes or robes that were dipped in the dye carried a strong odor, but because it was so expensive it was a status symbol (*Cultural Backgrounds Study Bible*, 2016).

> What does the murex marine snail look like? Are they purple? Do these animals still exist? Research online for the answers to these questions and more. (See smithsonianmag.com to get started. They have a short video clip – Tyrian Purple Dye) Write and discuss:

_____
_____
_____
_____
_____
_____

Olive trees were very important in the Mediterranean world of the first century. Olives were eaten as food and crushed for their oil. The oil was used as an ingredient in cooking and as fuel for oil lamps. Olive oil was considered a major source of wealth as far back as the time of Solomon (Wilson, 1989, pp. 13-14).

> Take a trip online to the Mediterranean and research more about olive trees. How long do they live? How are olives harvested? When are olives harvested? How are olives crushed and pressed? How does a person grow an olive tree? What kind of climate and types of soil are needed? Do the trees grow from olives or grafting? Write and discuss:

_____
_____
_____
_____
_____
_____

Questions for review and discussion

What is the theme of Luke Chapter 16?

After studying these last two chapters, what do you think is important to Yeshua?

What does Yeshua want people to do?

The Essenes studied Scriptures and prayed a lot, but were they doing what God wanted them to do? ____ How do you know?

What is the TANAK?

Is the TANAK the same thing as the "Old Testament?"

What do "Moshe and the Prophets" mean?

What is Yeshua saying about the Torah and TANAK?

Summarize the study notes from this chapter and discuss:

Summarize in one or two sentences the most important or the most interesting thing you learned in this chapter from your study:

_____

_____

What makes it important or interesting to you?

_____

_____

_____

Re-read Luke Chapter 16 from the *Hebrew Heritage Bible* translation used in this book. Discuss. Summarize Luke Chapter 16 in one paragraph and discuss:

_____

_____

_____

_____

_____

_____

_____

_____

_____

_____

_____

_____

_____

Choose one verse from Luke Chapter 16 that you think is the most important and write it here. Discuss why you think it is the most important verse:

_____

_____

_____

How did your understanding of Luke Chapter 16 change after you studied it and read it again? Discuss.

_____

_____

_____

_____

GOSPEL OF LUKE 251

How can you apply what you learned from Luke Chapter 16 to your life? Discuss.

___
___
___

What question or questions do you still have about Luke Chapter 16 that you don't understand or want to know more about? Discuss

___
___
___
___

Beit She'an
Yerushalayim
Qumran

Locate Qumran on the map. How far is it to Yerushalayim?
___
What is the climate like?
___
What does it look like?
___
Locate Beit She'an on the map. How far is it to Yerushalayim?
___
What is the climate like?
___

GOSPEL OF LUKE   252

THE GOSPEL OF LUKE CHAPTER SEVENTEEN

Lesson 19

Before you begin your study, read Luke Chapter 17 out loud (as a group) from your Bible.

In your own words, summarize Luke Chapter 17 in one paragraph and write at least two questions that you had about the chapter as you read the biblical text: (Discuss)

_____
_____
_____
_____
_____
_____
_____
_____
_____
_____
_____
_____
_____
_____

The continuing themes through Luke Chapter 17 are the importance of the TANAK and its mandate on how to live. Yeshua reminds His disciples about the significance of forgiveness. It is foundational to a person's relationship with other people and with God. Refer to Lesson 13 and the lesson on forgiveness.

What do you think forgiveness means?

_____
_____
_____

What have you learned about forgiveness as you have studied Luke?

_____
_____

Why is it important to forgive?

_____
_____
_____
_____

> "Studying the Bible has changed practically everything about me. Before I started reading the Bible every day, I would wake up and just not want to get out of bed or do anything. About a year ago, I made reading the Bible my top priority. I set reminders on my phone every day, and then it became something that I couldn't go through my day without doing. It changed my whole outlook on life and made me more joyful. I was able to fully love my neighbors because I was confident in my relationship with God. I find now that I wake up every morning excited to read the Bible and ready to face the day because God gives me this natural energy that makes me excited and prepared to learn and love. The Bible has given me a reliable, never-failing place to turn when I am struggling. There is no place that gives me more comfort than the Bible." Emma England – Class of 2021

Hebrew Names and their English Equivalents

Hebrew	**English**
Shomron	Samaria
Noach	Noah
Sedom	Sodom

Chapter 17

17:1) He taught His disciples, "Temptations to do wrong are sure to come, but severe retribution threatens the person who causes others to be tempted! 17:2) It would be better for that person to have a millstone tied around his neck and to be thrown into the sea than to cause one of these little ones to stumble. 17:3) Be on your guard for your own sakes! If your friend does wrong, correct him. If he repents, forgive. 17:4) If that person does wrong to you seven times during the day, but then turns to you seven times and says, 'I repent,' you must forgive him."

- Yeshua is telling His disciples not to put stumbling blocks in the way of others, and He is teaching about the importance of forgiveness (Marshall, 1978).
- A common ancient metaphor for sin is "stumble" (Cultural Backgrounds Study Bible, 2016).
- What is sin?
- The Hebrew word for sin is *chayt*, an archer's term. The archer aims but misses the mark. The archer might pull back too far on the bow and overshoot the target. The archer might not pull hard enough and fall short, or the archer might simply be off-line. That is what *chayt* is; it is missing the mark (Sherman, personal communication, September 4, 2014).
- There are bound to be causes of sin in the world, but people are morally responsible. One must not cause or lead another person to sin. So fearful is the judgement that it would be better to die first than to act as a stumbling block. This is probably a hyperbole, or exaggeration, but it emphasizes the extreme importance of one's responsibility to others.
- A millstone was a circular stone that was used to grind grain. There were smaller millstones used by women each morning to grind grain for preparing bread and larger millstones that were turned by donkeys. This is the larger (Archaeological Study Bible, 2005).
- Who are these "little ones?" Perhaps they are children, the poor, or other people who are present.
- Similar to the subject of not leading others into sin is helping them when they fall into sin.
- Here one particular type of sin, namely personal offence, is discussed (Marshall, 1978).
- The disciple has the duty to correct an offender so that they have the opportunity to repent (Marshall, 1978).
- Jewish custom required private correcting before exposing someone in front of a Jewish assembly (Archaeological Study Bible, 2005).

- The standard teaching within Judaism (based on Job 33:29-30; Amos 1:3, 2:6) was that three instances of forgiveness reflected a forgiving spirit. In Matthew 18:21, Kefa's (Peter) offering to forgive seven times may have reflected his desire of completeness and generosity. Yeshua's response in that circumstance was that one should forgive countless times (Archaeological Study Bible, 2005).
- Jewish tradition valued forgiveness. However genuine repentance should include restitution, and the sinner should have no plans to sin again (Cultural Backgrounds Study Bible, 2016).
- This indirectly forbids the holding of grudges and criticism of the offender behind his or her back.
- The hoped result is positive. It is one of repentance and forgiveness.
- Teshuvah is the process of effecting repentance, of turning one's life around, of getting back on target (Sherman, personal communication, September 4, 2014).
- The forgiveness that Yeshua is teaching here is more demanding than the traditional "three times" in Judaism. It is limitless.
- Forgiveness is not to be merely outward. It must be from the heart – genuine (Marshall, 1978) and accompanied by change.

> "To me, the Bible is a means of finding peace. It's like a gateway to knowledge. Through it, we can see all that God has for us, and what he will continue to do. The Bible isn't just a book, it's wisdom and guidance." Ethan Heiling – Class of 2020

The God of Justice and Mercy

The rabbis claimed that the term *elo-im* refers to God's attribute of justice and *adon-y* to His quality of mercy. Both of God's names and attributes are necessarily involved in His rule of the world. For example, when God tells Noah that He would bring a flood, the Torah uses the term *elo-im*, but when Noah is safely in the ark, it is **adon-y** who closes the door and secures him and his family. Similarly, when God tells Abraham to sacrifice his son Isaac, the term *elo-im* is used, but when he stops him from killing Isaac, it is "an angel of *Adon-y*." God waits for people to repent. God is a merciful and compassionate Father as well as a judge of justice. The rabbis taught that God created and governs the entire world through a combination of His attributes of mercy and justice (Eckstein, 1997, pp. 112-113).

Forgiveness is a call to action. In the Sermon on the Mount, Rabbi Yeshua teaches His disciples that reconciliation with one's brother or sister must be sought before reconciliation with God is possible. Hostility in relationships must be corrected *prior* to the act of worshiping God. "If you are offering your gift on the altar and there remember that your brother has something against you, leave your gift there in front of the altar. First go and be reconciled to your brother; then come and offer your gift" (Matt. 5:23-24). How is it possible to know if someone is genuinely penitent (sorry)? The rabbis believed that changed behavior, through consistency of life was necessary to demonstrate this (Wilson, 2014, p. 215). Imagine yourself as a member of Yeshua's audience in Galil, some eighty miles from Yerushalayim. Yeshua says that after making a long journey to the Temple and before you offer your gift to God, you must first make sure that you aren't holding unforgiveness in your heart. (Remember the concept of the "preservation of life," and in cases of physical or emotional abuse it might be too dangerous for a person to reconcile face-to-face. However, it is possible to forgive someone from a safe distance.)

What do you think about Yeshua's teaching on forgiveness in Matthew 5:23-24? How important is it to God that people forgive one another? Even one's enemy? Write and discuss:

_____

_____

_____

_____

17:5) Then the authoritative emissaries asked Him, "Cause our faith to grow strong!" 17:6) At that, the Lord said, "If you only had faith as small as a mustard seed, you would say to this mulberry tree, 'Be uprooted and be planted in the sea,' and it would obey you. 17:7) Who among you, who has a servant plowing dirt or herding sheep, when he comes back from the field, will say to him, 'Come in right now and sit down to eat'? 17:8) But will he not say to him, 'Prepare my supper for me, and properly clothe yourself. Serve me until I have finished eating and drinking, and then you may eat and drink'? 17:9) He does not thank the servant, just because he did everything he was required to do. 17:10) It is the same with you—when you merely do everything you were required to do, say, 'We are unworthy servants; we have done only that which we were obligated to do.'"

- The mustard seed is not the smallest seed known today, but it was the smallest seed used by farmers in the Holy Land 2,000 years ago. It could reach a height of up to ten feet at maturity (*Archaeological Study Bible*, 2005).
- The fig mulberry tree was very deep-rooted (Marshall, 1978), and its wide root system made it very difficult to uproot (*Cultural Backgrounds Study Bible*, 2016).

- The contemporaries of Yeshua taught that the person who knows the Torah and obeys it cannot be moved (Jeremias, 1972).
- "Be uprooted and be planted in the sea," is not to be taken literally. This word does not invite Christians to become conjurers or magicians but heroes whose deeds are celebrated like those mentioned in Hebrews 11.
- The wonders of God's presence must be translated into action. True faith leads to active involvement. Deeds of wonder are related to vigorous obedience that brings wholeness to others in need.
- Faith and trust – life in the Kingdom is filled with the wonder of God's goodness and grace.
- During the Second Temple period a religious revolution in Jewish thought occurred. The strong emphasis on divine grace, that is, serving God from the primary motivation of love, was emerging. The servants serve their master but not for a reward (Young, 1998).

A Foundation of Faith

Yeshua realized that true faith in God originates in a sense of wonder and amazement. Abraham's faith began with a sense of wonder and awe in God's presence. "All Abraham could achieve by his own power was wonder and amazement; the knowledge that there is a living God was given to him by God." Wonder and amazement are the first steps to encountering the Kingdom of Heaven. The word of faith in the Bible is comprehended through the wonder of God's presence. "God's light may shine upon us, and we may fail to sense it. Devoid of wonder, we remain deaf to the sublime. We cannot sense His presence in the Bible except by being responsive to it. Only living with its words, only sympathy to its pathos, will open our ears to its voice. Biblical words are like musical signs of a divine harmony which only the finest chords of the soul can utter. It is the sense of the holy that perceives the presence of God in the Bible" – Abraham Joshua Heschel (Young, 1995, p. 99).

Slavery in the Roman World

- The Roman empire was built on a foundation of slavery.
- People could become slaves through debt bondage.
- They could be born into slavery, or they could be captured in warfare.
- They could become slaves as a form of judicial punishment, piracy, or slave trade (*ESV Archaeology Study Bible*, 2017).

Slavery in the Roman World

- There was no racial element to slavery.
- About 20% of the population were slaves. However, approximately one out of every three people living in Rome was a slave.
- The slave was absolute property of the master. They had no legal rights. They had no rights to their own bodies.
- There were classes of slaves:
  - Public (there was more freedom, but it was more brutal and more dangerous)
  - Private
    - City slaves
    - Country slaves
- Slaves could be freed by a legal process and become "freedmen" (ESV Archaeology Study Bible, 2017).

- Without a break, Yeshua describes how a slave has just finished his daily work in the field and still has to perform his household duties. The performance of duty does not entitle one to receive a reward (Marshall, 1978).
- A home with just one multi-tasking slave was far from elite. Except during the harvest season, the slave would finish the work outside and be ready to serve an afternoon meal by 3:00 (Cultural Backgrounds Study Bible, 2016).
- Yeshua is not talking about slavery in this passage. He is only using slavery to illustrate a point about the Kingdom of God. Slavery was prevalent in society, and all of His audience would be aware of a slave's household duties.
- Yeshua's saying in verse 10 is an attack on the attitude that said performance of good works constituted a claim upon God for due reward.
- People cannot put God in their debt. The attitude that seeks reward and thinks they can lay claim on God is wrong.
- Yeshua is emphasizing divine grace (Marshall, 1978).
- God does not deal with a person only on the basis of good deeds.
- In Judaism a person cannot earn acceptance. It does not believe in salvation by works. God's grace is unlimited (Young, 1998).
- There is no righteousness by works; it is by grace and the response is gratitude – not to feel entitled to a reward or to be proud – just thankful. Humility, love, and gratitude is life in the Kingdom (Marshall, 1978).

> "Studying the Bible is critical to a relationship with God. It has the guidelines for living for God and obeying Him. And it's also a history book. It shows what has happened and what God has done in the past. It has helped me trust God and have faith in Him because we can see that He is perfect and trustworthy. As someone who finds a lot of comfort in knowing that God has a plan, it is very reassuring to me to read the Bible and see God's plan unfold." Kaylen Anderson – Class of 2021

17:11) Now as He was ascending up to Yerushalayim, He was crossing through the middle of Shomron and of Galil. 17:12) As He entered a village, ten men who had leprosy met Him, but stood away at a distance. 17:13) They lifted up their voices and said, "Yeshua, Lord, have mercy upon us." 17:14) When He saw them, He said, "Go and show yourselves to the priests." So it happened, as they were going, they were made clean [of their leprosy]. 17:15) Then one of them, when he realized that he was healed, turned around [and went back to Yeshua], praising God with a loud shout. 17:16) He threw himself down upon his face at the feet of Yeshua, giving thanks to Him. But he was a Samaritan. 17:17) Yeshua answered, "Were not ten made clean [of their leprosy]? Where are the other nine? 17:18) Was no one found to return and give glory to God except this foreigner?" 17:19) He said to him, "Rise up and go your way; your [chutzpah style] faith has healed you."

- Yeshua was headed to Yerushalayim. One always ascends to Yerushalayim because it is the Holy City. It was the location of the Temple of God. It is a spiritual ascent. The Psalms of Ascent, Psalms 120-134, were sung by people as they made their way up to the Holy City in antiquity.
- Yeshua and His followers are passing through a border region between Galil and Samaria. Both Jews and Samaritans would be encountered on this journey.
- Yeshua is approaching a village and is met by these ten lepers. They were on the outskirts of habitation. The lepers were conforming to the law by avoiding physical contact with others (Leviticus 13:45, Numbers 5:2), but they were staying close enough to receive help.
- It's not surprising that they had heard about Yeshua; He could cleanse the lepers. Healing leprosy was one of the six signs of the Messiah. Great prophets like Elijah and Elisha had also healed lepers.
- Being healed of leprosy was extremely rare, if not completely unheard-of (Marshall, 1978).
- One of the lepers was a Samaritan. The condition of leprosy apparently outweighed the usual hatred and prejudice between the Jews and the Samaritans since these men were together when they approached Yeshua (*Cultural Backgrounds Study Bible*, 2016).

GOSPEL OF LUKE

- The command to go to the priests was a test of faith and obedience. The Jews would go to the Jewish priests in Yerushalayim and the Samaritan would go to the Samaritan priests.

- Normally, a command to visit the priest would follow a cure so that the one who was cured of leprosy could officially resume their place in society (Leviticus 13:49). The cured leper would offer a sacrifice, and the priest would certify that they had been healed of the disease.

- The command to go implies that the completion of the healing took place at a distance without Yeshua touching them (Marshall, 1978).

- The ten trusted Yeshua enough to obey His command, "Go and show yourselves to the priests," knowing that the examination would occur only after they had been healed. And, they had not yet been healed when they began their journey.

- Only one showed gratitude to Yeshua and praise to God. His kind of faith not only healed him; it saved him (Stern, 1992).

Mount Gerizim was where the Samaritan Temple had been located in antiquity. In the story about Yeshua and the Samaritan woman at the well, the woman says to Yeshua, "Our ancestors worshiped upon this mountain, but you Jewish people claim that the proper place to worship is in Yerushalayim where people should worship" (John 4:20, *HHB*). She was talking about Mount Gerizim.

Take a trip online to Mount Gerizim in Yisrael. Explore the archaeological excavations and learn more about the history of this site. (Visit both "The Temple on Mount Gerizim" at Biblical Archaeology Society and "Mount Gerizim" at biblewalks.com.) Write and discuss:

_____
_____
_____
_____
_____
_____

17:20) Being asked by one of the spiritual leaders when the kingdom of God would come, He answered them, "The kingdom of God is not coming through signs that can be watched, 17:21) neither will it appear when they say, 'Look it is here' or 'over there.' Recognize it right now—because the kingdom of God is already among you."

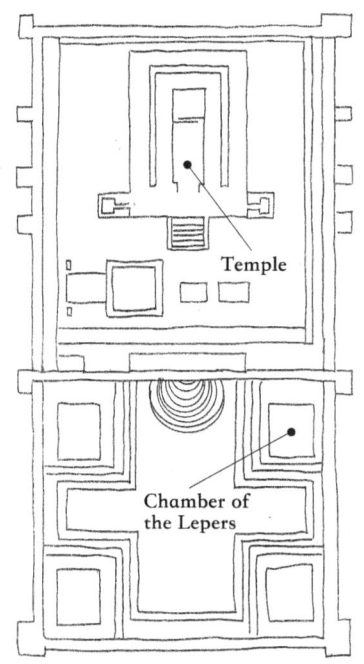

According to the law of Moses, when the leper was healed, he had to bring offerings to the Temple. He was shaved completely. He would leave and return on the eighth day. He had to bring additional sacrifices to the Temple and immerse himself in a mikveh in the Chamber of the Lepers. After his offerings and sacrifices were given and he was anointed with oil, he would be pronounced clean by the priests (Ritmeyer, 2006, pg. 352).

(Temple Diagram: Debbie Willey)

- When Yeshua says, "the kingdom of God is already among you" the understanding is that "kingdom" means God ruling in the lives of people. It is demonstrated through miracles, signs, and wonders. The kingdom was among them (Bivin & Blizzard, 1994).
- Yeshua is speaking of the presence of the Kingdom of God among people, possibly as something within their grasp if they will only take hold of it (Marshall, 1978).

17:22) He said to His disciples, "Look, the days are coming when you will long to see one of these days of the Son of Man but you will not see them. 17:23) Then they will say to you, 'Look there!' or 'Look here!' Do not go and run after them. 17:24) Because in the same way lightning strikes suddenly from one part of the sky, flashing over to the other part of the sky, so will be the coming of the Son of Man in His day. 17:25) But first, He must suffer many things and be rejected by this generation. 17:26) Just as it happened in the days of Noach, it will happen again in the days of the Son of Man. 17:27) They were eating, they were drinking, they were marrying, they were being given in marriage, until the day that Noach entered the ark. Suddenly the flood water came and destroyed them all. 17:28) The same thing happened in the days of Lot; they were eating, they were drinking, they were buying, they were selling, they were planting, they were building; 17:29) but on the day when Lot left Sedom, it rained fire and brimstone from heaven and destroyed them all. 17:30) The same will happen on the day when the Son of Man is revealed. 17:31) On that day, do not let the one who is on the housetop and whose goods are in the house go down to get them, and do not let the one who is in the field turn back. 17:32) Remember Lot's wife. 17:33) Whoever wants to save his life will lose it, and whoever loses his life will keep it alive. 17:34) I tell you, on that night, there shall be two in one bed; one will be taken, and the other will be left. 17:35) There will be two grinding at the same place; one will be taken, and the other will be left. 17:36) Two will be in the field; one will be taken, and the other will be left." 17:37) They questioned him, "Where Lord?" He explained to them, "Where there is a corpse, there also will the eagles flock together."

- In verse 22, Yeshua is again speaking to His disciples.
- Having established that the kingdom is already present, Yeshua deals with the unspoken question, "But what is still to happen?"
- The disciples are concerned about what is going to happen in the future. A time will come when they will want to see some visible evidence of the coming of the Son of Man, but there will be nothing to see.
- People will spread rumors, but the disciples must not be misled.
- When the Son of Man appears, there will be no mistaking it. His glory cannot be missed, and it will stand in absolute contrast to His suffering and rejection.
- The same generation will give itself up to worldly living, like the days of Noah and Lot. They will not listen to the Gospel.
- The day of the Son of Man will come suddenly, and people will be taken by surprise.
- It will bring judgment on the ungodly and redemption for God's people.
- The disciples should not be attracted to worldly desires that would keep them from being instantly ready. Only those prepared to lose their lives will survive the judgement.
- Don't ask for a map or a timetable. Just like a corpse can be found by spotting the vultures circling it; the Son of Man will appear in an unmistakable manner, and there will be no need to ask where He is. It will be obvious (Marshall, 1978).

Questions for review and discussion

What does *chayt* mean?

What does *teshuvah* mean?

What does Yeshua mean when He tells His followers not to cause others to "stumble"?

Explain "The God of Justice and Mercy" in your own words:

What could cause someone to become a slave?

What happened with the lepers?

What does Yeshua say about the coming Son of Man?

Summarize the study notes from this chapter and discuss:

Summarize in one or two sentences the most important or the most interesting thing you learned in this chapter from your study:

What makes it important or interesting to you?

Re-read Luke Chapter 17 from the *Hebrew Heritage Bible* translation used in this book. Discuss. Summarize Luke Chapter 17 in one paragraph and discuss:

_____
_____
_____
_____
_____
_____
_____
_____
_____
_____
_____
_____
_____
_____

Choose one verse from Luke Chapter 17 that you think is the most important and write it here. Discuss why you think it is the most important verse:

_____
_____
_____

How did your understanding of Luke Chapter 17 change after you studied it and read it again? Discuss.

_____
_____
_____

How can you apply what you learned from Luke Chapter 17 to your life? Discuss.

_____
_____
_____

What question or questions do you still have about Luke Chapter 17 that you don't understand or want to know more about? Discuss.

_____
_____
_____

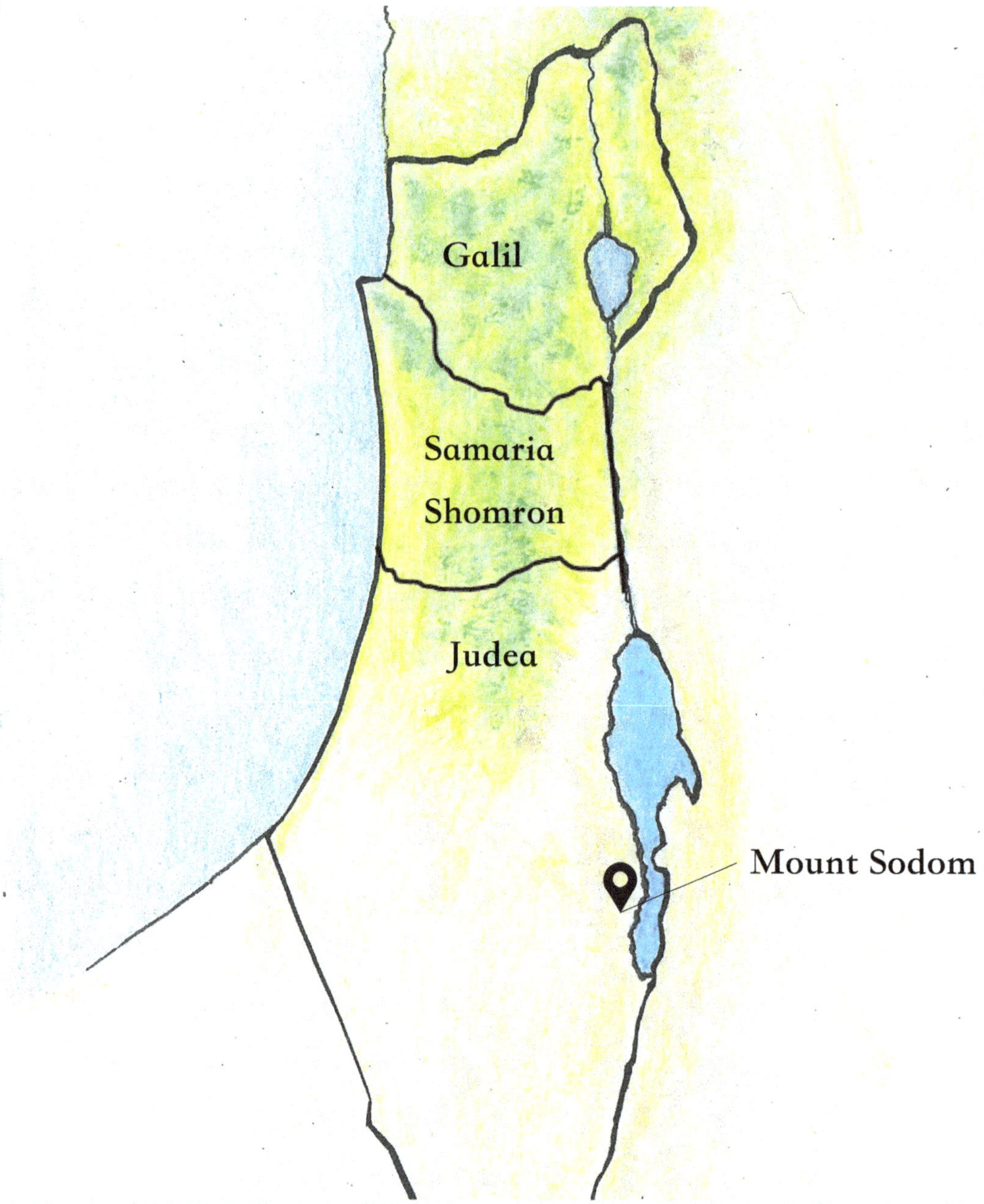

Notice the location of the region of Shomron (Samaria) on the map and how it is located between Galil and Judea.

 Mount Sodom (Sedom) is located near the western shore of the Dead Sea. Discover more about the salt cave located there. Is it the location of the story of Sodom and Gomorrah? Look at the Mount Sodom Hike online. Write and discuss:

___
___
___
___

GOSPEL OF LUKE   266

THE GOSPEL OF LUKE CHAPTER EIGHTEEN

Lesson 20

Before you begin your study, read Luke Chapter 18 out loud (as a group) from your Bible.

In your own words, summarize Luke Chapter 18 in one paragraph and write at least two questions that you had about the chapter as you read the biblical text: (Discuss)

_____
_____
_____
_____
_____
_____
_____
_____
_____
_____
_____
_____
_____
_____

Luke Chapter 18 opens with Yeshua again teaching about prayer. He tells a parable about persistence (chutzpah) in prayer and highlights the dependability and compassion of God. In the next story, Yeshua is emphasizing the importance of humility in prayer. Yeshua welcomes the children and encourages His disciples to be more like children in their wonder and amazement of God (See Lesson 19). He continues to teach about chutzpah, the Kingdom of God, and He heals the blind man.

 A beautiful practice is often followed in traditional Jewish homes on the eve of Shabbat. Putting their hands on the heads of their children, the parents bless their sons and daughters. For sons, they recite this blessing, "May God make you like Ephraim and Manasseh." For daughters, they recite, "May God make you like Sarah, Rebekah, and Leah." And over all of them they bless them with the priestly benediction found in Numbers 6:24-26 (Wilson, 1989, p. 218). The prayer ends with a blessing of shalom (peace). Research online and write more about the Jewish tradition of "Blessing the Children" at myjewishlearning.com. What do these prayers mean? When are the prayers said? Who says the prayers? What other traditions accompany the prayers? Write and discuss:

_____
_____
_____
_____
_____
_____
_____
_____

Chapter 18

18:1) He told them a parable to illustrate how they should pray at all times and not lose determination 18:2) by saying, "A judge who did not fear God or possess respect for other people lived in a particular city. 18:3) A widow lived in that city who kept on coming to him saying, 'Vindicate me against my accuser!' 18:4) Then he said to himself, 'Even though I do not fear God and do not respect other people, 18:5) this widow never stops bothering me. I will vindicate her so that she will not wear me out [with her unrelenting tenacity].'" 18:6) The Lord said, "Hear what the corrupt judge said. 18:7) Now will not God bring down justice for His elect ones who pray to Him day and night? Will He delay long over them? 18:8) I tell you that He will bring about justice for them speedily. However, when the Son of Man comes will He find faith [among the people] of the earth?"

- The parable Yeshua teaches in Luke 18:1-8 is a "twin parable" to the one He tells in Luke 11:5-8.
- In both of these parables Yeshua is teaching the importance of expectation and chutzpah in prayer.
- One should pray to God with bold determination because He is full of compassion and mercy.
- God is not like the corrupt judge or the contemptible friend (Luke 11:5-8).
- True faith requires bold perseverance and an understanding of the goodness of God.
- The Jewish view of a judge in the first century was that the judge would be fair and just. A judge represented God's authority on earth and was supposed make fair decisions based on evidence (2 Chronicles 19:6-7).
- The Jewish understanding of God was that He would be greatly concerned for the wellbeing of widows and orphans.
- The judge in this story does not behave in a manner Yeshua's audience would have expected. His behavior is quite the opposite.
- The judge is only concerned about himself. For the judge not to fear God is quite scandalous.
- The rabbis and the Jewish culture of the first century viewed chutzpah as a positive trait. Chutzpah was a valid expression of religious faith going all the way back to Abraham (Young, 1995, p. 174).
- This parable emphasizes the need for faithful perseverance in prayer (Young, 1995, p. 177).
- The widow represented the weakest and most vulnerable member of society. They were often exploited.
- The judge only granted her request because she was nagging him (Stern, 1992).
- If the corrupt judge will grant a poor widow's request just because of her persistence, how much more (al achat kamah vekamah) will the merciful God be moved by the prayers of His people (Young, 1995, pp. 177-178).
- The Jews were expecting a period of intense suffering, leading to a "falling away" (apostasy) before the day of God's judgement and vindication (Cultural Backgrounds Study Bible, 2016).

18:9) He also told this parable for certain individuals who put confidence in themselves that they were righteous and viewed others with contempt. 18:10) "Two men went up into the Temple to pray, one a spiritual leader, and the other a tax collector. 18:11) The spiritual leader stood and was praying to himself, 'God, I thank Thee that I am not like other people: swindlers, unjust, adulterers, or even like this tax collector. 18:12) I fast twice a week. I pay tithes of all that I receive.' 18:13) But the tax collector standing some distance away was unwilling even to lift up his eyes toward heaven. He was beating his breast saying, 'God be merciful to me the sinner!' 18:14) I tell you, this man went down to his house justified, rather than the other. Everyone who exalts himself shall be humbled [by God], but the one who humbles himself shall be exalted [by God]."

- This is a continuation of the theme of prayer.
- Later rabbis sometimes contrasted the spiritual leaders and tax collectors as the examples of piety (the religious leaders) and sin (the tax collectors).
- Thanking God for one's devoutness, was considered pious and humble. However, this religious leader looked down on everyone else (*Cultural Backgrounds Study Bible*, 2016).
- And, this religious leader was praying to himself and not to God. In spite of his addressing God, he wasn't in contact with God at all. He was only boasting and justifying himself (Stern, 1992).
- The Talmud speaks of one who would "undertake to fast every Monday and Thursday throughout the year" (Stern, 1992).
- People often looked to heaven when they prayed.
- The tax collector beat his breast as a sign of mourning because of his sins. The tax collector understands his dependence upon God's mercy, not on his own righteousness.
- The exalting of the humble and the humbling of those who exalt themselves is reminiscent of the principle of judgement found in the TANAK. Here it is applied to the religiously proud (*Cultural Backgrounds Study Bible*, 2016).
- All claims on self-righteousness are rejected.
- Even tax collectors can be accepted by Him if they repent.
- The tax collector dares to pray even in his unclean state as a tax collector. This is also chutzpah.
- The attitude of the heart is ultimately what matters to God (Marshall, 1978).

18:15) The people were bringing their young children to Him so that He might give them His touch [for spiritual blessing]. But when the disciples saw it, they started to turn them away with stern words. 18:16) But Yeshua called for them saying, "Allow the children to come to Me! Stop hindering them because the kingdom of God belongs to such as these. 18:17) I tell you the absolute truth, anyone who does not receive the kingdom of God like a child, will not enter it at all."

- In verse 15, the text "give them His touch [for spiritual blessing]" refers to the Jewish tradition of laying hands on the children. Here Luke, like Mark 10:13, explains the tradition using the verb "touch" while Matt 19:13 uses the actual Hebraic wording that says He laid hands on them and also prayed for the children. The reference in Luke to the "young children" that could be translated as "babies" likely recalls the blessings that the young Yeshua received in the Temple (Luke 2:27, 36). Even today on Shabbat, the father blesses his children at the table with the ritual of the laying on of hands (Young, 2019).

- Perhaps verses 15-17 reflect a Shabbat day-long teaching event.
- Children are filled with awe and faith in God's goodness.
- Wonder and amazement are the first steps to entering the Kingdom of God (Young, 1995).

18:18) A certain ruler questioned him saying, "Good Rabbi, what shall I do to attain eternal life?' 18:19) Yeshua said to him, "Why do you call Me good? No one is good, except God alone." 18:20) You know the commandments, "Do not commit adultery, Do not murder, Do not steal, Do not bear false witness, Honor your father and mother.'" 18:21) He replied, "All these things I have observed from my youth." 18:22) When Yeshua heard this, He said to him, "One thing you still lack: sell all that you possess and give it to the poor, and so you shall have treasure in heaven. Then come follow Me." 18:23) But when he heard this, he was filled with great sadness because he was extremely rich. 18:24) Yeshua looked at him and said, "How difficult it is for those who are wealthy to enter the kingdom of God! 18:25) It is easier for a camel to go through the eye of a needle than for a rich person to enter the kingdom of God." 18:26) They that heard this remarked, "How then is it possible for anyone to be saved?" 18:27) But he said, "What is impossible with human beings is possible with God." 18:28) Then Kefa pointed out, "Look, we have left our own homes and followed you." 18:29) He said to them, "I tell you the absolute truth, there is no one who has left house or wife or brothers or parents or children for the sake of the kingdom of God, 18:30) who will not receive many times more in the present time, as well as in the age to come, eternal life."

- These verses reinforce the earlier teaching: The way into the Kingdom is by loving God and one's neighbor. This is realized by obedience to the commandments and limitless charity.
- Good was used to describe God alone. True goodness is only attributable to God.
- "You know the commandments" is synonymous to an order to obey them.
- The man claims to have kept all of them. This statement is not unusual. Yeshua does not praise nor condemn him for keeping all of the commandments, probably because the man is just doing what he is supposed to do.
- Yeshua gives him an additional command: a call to discipleship (Marshall, 1978).
- The extremely rich man was filled with great sadness at the thought of losing his wealth in order to participate in the Kingdom of Heaven.
- Yeshua replies, "How difficult it is for the wealthy to enter the kingdom of God!" The statement appears to rule out all hope of salvation for anybody.
- Yeshua says that while this seems impossible from a human point of view, it is possible in terms of the power of God. God can work a miraculous change of heart even in the rich (Marshall, 1978).

- For "a camel to go through the eye of a needle" illustrates that salvation is impossible without God. This is a vivid and memorable illustration. Similar statements are found in later Jewish writings such as the Talmud.
- The term "needle's eye gate" came after Yeshua gave this teaching. The popularity of this name for a type of gate came from Yeshua's illustration here. Yeshua's contrast of the largest animal in the Holy Land with one of the smallest holes created (literally the eye of a needle) painted a powerful image of the power of God (*Archaeological Study Bible*, 2005).
- Only God can work a miracle in a human heart (Marshall, 1978).
- Yeshua clearly understood that uncompromising religious commitment sometimes results in the breaking of family ties. Yeshua's own family did not favor His mission (Flusser, 2001).

18:31) He took the twelve aside and said to them, "Look! We are going up to Yerushalayim, and all things which are written by the prophets about the Son of Man will be accomplished. 18:32) For He will be betrayed over to the Heathens. He will be mocked, tortured, and spit upon. 18:33) After they have scourged Him, they will kill him; but on the third day He will rise again." 18:34) They understood none of these teachings, and this saying was hidden from them. They did not comprehend the things that were said.

- Yeshua tells His disciples about His upcoming suffering, death, and resurrection. Prophecy will be fulfilled in these events.
- Yeshua will suffer in the same way as the righteous did in the TANAK.
- His disciples either couldn't believe or didn't understand (Marshall, 1978).

18:35) It happened that as He was approaching Yericho, a certain blind man was sitting by the road, begging. 18:36) Now hearing a crowd going by, he began to ask what was happening. 18:37) They told him, "Yeshua of Natzeret is passing by." 18:38) He started yelling out, "Yeshua, Son of David, have mercy on me!" 18:39) Those who were out front leading the way sternly rebuked him and told him to be quiet. But he kept on yelling at the top of his voice, all the more, "Son of David! Have mercy on me!" 18:40) Yeshua stood still and commanded that he be brought before Him. When he came near, He asked him, 18:41) "What do you want Me to do for you?" He said, "Lord, I want to see again!" 18:42) Yeshua said to Him, "Receive your sight; your [chutzpah style] faith has made you whole." 18:43) Instantly he recovered his sight, and began following him, glorifying God. When all the people saw [the miracle], they gave praise to God.

- The blind man is begging near the gate of the town.
- He hears the excitement and noise of the crowd and asks who is approaching. They respond, "It is 'Yeshua of Natzeret.'" His response is to yell out to Yeshua addressing Him as the "Son of David," which is clearly a reference to His being the Messiah of God (Marshall, 1978).
- The blind man was rebuked for yelling, but he continued crying out for mercy from Yeshua.
- Yeshua's response to the man's chutzpah was to ask the man what he wanted, and He healed the man.
- This man is added to the list of those who possessed great chutzpah or faith; the friends who tear a hole in the roof of the house, the woman with the issue of blood, the woman who anointed Yeshua's feet…"Your chutzpah faith has made you whole" (Young, 1998).
- Yeshua is approaching Yericho on His way to Yerushalayim.

Yericho is one of the oldest cities in the world. It was known as the "city of palms" because of its production of dates. Date palms have grown in this area of the Judean desert for thousands of years. In 2005, a 2,000-year-old date palm seed was discovered in the excavations at Masada (Herod the Great's ancient palace fortress near the Dead Sea). Scientists were able to germinate the seed and named the tree "Methuselah."

Take a trip online to Israel and discover more about this amazing tree. Begin with the article "Methuselah Palm 2,000-year-old Seed" at National Geographic.com. Where did the name Methuselah come from? Why would they choose that name? What did you learn about the tree? How were scientists able to germinate the seed? What is unique about the tree? Has it produced dates? Have they been able to germinate other ancient seeds? Write and discuss:

___
___
___
___
___
___
___

GOSPEL OF LUKE

> "For me studying the Bible has been very big in my walk with God. Before I would read the Bible without really tapping into the meaning behind the words. By actually really digging into the Bible and the deeper meaning of it, I can much more easily feel the power and presence of God. I can sense the fight and the struggle that many faced creating our Bible. I feel that if I had never begun studying the Bible like we do now, I do not think I would be as close to God as I feel now. I would suggest digging deeper into the Bible every time you get into it and try to understand the deeper meaning." Ben Brown – Class of 2021

Questions for review and discussion

What is the main theme of this chapter?

What does Yeshua teach about prayer?

What is chutzpah?

Was having Chutzpah considered rude behavior?
How do you know?

What did Yeshua say about children?
What did He do when He blessed them?

What did Yeshua say to the very wealthy man when the man said he kept all the commandments?

What does that mean?

How did the very wealthy man feel when Yeshua told him to sell his possessions and give it to the poor and follow Him?

Does that mean you can't have money and follow Yeshua?

Explain:

What does the expression "easier for a camel to go through the eye of a needle" mean?

What does all of this mean to you?

Summarize the study notes from this chapter and discuss:

Summarize in one or two sentences the most important or the most interesting thing you learned in this chapter from your study:

What makes it important or interesting to you?

Re-read Luke Chapter 18 from the *Hebrew Heritage Bible* translation used in this book. Discuss. Summarize Luke Chapter 18 in one paragraph and discuss:

Choose one verse from Luke Chapter 18 that you think is the most important and write it here. Discuss why you think it is the most important verse:

How did your understanding of Luke Chapter 18 change after you studied it and read it again? Discuss.

How can you apply what you learned from Luke Chapter 18 to your life? Discuss.

What question or questions do you still have about Luke Chapter 18 that you don't understand or want to know more about? Discuss

THE GOSPEL OF LUKE CHAPTER NINETEEN

Lesson 21

Before you begin your study, read Luke Chapter 19 out loud (as a group) from your Bible.

In your own words, summarize Luke Chapter 19 in one paragraph and write at least two questions that you had about the chapter as you read the biblical text: (Discuss)

_____
_____
_____
_____
_____
_____
_____
_____
_____
_____
_____
_____
_____
_____

At the end of Luke Chapter 18, as Yeshua approaches the gate to the city of Yericho, He heals the poor blind man, a beggar, who had been an outcast in his community and perhaps had been considered a sinner by many. When Yeshua enters Yericho at the beginning of Luke Chapter 19, He is approached by another outcast. This time the outcast is a much hated very wealthy unscrupulous tax collector. Yeshua continues to bring healing as He teaches about the Kingdom of God. He enters Yerushalayim on a donkey and finally arrives at the Temple.

Yeshua continues to heal those who are sick and bring hope to those who are discouraged. Zakhai (Zacchaeus) was a corrupt tax collector whose life was radically changed by Yeshua at the beginning of chapter nineteen. He had a powerful testimony. What is your testimony?

_____
_____
_____
_____
_____
_____
_____
_____
_____
_____

Hebrew Names and their English Equivalents

Hebrew	English
Zakhai	Zacchaeus
Yericho	Jericho
Beit Pagei	Bethphage
Beit Anyah	Bethany

Hebrew Names

Interestingly, the word in Hebrew for **"salvation,"** **yeshuah**, is essentially the same as the name of **Yeshua** (Young, 2019).

Chapter 19

19:1) He entered Yericho and was passing through. 19:2) Look, there was a man named Zakhai. He was a principal tax collector and quite wealthy. 19:3) He wanted to see who Yeshua was, but could not on account of the crowd, because he was small of stature. 19:4) So he ran on ahead and climbed up high into a sycamore tree in order to see Him, for He was about to pass through that way. 19:5) When Yeshua came to the place, He looked up and said to him, "Zakhai, hurry up and come down; because I must stay at your house today." 19:6) He came down as fast as he could and welcomed Him as his guest with great joy. 19:7) But when they saw what had happened, they all began to complain saying, "He has gone off to be entertained by a man who is a sinner!" 19:8) But Zakhai stood still and said to the Lord, "See this, Lord, half of all my possessions I will give to the poor, and if I have cheated anyone of anything, I will pay back each one four times as much." 19:9) So Yeshua said to him, "Today salvation has come to this family because he too is a son of Avraham. 19:10) For the Son of Man has come to seek and to save the person who is lost."

- Yeshua associates Himself with the notorious tax collector Zakhai and others of ill repute. Everybody knew Zakhai was dishonest. He was a wealthy principal tax collector.
- Yeshua is searching diligently for the lost. He was equally comfortable in the home of the honorable Simon the Pharisee and the dishonorable Zakhai the principal tax collector (Young, 1998).
- All of them were Jewish including Zakhai – "members of the people to whom salvation was promised by God in the coming of the Messiah" (Marshall, 1978, p. 694).

Yericho (Jericho) was a wealthy city in antiquity. It was a winter residence for Herod and his sons and members of the Hasmonean dynasty (see Lesson 2). It also became a distribution hub for spices, salt, and expensive balsam. The main source for balsam and salt was the Dead Sea (*ESV Archaeology Study Bible*, 2017). It was home to many wealthy priests, and because of its strategic location on the border between Judea and Perea, the customs duties and taxes collected there would have been significant (*Cultural Backgrounds Study Bible*, 2016).

Take a trip online to Yericho (Jericho). Jericho at BiblePlaces.com. What did you learn about the excavations and the city of Jericho?

___

___

___

Research more about the modern city of Jericho. What is the population? Who lives there? What is the economy like? What is the predominant religion there?

___

___

___

- Because Yericho was a distribution hub for expensive products and a strategic tax center, Zakhai would have been very wealthy as a principal tax collector even if he had been ethical.
- After he met Yeshua, he confessed his sins and made restitution. The Torah required that he return the amount stolen plus 20 percent (Lev. 5:20-24). An apprehended thief had to pay the victim double (Ex. 22:3). A man caught stealing essential items was required to pay back fourfold (Ex. 21:37). He voluntarily self-imposed the entire amount required by the Torah for such acts (Stern, 1992).
- As a principal tax collector Zakhai was stationed at the center of commercial activity to collect toll on personal property for Rome. Principal tax collectors in Judea were chosen from the local population by the prefects (in this case: Pilate).
- As a Jew, Zakhai would have been considered a traitor by his fellow Judeans.
- The principal tax collectors would keep a percentage of what they collected. There was no limit on what they could keep for themselves although Emperor Tiberius had tried unsuccessfully to limit corruption.
- These tax collectors were notorious for taking bribes, granting favors, and were viewed as robbers (ESV Archaeology Study Bible, 2017).
- Yeshua was teaching His disciples to reach out to everyone, unlike the Essenes who believed everybody except them was predestined to damnation.
- On this day, Yeshua – yeshuah (salvation) came to Zakhai's house.
- Yeshua encourages His followers to trade with the unbelievers and associate with the outcasts.
- They are to love each other more than they love money, and almsgiving is to become a way of life.
- Yeshua's followers must reach beyond their group affiliation and move past their self-righteous prejudices (Young, 1998).

"Studying the Bible has really made an impact on me. Up until my junior year I was living for the wrong reasons. I was selfish, lazy, and arrogant. And, when God hit me over the head one day with trouble, I turned to Him and studied along with my Bible classes. Since then, I changed my look on life and am living for Him. So, study! There's plenty of things for you." Braden Marsh – Class of 2020

Zakhai climbs a sycamore tree so he can see Yeshua. This tree *(Ficus Sycomorus)* is a type of fig tree. The fruit is small and inferior in taste and smell to true figs. In antiquity only poor people ate sycamore figs. The tree has large, low-spreading branches and grows in the lower, warmer elevations of Israel including the Yarden (Jordan) River valley. The tree was used for its wood (ESV *Archaeology Study Bible*, 2017).

Research online and learn more about this tree. Does this type of tree still grow around Jericho? What does it look like? How is it used today?

___

> "Studying the Bible has shown me it is so much deeper that what I thought, and truly every little detail is put into place by God. I love how you can see little things in one part and see where it is coming from in other parts — as if it is all one picture."
> Caillum Ward – Class of 2020

19:11) While they were listening to these teachings, He went on to tell a parable because He was near Yerushalayim, and they supposed that the kingdom of God was going to appear immediately. 19:12) Therefore He explained, "A certain nobleman went to a faraway country to be crowned as king and then return. 19:13) He called ten of his servants and entrusted them with ten deposits of money and said to them, "Do business with this money until I come back." 19:14) But his subjects despised him and sent a delegation after him to say, 'We do not want this man to reign over us.' 19:15) When he returned after being appointed king of the kingdom, he ordered these servants to whom he had entrusted the money to be summoned before him. He wanted to find out what profit they had gained by trading. 19:16) The first one appeared saying, 'Master, your deposit has made ten times more.' 19:17) He said to him, 'Well done, good servant; because you have been faithful in a very little thing, you will receive authority over ten cities.' 19:18) The second one came in saying,

'Your deposit, Master, has made five times more.' 19:19) So he said to him, 'You also will be given authority over five cities.' 19:20) Then another came in to say, 'Master, here is your deposit which I kept put away in a handkerchief. 19:21) I was afraid of you because you are a severe man. You pick up what you never put down and reap what you did not sow.' 19:22) He said to him, 'By your own words I will judge you! You worthless servant! You knew that I am a severe man who picks up what I did not put down and that I reap what I did not sow. 19:23) Then why did you not put the money in the bank? When I came back, at least I would have collected the deposit with interest.' 19:24) He said to the bystanders, 'Take the deposit away from him, and give it to the one who made ten times more.' 19:25) They said to him, 'Master, he already has ten times the deposit!' 19:26) 'I tell you, that to everyone who has, shall more be given, but from the one who does not have, even what that person does have shall be taken away. 19:27) But as for these enemies of mine who did not want me to rule over them, bring them here, and kill them in front of me.'"

- Yeshua is continuing to travel from Yericho to Yerushalayim. It is about 17 miles from Yericho to Yerushalayim along the road made famous as the location of the Parable of the Good Samaritan (Luke 10:25-37). It is uphill all the way from Yericho to Yerushalayim with an elevation change of about 3500 feet.

- Yeshua is telling this parable to those who were present in the previous verses.

- They were believing that when Yeshua came to Yerushalayim the Kingdom of God would appear. Yeshua's disciples understood that the Kingdom of God had in some sense arrived, and it was a natural thought of theirs that its completion or implementation would follow once the activity of Yeshua reached the capital city.

- He is telling this parable in order to dispel (dismiss) such hopes (Marshall, 1978).

- In verse 12, Yeshua may be referencing Archelaus, the son of Herod the Great, who traveled to Rome to receive the approval of Emperor to rule Judea after Herod died.

- The descriptions of the nobleman in the parable ("we do not want this man to reign over us" and "I was afraid of you because you are a severe man") fit the attitudes of the Jews toward Archelaus. Archelaus had made extravagant additions to Herod's palace at Yericho (ESV Archaeology Study Bible, 2017). Therefore, the location is appropriate for the story.

- Archelaus was exceptionally cruel and brutal. The people wanted change and had sent a delegation of Jews and Samaritans to Rome to try to persuade the Roman officials to appoint someone other than Archelaus (Young, 1998).

- The theme of the parable is "faithful stewardship of God's gracious gifts" (p. 82). What will the servants do while the nobleman is away? Even though the nobleman leaves, he will return (Young, 1998).

- Each deposit of money was about 100 days wages for a common worker. Thus, the ten deposits of money equaled about three years' pay (ESV Archaeology Study Bible, 2017).

- Each servant received the same amount of money (3 months' wages), and they each had the same opportunity to gain by trading (Marshall, 1978).

- Two of the servants have made more money. The third laid it away in a handkerchief. He behaves with an inexcusable irresponsibility. He wrapped it in a handkerchief, "neglecting the most elementary safety measure. According to rabbinical law, if anyone tied up entrusted money in a cloth, he was responsible to make good any loss through inadequate care" (p.61). The handkerchief was a woven head-covering that was about a yard square (Jeremias, 1972, p. 61). It was worn as a scarf or neckcloth to protect the back of the head from the sun (Marshall, 1978).

- Because of fear, the servant sought to avoid failure. "His attempt to preserve capital brought about his ruin. Instead of faith, he had fear" (Young, 1998, p. 95).

- The message of the parable focuses on decisive action. God is good, and the stewards of His divinely given abilities must use them creatively to achieve maximum results (Young, 1998).

- The lesson is one of reward for the faithful and loss for the unfaithful.

- In verse 27, the fate of the enemies who refuse to accept the nobleman's rule is that of ancient rebels. The language would have made sense to Yeshua's audience (Marshall, 1978).

- The language used in verse 27 underscores the seriousness of the situation (Marshall, 1978).

- The final judgement will bring recompense in line with divine standards difficult to comprehend (Young, 1998).

19:28) When He had said these things, He made the ascent, going up to Yerushalayim. 19:29) When He came to Beit Pagei and Beit Anyah, which is located near the Mount called Olives, He sent two of His disciples on ahead 19:30) saying, "Go into the next village facing us, where as you go in, you will find a donkey colt hitched, upon which no one has ever yet ridden. Untie him and bring him here. 19:31) If anyone asks you, 'Why are you untying him?' You say this, 'The Lord has need of him.'" 19:32) So those who were designated to go went off and found everything exactly as He had told them. 19:33) Moreover, as they were unhitching the donkey colt, its owner said to them, "Why are you untying the colt?" 19:34) They said to him, "Because the Lord has need of him." 19:35) They led it to Yeshua. Then throwing some of their robes on the colt, they set Yeshua on his back. 19:36) As He rode along, they were throwing down their robes on the road. 19:37) As He was now coming near the descent of the Mount of Olives, everyone of the whole throng of the disciples in their joy began to praise God with a loud voice because of the miracles they had witnessed 19:38) saying, "Blessed is the King who comes in the name of the Lord! Shalom in heaven and glory in the highest!" 19:39) Some of the spiritual leaders in the crowd said to Him, "Rabbi, rebuke your disciples." 19:40) He answered, "I tell you, if these become silent, the very stones would cry out."

Hebrew Names

Beit Pagei – "Beit" means "house" and "Pagei" means "unripe figs"
Beit Anyah – "Beit" means "house" and "Anyah" "the poor" or "dates" (Marshall, 1978).

- In verse 33, the Greek has the plural form "owners," but it should be translated in the singular. See R. Buth, "Luke 19:31-34," JBL 104 (1985), 680-685. In Biblical and Mishnaic Hebrew, the plural "owners" is used with a singular verb. See also, D. Bivin, "Syndicated Donkey," JP (Feb. 1988) (Young, 2019).

- Yeshua is making His final ascension to Yerushalayim.

- He approaches Yerushalayim from the east and comes first to the villages of Beit Pagei (Bethphage) and Beit Anyah (Bethany). He would have reached Beit Anyah first.

- Beit Pagei was a walled suburb outside the walls of Yerushalayim and about three quarters of a mile east of the peak of the Mount of Olives. Beit Pagei was located between Beit Anyah and Yerushalayim.

- Beit Anyah was about two miles east of Yerushalayim on the eastern side of the Mount of Olives (Cultural Backgrounds Study Bible, 2016).

- People probably knew Yeshua in the area of Beit Anyah because He had friends who lived there (Lazarus, Mary and Martha were from Beit Anyah. See John 11:1).

- In verse 30, Yeshua sends His disciples to the village of Beit Pagei to get the donkey colt. Beit Pagei marked the outer limit of the area which ritually belonged to Yerushalayim itself.

- Animals would have been kept for the benefit of travelers who might borrow or hire them to aid them on their journeys.

- The animal is described as tied up and not previously ridden. This is very important because animals for sacred use could not be put to ordinary use (this donkey had never been ridden nor used in an ordinary manner), and the same was true for animals to be used for royalty.

- This occasion is very solemn. A question might arise about the donkey because of the odd action of the disciples taking a colt that was not used for riding.

- When the animal had been brought to Yeshua they threw garments upon it and seated Yeshua on it. This act was one of honor and a sign of kingship.

- The placing of garments for an animal to walk over is another expression of respect, perhaps indicating willingness to let a ruler trample on one's own property (Marshall, 1978, p. 714).

- As Yeshua reaches the peak of the Mount of Olives and begins His descent, Yerushalayim is in clear view.

- Yeshua was coming to Yerushalayim to celebrate the Passover Feast. As he enters Yerushalayim on Sunday, he is followed by a large crowd of Jewish pilgrims traveling from Galil and other parts of Yisrael. They had either witnessed or heard about how Yeshua had healed the lepers, given sight to the blind, how the deaf could hear, the lame could walk, and the dead had been raised to life. Yeshua had fulfilled all the signs prophesied about the Messiah. The people were looking for a messiah to deliver them from the Romans.

- As Yeshua rides on a donkey that had never been ridden (animals for sacred use could not have ever been used for ordinary purposes) the people placed their cloaks on the road as a symbol of respect and submission. The leafy branches were symbols of Jewish nationalism and victory.
- Yeshua rides a donkey in fulfilment of prophesy (Zechariah 9:9) and to show that he was the Messiah of peace – not war – a warrior would have ridden a horse (*Cultural Backgrounds Study Bible*, 2016).
- What the crowds shout is reminiscent of the praises from the angels and the shepherds who greeted Yeshua's entry into the world when He was born in Beit Lechem.
- "Blessed is the King who comes in the name of the Lord" is based on Psalms 118:26. In the Psalms, it appears to have been originally a greeting addressed to the king as he approached the Temple to worship God.
- The spiritual leaders are probably trying to help Yeshua, and their actions should be considered friendly as elsewhere in Luke (7:36; 11:37; 13:31-33; and 14:1). They may have feared for Yeshua's safety (and their own) if such outbursts led to a messianic demonstration (Marshall, 1978, p. 716).
- The Targum and rabbinic writings interpret Hab. 2:11 to mean that the stones could cry out against those who do evil. This may be taken to refer to those who would sin by keeping silent.
- This serves to underline the truth of the statements (Marshall, 1978).

Beit Anyah and Beit Pagei (Bethany and Bethphage) were two villages on the upper east slope of the Mount of Olives. They were the first permanent villages one would encounter on the road from Yericho to Yerushalayim. They were a good place to rest before entering Yerushalayim. Yeshua used Beit Anyah as His home-base when visiting the Holy City (*ESV Archaeology Study Bible*, 2017).

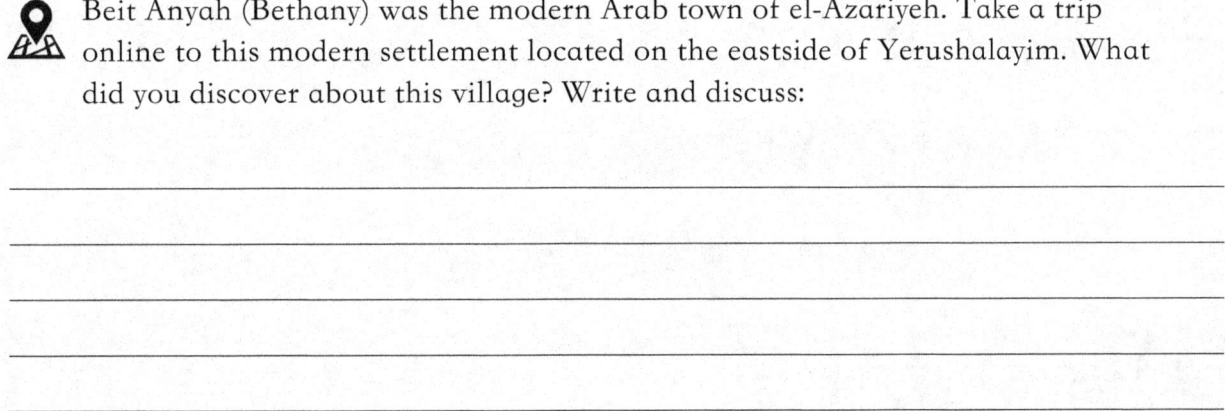 Beit Anyah (Bethany) was the modern Arab town of el-Azariyeh. Take a trip online to this modern settlement located on the eastside of Yerushalayim. What did you discover about this village? Write and discuss:

_____

_____

_____

_____

GOSPEL OF LUKE

📍 Beit Pagei (Bethphage) may have been the modern village of at-Tur at the southern end of the Mount of Olives. There is some archaeological evidence of settlement at this location during the Roman period. Take a trip online to at-Tur. What did you learn about this village? Write and discuss:

_____
_____
_____
_____
_____

"There is a huge impact I've experienced while studying the Bible. This Holy Book has taught me to always look to God and know he is in control at all times. God always has a plan and that plan is always for the good." Miles Bonine – Class of 2020

Photo: A view of the Temple Mount (Yerushalayim) from the southern end of the Mount of Olives (Credit: David Anderson, 2018)

The Mount of Olives is a ridge on the east side of Yerushalayim separating the Holy City from the Judean wilderness. The Kidron Valley lies between the Mount of Olives and Yerushalayim. The Mount of Olives is higher in elevation than Yerushalayim.

> Take a trip online to the Mount of Olives in Yerushalayim. What is its elevation? How long is the ridge? Where is Mount Scopus? What else did you learn? Write and discuss:

_____
_____
_____
_____
_____

19:41) When He came nearer and saw the city, He broke down in tears weeping over it 19:42) saying, "If you could only know this day what actions you could take to make shalom! But for now, they have been hidden from your eyes. 19:43) For the days will come upon you when your enemies will throw up a bank before you. They will surround you, and hem you in on every side. 19:44) They will beat you and your children into the ground. They will not leave in you one stone upon another—because you did not recognize the time of your visitation."

- Yeshua weeps over Yerushalayim when He sees it spread out before Him. He weeps over the destruction that is to come in AD 70 when the Romans surround the city, breach its walls, murder its residents, and destroy its Temple.
- The city could have learned the way of shalom from Him, to love even their enemies, but many became entangled in the military revolt against Rome which led to the destruction of the Holy City and its Temple. As a result, hundreds of thousands would be enslaved, dispersed, or murdered. See Luke 21:6.
- Archaeological evidence shows that the destruction was massive in scope (*ESV Archaeological Study Bible*, 2017).

19:45) He entered the Temple and began to bring out those who were selling, 19:46) saying to them, "It is written 'My house shall be a house of prayer' (Isa 56:7), but you have turned it into 'a den of robbers'" (Jer. 7:11). 19:47) Day by day, He was teaching in the Temple; but the chief priests and the scribes and some of the leading men among the people were trying to stop Him. 19:48) They could not find anything that they could do because all the people were hanging upon His words.

- Yeshua is entering the Temple Mount, not the Temple building itself. Only priests could enter the Temple.
- The Royal Stoa, which was located along the southern end of the Temple Mount, functioned as the financial center of the Jewish population of Judea and Galil. This is where animals were sold for sacrifice, and money was exchanged (*ESV Archaeology Study Bible*, 2017).
- The Temple currency was the Tyrian Shekel. Therefore, those entering Yerushalayim for worship had to have their currency exchanged for Tyrian Shekels (Jeremias, 1975).
- The Tyrian Shekel was 99 percent silver and was vastly superior in quality compared with other money in the Roman empire. The quality and metals of coinage within the empire varied widely.
- Scales weighed differently in Yerushalayim than they did in other areas, and prices were drastically inflated. "Once a pair of doves sold for two gold dinars (fifty silver dinars) by the Temple. 'I will not rest this night until I have made it so that they can be bought for one silver dinar!' said Simeon Gamaliel." That day, the Sanhedrin reduced the price so that the poor could participate in the Temple offerings (Jeremias, 1975).
- The cleansing of the Temple was expected in the end times. See Malachi 3:1; Jeremiah 7:11; and Ezekiel 40-48.
- Yeshua was teaching in the Temple area. His teaching received much popular support. The people were favorable toward Yeshua (Marshall, 1978).

Photo: Front and back of a Tyrian Shekel from the time of Yeshua.
(Private collection)

"I think it is important to study the Bible and to understand the culture that was behind the writing of it. Knowing the Bible and understanding the culture really brings a lot of things into context, like how or why certain words were used, and how they would affect a story in the Bible. Studying the Bible also grounds us in our faith. Knowing the Bible allows us to defend our faith and share it with others." Traci Palmer – Class of 2021

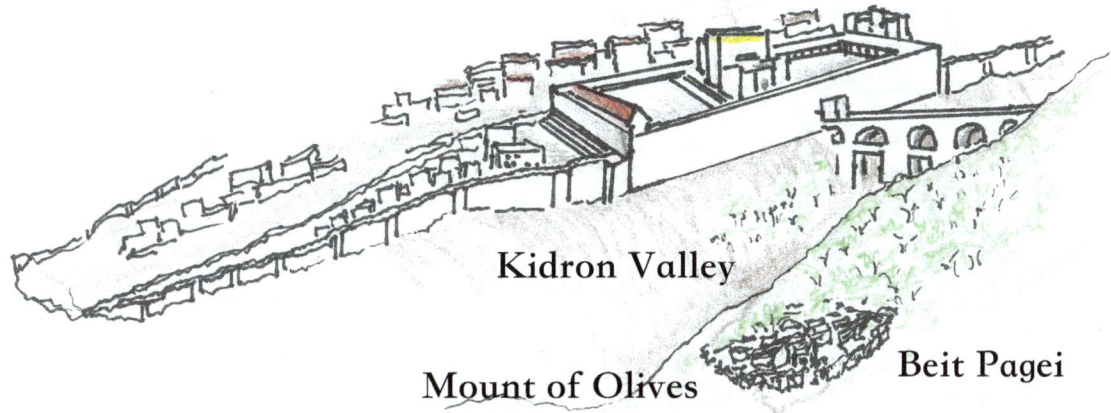

The view approaching Yerushalayim from Yericho. Beit Anyah is located about two miles from Yerushalayim and Beit Pagei was about three-quarters of a mile. Beit Pagei was at the crest of the Mount of Olives. Yeshua would have approached Yerushalayim from this direction looking at Yerushalayim before descending into the Kidron Valley and then ascending as He entered the Holy City.

Targums were paraphrases or interpretations of Scriptures written in Aramaic (Hoffmeier, 2008).

Rabbinic writings include rabbinic parables, commentaries, the Mishnah, and Midrash (Wilson, 1989).

Questions for review and discussion

Look up these friendly encounters between Yeshua and the spiritual leaders elsewhere in Luke (7:36; 11:37; 13:31-33; and 14:1). Comment on each one here:

_____

_____

_____

_____

Look up and comment on Malachi 3:1 and Jeremiah 7:11, as related to Yeshua's activities in Luke 19:46.

___

How did Zakhai's life change?

___

Who would Yeshua associate with?

___

Why?

___

What does Yeshua encourage His followers to do?

___

What does that mean you are supposed to do?

___

Explain what you think Yeshua is teaching in the parable that begins in verse 11, in your own words:

___

Why is that important?

___

Explain the significance of Yeshua's entrance to Yerushalayim:

___

Why does Yeshua "Bring out those who were selling" in verse 45?

___

The Romans mastered the art of siege warfare, training engineers in their armies to construct siege works. Their siege techniques included trenches, embankments, and walls with military camps surrounding a besieged city. The best-preserved Roman siege works are at Masada, Herod's palace fortress on the eastern side of the Dead Sea. The Romans surrounded Masada and built a siege ramp there after the destruction of the Temple at the end of the First Jewish Revolt (*ESV Archaeology Study Bible*, 2017). (The 1981, ABC mini-series *Masada* is a fictionalized account of the events that happened at Masada.)

Take a trip online to Masada, Israel and learn more about the tragic events that happened there at the end of the First Jewish Revolt. Write and discuss:

_____
_____
_____
_____
_____

The Royal Stoa was located on the southern end of the Temple Mount.
(Photo: Second Temple Model, Israel Museum, Jerusalem)

Summarize the study notes from this chapter and discuss:

_____
_____
_____
_____
_____
_____
_____

Summarize in one or two sentences the most important or the most interesting thing you learned in this chapter from your study:

_____

_____

Re-read Luke Chapter 19 from the *Hebrew Heritage Bible* translation used in this book. Discuss. Summarize Luke Chapter 19 in one paragraph and discuss:

_____

_____

_____

_____

_____

_____

_____

_____

_____

Choose one verse from Luke Chapter 19 that you think is the most important and write it here. Discuss why you think it is the most important verse:

_____

_____

How did your understanding of Luke Chapter 19 change after you studied it and read it again? Discuss.

_____

_____

_____

How can you apply what you learned from Luke Chapter 19 to your life? Discuss.

_____

_____

_____

What question or questions do you still have about Luke Chapter 19 that you don't understand or want to know more about? Discuss.

_____

_____

_____

_____

THE GOSPEL OF LUKE CHAPTER TWENTY

Lesson 22

Before you begin your study, read Luke Chapter 20 out loud (as a group) from your Bible.

In your own words, summarize Luke Chapter 20 in one paragraph and write at least two questions that you had about the chapter as you read the biblical text: (Discuss)

_____
_____
_____
_____
_____
_____
_____
_____
_____
_____
_____
_____
_____
_____

Yeshua has arrived in Yerushalayim and is teaching at the Temple Mount. He continues to teach by using parables to illustrate the truths about the Kingdom of God. He is questioned by some of the Jewish leaders.

 While Yeshua is in Yerushalayim teaching at the Temple Mount, He is questioned by the chief priests, the Sadducees and the elders. It is important to remember who they were and what they believed. Refer back to Lesson 2 in this book and identify the following and explain what they believed. Write and discuss.

Sadducees:
___
___
___

Priests:
___
___
___

Pharisees (spiritual leaders):
___
___
___

In verses 27-40, explain the dialog that Yeshua is having with the Sadducees. What kind of question were they asking Him?
___
___

What do you think this is about?
___
___
___

Several places where teaching occurred have been identified at the Temple Mount. They include: Solomon's Portico, the Terrace (Ritmeyer, 2006), and the Huldah Stairs along the Southern Wall (Hoffmeier, 2008). Solomon's Portico (Colonnade) was located along the length of the eastern side of the Temple Mount. This covered area where people could meet provided protection from the weather (See John 10:23; Acts 3:11).

The Huldah Stairs are located along the Southern Wall of the Temple Mount and were the main entrance for the Jewish people during the time of Yeshua. Many mikva'ot (ritual immersion baths) were excavated after the Six-Day War in 1967 at the base of these stairs. "The Midrash (the authoritative rabbinic interpretation of the Torah) refers to the great Rabbi Gamaliel 'and the elders who were sitting on the stairway in the Temple.' An incomplete Hebrew inscription was found on the stairs which preserves the Hebrew word zeqenim (elders) on it, suggesting that this was the area where elders and teachers of the Law met to discuss the finer points of the Torah" (Hoffmeier, 2008, pp. 139-140). Yeshua may have been teaching on these stairs when He tells the parable recorded in this chapter.

 Take a trip online to the Southern Wall and the Huldah Stairs in Yerushalayim. What did you learn?

_____
_____
_____

 Neil Armstrong visited these famous stairs after he was the first man to walk on the moon. What did he say when he visited? (See "Neil Armstrong Walks on Jerusalem," tabletmag.com)

_____
_____

Communion and teaching on the Huldah Stairs at the Huldah Gates in Yerushalayim 2018. Notice the Mount of Olives in the background.
Photo: David Anderson

GOSPEL OF LUKE 295

The Events of Holy Week

Sunday: Yeshua enters Yerushalayim on the colt of a donkey: Luke 19:35-40.

Monday: Yeshua drives out all of those who were buying and selling, overturned the tables of the money changers and rebukes them: Luke 19:45-47.

Tuesday: Yeshua is teaching at the Temple Mount in Yerushalayim: Luke 20:1-21:36. The widow's offering event occurs in the Court of the Women on the Temple Mount: Luke 21:1-4. Yeshua prophesizes about the destruction of the Temple and the signs of the End Times: Luke 21:12-17

Wednesday: The Bible does not say what Yeshua does on Wednesday of the Passion Week. He may have remained in Beit Anyah with his disciples.

Thursday: Yeshua had the "Last Supper" with his disciples. It was a Passover Seder. Afterward they went to a place called Gethsemane where Jesus prayed and was arrested: Luke 22:7-23

Friday: Late Thursday night into the early hours of Friday morning while Yeshua "was still speaking a crowd came up, and the man who was called Judas, one of the Twelve, was leading them..." Luke 22:47. Then seizing Yeshua, they lead him away: Luke 22:54 Yeshua appears before the Council, Herod (Antipas) and Pilate. Yeshua is crucified, He dies and is buried before Shabbat begins: Luke 22:66-23:56.

Saturday: Shabbat

Sunday: Resurrection morning. The empty tomb is discovered: Luke 24:1-12. In the afternoon, Yeshua appears to two on the road to Emmaus: Luke 24:13-35. Later that same day, Yeshua appears to His disciples in Yerushalayim: Luke 24:36-43.

Chapter 20

20:1) One day, as He was teaching the people in the Temple and proclaiming good news, the chief priests and the scribes, along with some of the elders, came up 20:2) and questioned Him, "Tell us by what authority You do these miracles, and who it is that gave You this power." 20:3) He answered them, "I also will ask you a question. Now tell Me, 20:4) was the ritual immersion in water of Yochanan from heaven or by human design?" 20:5) They discussed it with one another, saying, "If we say, 'From heaven,' then He will ask, 'Why then did you not believe him?' 20:6) But if we say, 'By human design,' all the people will stone us; because they are convinced that Yochanan was a prophet." 20:7) So they answered that they did not know from where it originated. 20:8) Yeshua said to them, "Neither will I tell you by what authority I do these things."

- Yeshua is taking His ministry to the Jews in Judea and teaching at the Temple Mount.
- A representation of the Sanhedrin (the Jewish "Supreme Court") question Him.
- Perhaps they have witnessed His activities concerning the money changers (Marshall, 1978).
- Is Yeshua a prophet?
- Yeshua's response is very Jewish. "The counter-question, especially as a means of avoiding a question already asked, is found frequently in rabbinic literature" (Lachs, 1978, p.352).
- The people were convinced Yochanan (John the Baptist) was a prophet from God.
- The problems for the leaders were these: If Yeshua were a prophet from God, they had failed to realize and accept His message, and they feared the people. The Jewish people were favorable toward Yeshua and His ministry.
- The penalty for a false prophet was stoning.
- The penalty for denying a true prophet was stoning.
- The leaders can't solve their dilemma, so they take refuge in ignorance. However, they do take note as to what is happening (Marshall, 1978).

> "It is important to study the Bible in the historical and cultural context. Looking deeper into passages and beyond the face value of Scripture allows us to understand the true significance of the story." – Alex Hart Class of 2021

20:9) He began to tell the people this parable: "A man planted a vineyard and leased it out to share-croppers. Then he went away on a journey for a long time. 20:10) At the harvest time, he sent a servant to the share-croppers, in order that they might give him some of the produce of the vineyard. But the share-croppers beat him and sent him away empty-handed. 20:11) Then he determined to send yet another servant. They beat him up also, tortured him shamefully, and sent him away empty-handed. 20:12) So he made up his mind to send a third. After wounding this one, they threw him out. 20:13) Finally the owner of the vineyard said, 'What shall I do? I will send them my only son; perhaps they will honor him.' 20:14) But when the share-croppers saw him, they reasoned with one another saying, 'This is the heir! Let us kill him so that the inheritance may belong to us.' 20:15) So they threw him out of the vineyard and murdered him. What therefore will the owner of the vineyard do to them? 20:16) He will come and destroy these share-croppers and will give the vineyard to others." And when they heard it, they said, "May God prevent it!" 20:17) But He looked at them and said, "What then is this that is written, 'The stone which the builders rejected, this one has become the chief corner stone'? (Ps 118:22) 20:18) Everyone who falls on that stone will be broken to pieces; but on whomever it falls, it will crush him."

- This parable is against an elite group of religious leaders, not the Jewish people.
- The owner farmed out his property to share-croppers or tenant farmers. He was an absentee landlord. Many estates in Galil were owned by landlords like this. The people would be very familiar with this type of situation.
- A servant visits the share-croppers once a year at harvest time.
- It would take four years for a vineyard to reach maturity and produce a profit (Marshall, 1978).
- The share-croppers or tenant farmers live on the land and have tremendous control over the operation. They might pay up to 40 percent of the produce to the owner for the right to farm the land.
- He finally sends his only son. This is important because most families would have had many children. This increases the suspense of the parable.
- The share-croppers reason that if they kill the only heir, they will possess the vineyard since they already live on the land. The landowner is absent, and the only son is dead. They can claim ownership (Young, 1995).
- The stone is compared to the Messiah (Lachs, 1987).
- The stone is Yeshua, the son of David. This is confirmed by the Jewish interpretation of Psalm 118:22-23 in light of King David's life. At the beginning, young David was rejected by the builders. The builders refer to Samuel and Jesse. David became the "head" or the greatest of all the kings of Israel.
- King David was small and had red hair. His brothers were stronger and more handsome. However, David's strength was from within. When he finally became king, he was the greatest of all time, but he wasn't their first choice. David, the stone that was rejected, became the chief cornerstone.
- God saw David's heart. The builders accepted the word of the Lord and anointed David (Young, 1995).
- The parable is about the son of David. The son of David is the Messiah.
- The death of the son will not hinder his ultimate success.
- The rabbis taught, "If a stone falls on a pot, woe to the pot! If a pot falls on a stone, woe to the pot! In either case woe to the pot! So, whoever ventures to attack them [the people of Israel] receives his deserts on their account" (Young, 1995, p. 221).
- The stone remains intact. The stone is the chosen people surviving with strong faith and clear identity. They remain victorious.
- The builders who rejected Yeshua were the Sadducees (the priests and the Temple leaders) and the Romans (Young, 1995).

- Yeshua's cleansing of the Temple and claiming to be the son of David was provocation for the Romans' threat to them and their allies among the Sadducees.
- Pilate thought Barabbas was more dangerous.
- Pilate sentenced Yeshua and the Romans crucified Him.
- This parable shows Yeshua's absolute confidence in His special mission; however, it gave Him great pain because of His love.
- Many Jews at the Temple supported Him, "May God prevent it!" Some of them were the spiritual leaders (Pharisees) who had warned Yeshua about Herod Antipas (Luke 13:31).
- The Stone remains. Death cannot defeat. He is the Stone that became the corner (Young, 1995).

"Studying the Bible has given me a peace. Having a Bible to be able to study from means that I do not have to blindly believe what others tell me is correct. I have the ability to research and find out what is actually true. This allows me to be so much more secure in my faith because I know what I've read and researched is true. I no longer have to worry about the authenticity of what other people have told me." Noah Keys – Class of 2021

20:19) At that very hour, the scribes and the chief priests wanted to arrest Him, but they feared the people. They understood that He told this parable against them. 20:20) So they watched Him and sent spies who pretended to be righteous, in order that they might catch Him making some statement, so as to deliver Him over to the power and the authority of the governor. 20:21) These questioned Him saying, "Rabbi, we know that You speak and teach the straightforward truth, and that You do not betray a partiality to any, but You teach the way of God in sincerity. 20:22) Is it really permissible according to the Torah for us to pay taxes to Caesar or not?" 20:23) He detected their entrapment, however, and said to them, 20:24) "Show me a denarius coin. Whose image and likeness is inscribed upon it?" They answered, "Caesar's." 20:25) With that, He said to them, "Then give back to Caesar the things that belong to Caesar, but give to God the things that belong to God." 20:26) They were unable to trap Him into making a statement in the presence of the people. Marveling at His answer, they were silenced.

- The silver denarius coin had a likeness of Tiberius Caesar wearing a wreath and was inscribed, "Augustus Tiberius Caesar son of the deified Augustus." On the reverse side was Livia, the mother of the emperor and was inscribed, "Pontifex Maximus" highest priest "[of Rome]" (ESV Archaeology Study Bible, 2017).

- One silver drachma or denarius was a day-wage for a common laborer (ESV *Archaeology Study Bible*, 2017).
- This particular coin was required for payment of Roman taxes.
- The coin symbolized the power of the Roman emperor and made religious claims about him that the Jews would consider blasphemous.
- The Jewish Temple tax was paid using a different coin – the Tyrian Shekel.
- Was paying the tax to the Romans lawful for the Jews? A poll tax was paid to a foreign ruler. The Jews hated this tax imposed by Rome. They had rioted against the tax.
- If Yeshua answered, "No, it is not legal," Rome would have a case against Him. If Yeshua answered, "Yes," He would lose support from some of the people (Marshall, 1978).
- An earthly king stamps every coin with his image, and all the coins look exactly alike.
- Not so in regard to God Himself! The rabbis teach, "The King of Kings, the Holy One, Blessed be He, has stamped every human being with the likeness of the first human and there is not a single individual who looks the same as another."
- The Haggadah (Jewish text) reveals that the ones crafted in God's image are the faces of all humanity. Anyone who kills another has murdered an entire world and diminished the divine image. The rabbis warned that causing one soul to perish from Yisrael is like wiping out an entire nation.
- Caesar's image was stamped on the coins he minted; the divine image is stamped on each person.
- Yeshua was calling on each person to give everything to God – the Creator of every human being (Young, 1998, p. 10).

"The Bible isn't some fiction book; it's history. We base our governments and our lives off of the Bible. It's God's word on paper. It is beyond important to study and understand the Bible." Gunner Evans – Class of 2021

20:27) Some of the Sadducees [of the priestly aristocracy], who teach that there is no resurrection, approached Him. 20:28) They questioned Him saying, "Rabbi, Moshe wrote us that, 'If a man's brother who has a wife dies, and he is childless, then his brother should marry the wife and raise up children for his brother' (Deut. 25:5). 20:29) Now there were seven brothers. The first took a wife and died without any children. 20:30) Also the second, 20:31) and the third married her, and in the same way, all seven died and left no children. 20:32) Finally the woman also died. 20:33) In the resurrection, therefore, whose wife will the woman be? After all, [each of] the seven had her as [his] wife." 20:34) At that, Yeshua answered them, "The children of this age marry and are given in marriage, 20:35) but the ones who are considered worthy to attain to that age and to the resurrection from the dead neither marry nor are given in marriage, 20:36) because they cannot die. They are like the angels and are the children of God in the resurrection. 20:37) But that the dead are raised, even Moshe revealed in his experience at the burning bush, where he calls the LORD the God of Avraham, and the God of Yitzchak, and the God of Yaakov. 20:38) Now He is not the God of the dead, but of those who live, because all are living for Him." 20:39) Some of the scribes answered and said, "Rabbi, you have answered well." 20:40) No longer did they have the boldness to question Him.

- The Sadducees believed that "the soul perishes along with the body.... As for the persistence of the soul after death, penalties in the underworld and rewards, they will have none of them" (Lachs, 1987, p. 41).
- It is the Sadducees who are questioning Yeshua. They do not believe in resurrection, but they are asking a question about it.
- Moshe is Moses, who authored the first five books of the TANAK including the commandments.
- Their questions are irrelevant and misconceived.
- The starting point is what Moshe (Moses) wrote in the Law about levirate marriage. "A levirate marriage is the obligation of a surviving brother to marry the widow of his brother if he died without having children (Deuteronomy 25:5-6). The idea is that the widow must marry a brother-in-law rather than anyone outside the family. The oldest of the surviving brothers had the first obligation, which also allowed him to inherit all of his deceased brother's property" (Eisenberg, *Levirate Marriage and Halitzah*, myjewishlearning.com).
- The purpose was to keep the property in the family by raising up an heir to inherit it. None of the brothers could claim to be the real husband in terms of having had a child (Marshall, 1978).
- In rabbinic literature from around this time period stated that "a woman who had been widowed several times was not permitted to remarry, since she was considered to be dangerous and was called 'a killer' and another marriage was deemed inadvisable... Twice or three times were enough to establish the presumption...and a fourth was prohibited" (Lachs, 1987, p. 361).
- The point here is that in the resurrection people are not involved in marriage relationships. The relationship is transcended in a new level of personal relationships, and the basic point being made is that marriage as a means of having children is no longer necessary (Marshall, 1978).
- The Sadducee's objection to the possibility of resurrection life has now been proven invalid since it wrongly assumes that earthly conditions persist into the heavenly world.

- In the burning bush story, God is the savior of the Patriarchs Avraham (Abraham), Yitzchak (Isaac), and Yaakov (Jacob). God will raise the dead because He cannot fail to keep His promises to them that He will be their God.
- God cannot be the God of dead people; only living people can have a God, and therefore God's promise to the Patriarchs that He is/will be their God requires that He maintain them in life (Marshall, 1978, p. 743).
- They do not die to God but live to God because God gives them life.
- The event closes with a "choral" response from some of the scribes who are assumed to be Pharisaic (Pharisee) scribes, and they accepted the viewpoint of Yeshua. They already believed in the resurrection (Marshall, 1978).

The Scribes

The Pharisees and the Scribes were two closely related classes of scholars. The Pharisees arose during the period of time between the "Old" and "New" Testaments. They taught and applied the Jewish religious law to everyday life. Josephus called them "the most accurate interpreters of the laws" of Moses. They believed in the resurrection and life after death. The Scribes were also Torah scholars. They came from a variety of backgrounds and could be associated with either the Pharisees or Sadducees. Many had regular jobs and were highly educated. The Pharisees and the Scribes associated with the them lived in Jewish villages. Their activities focused on synagogue and not the Temple (ESV Archaeology Study Bible, 2017, p. 1410).

20:41) He said to them, "How is it that they say the Anointed One is the son of David? 20:42) After all, David himself said in the scroll of the Psalms, 'The LORD said to my Lord, sit at My right hand 20:43) until I make Your enemies a footstool for Your feet' (Ps 110:1). 20:44) Hence, David calls Him Lord. So how can he be His son?" 20:45) While all the people were listening, He said to His disciples, 20:46) "Beware of the scribes who like to walk around in distinctive robes. They love respectful greetings in the market places, the distinguished seats for recognition in the Jewish learning centers, and positions of honor at banquets. 20:47) They take homes away from the widows but say long prayers to make themselves look good. These will receive a more severe decree of judgment."

"In this secular society, knowing and studying Scripture is important to me. Simply knowing the text and being able to read between the lines has been helpful not only for my faith, but also being able to defend it. Often, when I make my faith known in secular spaces, I receive malicious commentary and backhanded questions." Kristina Thompson – Class of 2021

- Yeshua is asking a theological question (Marshall, 1978).
- Jewish people who awaited a royal messiah expected him to be a descendant of David (Cultural Backgrounds Study Bible, 2016).
- Davidic descent of the Messiah is so clearly attested to in the TANAK and in Judaism that it is impossible that Yeshua or the early believers could have ever denied it. The "Son of David" is the regular title for the Messiah in rabbinic texts (Marshall, 1978, p. 744, 747).
- Again, Yeshua is addressing religious leaders and not the Jewish people in verse 46.
- He is speaking only about those leaders who are using their positions to further their prestige and making financial gains by abusing their positions of trust as guardians of property (Marshall, 1978).
- In verse 47, this could be a passage where "homes" may refer to families. F. Fenton (HBME) translates, "who devour the families of widows, and for a disguise offer up long prayers" (Young, 2019).

Questions for review and discussion

Yeshua is in Yerushalayim for Pesach or Passover. He arrives on the colt of a donkey and then visits the Temple Mount and begins to teach. What do you think Yeshua is teaching about in the parable in verses 9-18?

Why is this important?

Why do you think the priests and the scribes associated with them wanted to arrest Yeshua?

What is Yeshua talking about in verses 27-44?

Who is His audience?

Why is it important to identify the audience?

Who were the Scribes?

Is He talking about all scribes in verse 46? _____ How do you know? _____

Summarize the study notes from this chapter and discuss:

Summarize in one or two sentences the most important or the most interesting thing you learned in this chapter from your study:

What makes it important or interesting to you?

_____
_____

Re-read Luke Chapter 20 from the *Hebrew Heritage Bible* translation used in this book. Discuss. Summarize Luke Chapter 20 in one paragraph and discuss:

_____
_____
_____
_____
_____
_____
_____
_____

Choose one verse from Luke Chapter 20 that you think is the most important and write it here. Discuss why you think it is the most important verse:

_____
_____

How did your understanding of Luke Chapter 20 change after you studied it and read it again? Discuss.

_____
_____
_____
_____

How can you apply what you learned from Luke Chapter 20 to your life? Discuss.

_____
_____
_____
_____

What question or questions do you still have about Luke Chapter 20 that you don't understand or want to know more about? Discuss.

_____
_____
_____
_____

Additional Notes

THE GOSPEL OF LUKE CHAPTER TWENTY-ONE

Lesson 23

Before you begin your study, read Luke Chapter 21 out loud (as a group) from your Bible.

In your own words, summarize Luke Chapter 21 in one paragraph and write at least two questions that you had about the chapter as you read the biblical text: (Discuss)

_____
_____
_____
_____
_____
_____
_____
_____
_____
_____
_____
_____
_____
_____

Luke Chapter 21 begins with Yeshua on the Temple Mount and specifically in the Court of the Women. The events in this chapter are a continuation of Yeshua's activities and teachings in and around Yerushalayim during the Holy Week.

This chapter includes Yeshua's ominous prophecy concerning the destruction of the Temple. Yeshua's disciples may have been shocked by His words because construction on the Temple Mount had taken years, and it had just been completed or was nearing completion when Yeshua spoke about its ruin. About 40 years after Yeshua speaks these tragic words, in AD 70 the Temple was burned under the command of Titus, Yerushalayim fell, hundreds of thousands of Jews were dispersed, multiple thousands of Jews lost their lives, and thousands of Jewish men were carried off to Rome as slaves. The loot from the Jewish Temple financed the construction of the Colosseum in Rome, and Jewish slaves were among those who were forced to build it.

To commemorate the event, Titus (who would later become emperor) built a monumental arch in Rome. Take a trip online to Rome. Research the Arch of Titus. What event is depicted on this structure? What items are included in the story it tells? Where is it located in Rome?

_____
_____
_____
_____
_____
_____
_____
_____
_____
_____
_____
_____

Chapter 21

21:1) He looked up and saw the wealthy putting their gifts into the Temple treasury. 21:2) Then He saw a certain impoverished widow putting in two penny coins. 21:3) He taught, "I tell you the absolute truth, this impoverished widow put in more than all of them. 21:4) After all, they gave offerings out of their surplus of wealth, but out of her poverty, she put in all that she had to live on."

The Court of the Women was surrounded by porticoes (colonnades). Thirteen collection boxes were placed inside these porticoes. They were called shofar-chests because of the funnel-shaped bronze receptacles which guided the coins into the wooden collection boxes. From the sound made by the coin when it dropped into the box, one could detect what type of coin had been placed inside. Each box had an inscription indicating the designation of that box's offering. Six boxes were free-will offerings, one box was for the wood, etc. (Ritmeyer, 2006, p. 350). (Illustration: Court of the Women, Debbie Willey)

GOSPEL OF LUKE

The lepton or widow's mite (two penny coins) was the smallest coin in use during the first century AD. It was equivalent to four minutes' wages (*ESV Archaeology Study Bible*, 2017). Photo: Numerous lepton coins from the time of Yeshua. Notice their size compared to the quarter, dime, and penny. (Private collection)

The Economy of the Jewish People

- The very wealthy. During the time of Yeshua's ministry, very few people belonged to the wealthy class. They included
  - The rich urban priests
  - The aristocrats
  - The high-level bureaucrats
- The middle class. There was a small middle class. They included
  - Larger landowners
  - Some merchants
  - Skilled artisans
- The very poor. Most people belonged to this class. They included
  - Small landowners
  - Tenants
  - Day laborers
  - Servants
  - Slaves
  - Widows
  - Orphans
- There were great crowds of the very poor – am Haaretz – "people of the land" or peasants. They were looked upon with disfavor. They had no skills. They were living hand-to-mouth and paying heavy tax burdens and obligations. Many were financially unable or unwilling to follow the Jewish ritual laws (*ESV Archaeology Study Bible*, 2017).

"When I study my Bible in the morning before my family wakes up, it gives me peace and purpose for that day. It gives me the ability to continue walking on the path to righteousness, so that my relationship with the Lord strengthens. Reading and studying the Bible daily has made me happier and made me a better friend, daughter, and student to everyone around me." Jensyn McCain – Class of 2021

Photo: A Columbarium at Tel Maresha, Israel.

This is one of eighty-five caves where doves were raised. (Many were used as sacrifices at the Temple.)

Doves and pigeons were the poor man's offering at the Temple. Rabbi Elazar said, "The poor man's offering is the lightest, because his heart is broken" (Chabad.org).

Photo Credit: David Anderson

Take a trip online to Beit Guvrin-Maresha, Israel and visit the fascinating tel. It is one of Israel's newest UNESCO sites. (Read the article "Land of a Thousand Caves" at israel21c.org and visit either biblewalks.com or Biblical Archaeology Society for more information.) What did you learn? Where is this site located? What else can be found at this site? Write and discuss:

_____
_____
_____
_____
_____

GOSPEL OF LUKE 311

Read the article "Doves and Pigeons: Reading Between the Lines" by Michael Gerbitz at unitedwithisrael.org. Summarize the article. Why should a woman choose option (a)?

_____
_____
_____
_____
_____
_____

- The widow offers all she has.
- "The importance of this passage is best summed up in the rabbinic saying, 'It does not matter whether your offering be much or little, so long as your heart is directed to Heaven.' A close parallel to the widow's offering is the following based on Lev. 2:1: 'There is a story of a woman who brought a handful of meal as an offering. A priest despised it and said, 'See what they offer! What is in it that one could eat, and what is in it that can be sacrificed?' It was shown to him in a dream 'Do not despise her; it is as if she has sacrificed herself [Heb. *Nafshah*] as the sacrifice'" (Lachs, 1987, p. 375).

21:5) While some were talking about the Temple, how that it was adorned with impressive stones and with lavish gifts, He said, 21:6) "As for all this which you look at [with admiration], the days are coming when there will not be left one stone upon another which will not be torn down."

21:7) They questioned Him saying, "Rabbi, but when will these events happen? What will be the sign when these events are soon to take place?" 21:8) He explained, "Do not be fooled! Do not be led astray! After all, many will come making use of my name claiming, 'I am he; the time is now here.' Do not follow after them. 21:9) When you hear of wars and revolutions, moreover, do not be afraid because these events must take place first, but the end does not follow at once." 21:10) Then He went on to say to them, "Nation will make war against nation, and kingdoms will attack each other' (Isa 19:2). 21:11) In many places, there will be terrible earthquakes, plagues, and famines. Fearful sights and great signs will appear in the sky.

21:12) "But before all these things take place, they will seize you and persecute you, delivering you up to the meeting places and prisons, taking you before kings and governors because you reverence My name. 21:13) This will make an opportunity for you to share your testimony. 21:14) So decide in your hearts not to prepare beforehand how to defend yourselves. 21:15) I will tell you what to say and give you wisdom which none of your opponents will be able to resist or refute. 21:16) But you will be turned over to enemies by parents and brothers and relatives and friends. They will put some of you to death. 21:17) You will be hated by many because you reverence My name. 21:18) Even so, not a hair of your head will be lost. 21:19) By your unrelenting determination you will keep yourselves.

21:20) "But when you see Yerushalayim surrounded by armies, then recognize that her desolation has come near. 21:21) At that time, let those who are in Yehudah escape to the mountains. Let those who live in the city evacuate. Do not allow those who live in the country to enter the city. 21:22) After all, these are 'the days of retribution' (Hos 9:7), in order that all events which were predicted in Scripture may come true. 21:23) In those days, it will be miserable for pregnant women and mothers who nurse their babies. There will be horrible suffering throughout the land, and severe punishment will come down upon this people. 21:24) They shall die by the sharp blade of the sword and will be taken away as prisoners being dispersed among the pagan nations. Yerushalayim will be overrun by the Heathens until the time given to the Heathens will expire.

- The location of this discourse is the Temple Mount. Its enormous size and magnificent décor were awe inspiring.
- "Herod's Temple was of striking beauty. 'They say, that he who has not seen the building of Herod has never seen a beautiful building in all his days'" (Lachs, 1987, p. 377).
- Verse 6 describes the destruction of the Temple by the Romans in AD 70 (ESV Archaeology Study Bible, 2017).
- A small minority of Jews (including the Essenes) denounced the Temple as impure and pronounced judgement on it and the establishment that ran it. Some believed (including the Essenes) that God would send a new Temple. More commonly, the Jews believed that the Temple was indestructible.
- The Temple was destroyed, but some of the stones of the retaining wall of the Temple Mount remain. These stones are massive. One stone is nearly 40 feet long and weighs 400 tons. Smaller stones weigh between 2-5 tons (Cultural Backgrounds Study Bible, 2016).
- In verse 8, Bar Kokhba claimed to be messiah and led a revolt against Rome that began in AD 132. He is the most well known of the false messiahs, but there were several deceptive claims made which deceived the people.
- "Throughout the apocalyptic literature universal fighting is considered a sign that the end is approaching. 'When you see the kingdoms fighting against one another look and expect the feet of the Messiah'" (Lachs, 1987, p. 379).
- In the TANAK the famines and earthquakes are manifestations of divine punishment. See Isaiah 8:21 (hunger), 13:13 (earthquake), 14:30 (famine). "The biblical material abounds with passages describing troubles, woes, breakdown of family, and general moral decline which will precede the coming great age and time of redemption. These are also found in rabbinic sources" (Lachs, 1987, p. 380).

- In verses 12-19, Yeshua is telling His disciples they will be persecuted, and during this time they must rely on the help Yeshua will give them and persevere faithfully to the end (Marshall, 1978).

- Persecution of the believers and hatred will be rampant (Lachs, 1987).

- Verse 19 more literally the verse is translated, "Through your endurance you will gain your souls" (Young, 2019).

- Verse 20 connects with verse 6 in the discussion concerning the destruction of the Temple and the fall of Yerushalayim which happened in AD 70. The encircling of Roman troops will be a sign that its prophesied fate is at hand. There will be terrible suffering for the Jews, and Yerushalayim will remain in the power of the Heathens (Gentiles) for an indefinite period (Marshall, 1978).

- AD 70 marked the beginning of the end of the Zealot, Sadducean, and Essene sects of Judaism. It was mostly the Pharisees and the believers in Yeshua who remained (Wilson, 1989).

There was indeed great suffering on Tisha B'Av (9th of Av) in AD 70 as the Romans destroyed the Temple, and the Jews who were still alive were dispersed and enslaved.

What is Tisha B'Av? What else happened on this day in Jewish history? What do today's Jews do to remember Tisha B'Av? Write and discuss:

_____
_____
_____
_____
_____
_____

The Temple construction was ordered by Herod the Great just before Yeshua was born.

The Temple was adorned with gold and marble. It was more than twice as tall as the Golden Dome of the Rock (which probably stands where the Jewish Temple stood 2,000 years ago).

Josephus wrote this about the Temple, "To strangers as they approached it seemed in the distance like a mountain covered with snow; for any part not covered with gold was dazzling white" (Whitson, 2016, p. 153).

The Temple Mount was the largest man-made structure in the world. It was inconceivable that anything or anyone could destroy it.

However, Yeshua prophesied its destruction, and it was destroyed by the Romans under Titus' command.

Top Photo: Computer graphic of the destruction of the Temple in AD 70 (Western Wall Tunnels, Jerusalem, 2015)

Lower Photo: The ancient street below the southwest corner of Temple Mount. The stones are from the Roman destruction in AD 70.

GOSPEL OF LUKE

Slowly Titus and his army approached Yerushalayim, reaching it early in the spring of the year 70. Only then did the fighting [among the Jewish sects] within the city cease, and the three rivals for power became rivals for glory. The Romans made their camp on Mount Scopus and began their siege of the city and their work with the battering rams. Time and time again the Jews would rush out of the city and attempt to destroy the military machine of the Romans. Nevertheless, within fifteen days a breach was made in the outermost wall... the middle wall did not last much longer. It was behind the first and oldest wall that the Jews made their longest stand. The Romans faced it with a wall of their own from the top which they hurled stones and arrows at the defenders. The Jews repulsed their attacks...made sorties and routed portions of the enemy force. But their food and their forces were growing insufficient...From the beginning of the siege Titus would not permit the civil population to leave the city, lest they relieve the pressure of hunger within. Such people would be crucified within sight of the defenders...The fighters would not give up. The time had come to redeem the oath every Zealot had taken, to die fighting rather than surrender to Rome...Finally the Fortress of Antonia fell, and all that was left for the Jews to defend was the Temple area... This was the last stand for Yerushalayim. Here the Jews felt they would be invincible, since God would not permit His Holy Place to be destroyed. Regardless of war and famine, the sacrifices in the Temple had been going on as usual, until there was nothing to sacrifice. The 17th of Tammuz, when the sacrifices were discontinued, is still observed as a fast day by many Jews. For three more weeks the defenders held out. On the 9th of Av, Titus ordered that the gates be set on fire, and, as soon as these were consumed, his soldiers rushed in. The slaughter which then commenced is beyond description. To the Jews, life was no longer worth living, now that they were sure that God had abandoned them, that His sacred building, the Shrine of His people, was in flames.

(Grayzel, 1947, pp. 169-171)

(It is no wonder that Yeshua had wept over the city...)

- What happened to the Jews living in Yerushalayim who were known as the believers in the Messiah of Nazareth? During the rebellion the believers in Yeshua, who had until then used Yerushalayim as their center of activity, moved out of the city to a small town on the other side of the Yarden River (Grayzel, 1947, p. 178).

- Sometime before the fall of Yerushalayim – probably between AD 66 and 68 – the Jewish believers in Yeshua fled to Pella in Perea (Luke 21:20-21). Located about 60 miles northeast of Yerushalayim, it became an important city for the early believers (Wilson, 1989, p. 76).

21:25) "Signs in the sun, moon, and stars will appear. Upon the earth, nations will be thrown into deep anguish and perplexity at the roaring of the sea and the waves, 21:26) with people fainting from intense fear and apprehension because of what is happening to the inhabited world.

Consequently, 'The powers of the heavens will be shaken' (Isa 34:4). 21:27) Then they will see 'The Son of Man coming in a cloud' (Dan 7:13) with power and great glory. 21:28) But when these things begin to take place, stand up straight and lift up your heads because your redemption is drawing near."

21:29) He told them a parable, "Consider the fig tree and all the trees. 21:30) As soon as they bud with leaves, you see it and recognize for yourselves that the summer is now near. 21:31) Even so you, when you see these events happening, recognize that the kingdom of God is near. 21:32) Truly I say to you, that generation will not pass away until all events take place. 21:33) Heaven and earth will pass away, but My words will not pass away. 21:34) Be on guard that your hearts may not be weighted down with corruption, drunkenness, and the worries of life, and that day spring on you suddenly like a trap; 21:35) for it will come upon all those who live on the face of the entire earth. 21:36) But keep on the alert at all times, praying in order that you may have strength to escape all these events that are about to take place and to stand before the Son of Man."

- Verse 25 begins the discussion of things that will happen after the destruction of the Temple during the "time given to the Heathens."
- These signs will be accompanied by panic on earth. There will be great dismay. The uncertainty shifts to fear...literally "to stop breathing" (Marshall, 1978).
- In verse 27, the cloud is the presence of God. It is His glory (Marshall, 1978).

21:37) During the day, He was teaching in the Temple, but at evening He would go out and spend the night on the mountain that is called Olives. 21:38) All the people would get up early in the morning to come to Him in the Temple to listen to Him.

- In verse 30, the word "summer" and the word "end," in Hebrew, are spelled and even sound alike. The letter *kof* and the letter *tzade*, appear in both words. As nature's signs indicate that summer is coming, the appearance of the signs signals the end for Jerusalem. Another interpretation is the end of the world and the last judgment. The text probably contains a play on words using the double meaning. That generation saw fulfillment in the destruction of Jerusalem which prefigures the final judgment (Young, 2019).
- Yeshua teaches during the day while the Temple is open.
- He spends the night on the Mount of Olives either at Gethsemane or Beit Anyah or both.
- Tens of thousands to hundreds of thousands of Jews would be in Yerushalayim for Passover (Pesach). Many would be staying in tents or out of doors in the evenings.

Questions for review and discussion

Where do the events discussed in this chapter occur?

Yeshua and many other Jews are in Yerushalayim getting ready to observe what holiday?

What does Yeshua say about the widow?

Where does the widow put her money?

What does *am Haaretz* mean?

How did Josephus describe the Temple?

What does Yeshua say is going to happen to the Temple and Yerushalayim?

Why do you think Yeshua wept over Yerushalayim?

What does Yeshua say about persecution?

What did the believers in Yeshua do when the rebellion began?

What is the cloud in verse 27?

Summarize the study notes from this chapter and discuss:

Summarize the study notes from this chapter and discuss continued:

___

Summarize in one or two sentences the most important or the most interesting thing you learned in this chapter from your study:

___

What makes it important or interesting to you?

___

Re-read Luke Chapter 21 from the *Hebrew Heritage Bible* translation used in this book. Discuss. Summarize Luke Chapter 21 in one paragraph and discuss:

___

Choose one verse from Luke Chapter 21 that you think is the most important and write it here. Discuss why you think it is the most important verse:

___

How did your understanding of Luke Chapter 21 change after you studied it and read it again? Discuss.

How can you apply what you learned from Luke Chapter 21 to your life? Discuss.

What question or questions do you still have about Luke Chapter 21 that you don't understand or want to know more about? Discuss.

THE GOSPEL OF LUKE CHAPTER TWENTY-TWO

Lesson 24

Before you begin your study, read Luke Chapter 22 out loud (as a group) from your Bible.

In your own words, summarize Luke Chapter 22 in one paragraph and write at least two questions that you had about the chapter as you read the biblical text: (Discuss)

_____
_____
_____
_____
_____
_____
_____
_____
_____
_____
_____
_____
_____

Before you begin, refer back to Lesson 22 and review the events of Holy Week. On which days are the events in this chapter happening?

_____

The beginning of this chapter shows Yeshua preparing for and participating in a Passover Seder. The story of Moses and the Passover is told in Exodus chapters 1-13:10. Read and write a summary paragraph for each chapter. Discuss:

(See pages 363-365 "Additional Notes" if you need more space for your answers.)

_____
_____
_____
_____
_____
_____
_____
_____
_____
_____
_____
_____
_____
_____
_____
_____
_____
_____
_____

Hebrew Names and their English Equivalents

Hebrew	**English**
Matzah Bread	Unleavened Bread
Pesach	Passover
Yehudah	Judas
Kariyot	Iscariot
Kefa	Peter
Yochanan	John
Shimon	Simon

Before you begin your study, it is important to understand more about the Passover Seder Yeshua will be celebrating with His disciples in Luke Ch. 24.

 Watch and take notes from "Jesus, Passover, and Judaism Copy 1" on YouTube. https://www.youtube.com/watch?v=qISJ8TiR3FM

Dr. Brad Young explains more about this ancient Jewish Holiday (length 34 minutes). What did you learn? What do these words mean: Pesach, Maror, and Matzah? What was the most interesting thing you learned? What questions do you have? Write and discuss:

___

Chapter 22

22:1) Now the Feast of Matzah Bread, which is called Pesach, was approaching. 22:2) Because they were afraid of the people, the chief priests and the scribes were seeking how they might put Him to death. 22:3) Satan entered into Yehudah who was called man of Kariyot. He belonged to the number of the twelve disciples. 22:4) He slipped away and discussed with the chief priests and officers how he might betray Him to them. 22:5) They were glad and made a bargain to give him money. 22:6) He accepted the offer, and he began to seek a good opportunity to betray Him to them when He would be away from the crowds.

- Passover and the Festival of Unleavened Bread (Matzah) were often celebrated together as parts of a single festival (*Cultural Backgrounds Study Bible*, 2016).
- The Feast of Matzah (Unleavened Bread) was held from Nisan 15th - 21st (or 22nd) during the barley harvest (March/April). During the time of Yeshua, it was closely linked with the Passover held on Nisan 14th-15th.

- The Festival of Matzah is the Festival of Redemption and the redemptive element is the interpretation of the crucifixion (Lachs, 1987).
- The approach of the festival of Passover was the signal to the chief priests and their scribes to plan to do away with Yeshua. The plot does not include the elders (Marshall, 1978).
- The hostile portrayal of the chief priests was not limited to the Gospels. Josephus, the Dead Sea Scrolls, and rabbinic writings depict members of this group exploiting their power (Cultural Backgrounds Study Bible, 2016).
- The chief priests were in charge of worship in the Temple. They included the ruling high priest, Caiaphas; the former high priest, Annas; and the high priestly families. All of them were included in the Sanhedrin (the ruling Jewish Council) (Archaeological Study Bible, 2005).
- In verse 3, the words, "man of Kariyot," represent "Ishkariyot," which is probably derived from the Hebrew word for man, Ish, and the town name, Kariyot. In English translations, the surname of Judas is Iscariot (Young, 2019).
- The "officers" in verse 4 refers to the "officers of the Temple guard." The Temple guard consisted of Levites designated as the Temple police force who kept order in the Temple (Cultural Backgrounds Study Bible, 2016).
- The "captain of the Temple guard was referred in rabbinical literature as the sagan." He belonged to one of the chief-priestly families, and in the Temple, he ranked next to the high priest (Bruce, 1988).
- In verse 4, the meeting is informal perhaps to maintain secrecy (Lachs, 1987).
- Yeshua is very popular with the Jewish people (Flusser, 2001).

22:7) Then came the day of Matzah Bread on which the Pesach lamb had to be sacrificed. 22:8) Yeshua sent Kefa and Yochanan saying, "Go and prepare the Pesach lamb for us that we may eat it." 22:9) They asked Him, "Where do You want us to prepare it?" 22:10) He said to them, "Pay attention when you go into the city. A man will meet you carrying a pitcher of water. Follow him into the house that he enters. 22:11) You shall say to the owner of the house, 'The Rabbi says to you, "Where is the guest room in which I may eat the Pesach lamb with My disciples?"' 22:12) He will show you a large furnished upper room. Prepare it there." 22:13) They left and discovered everything exactly as He had described to them. They prepared the Pesach lamb.

- The (Pesach) Passover meal was eaten after sundown on the evening of the fourteenth day of Nisan. The lamb was sacrificed at the Temple just a few hours prior to the meal (ESV Archaeology Study Bible, 2017).
- A man carrying a jar with water would have been an unusual sight, since men usually carried leather bottles and women carried jars or pitchers (Marshall, 1978).

> "Faith without knowing what you have faith in is going to be unstable and weak. Accepting Christ is the first step in joining the Christian faith. We are called to study why we believe in what we believe and bring others to the faith. Without careful study of the Bible, we could easily be thrown off the right path. We need the full armor of God to keep us steady and firm in His way." Corbin Smith – Class of 2021

Preparing for Pesach

Celebrating Pesach (Passover) during the time of Yeshua was a great spectacle of excitement and devotion. Jews near and far ascended to the Holy City of Yerushalayim in large numbers. Many pilgrims were also merchants, and they would arrive early to sell or barter their products. Beggars would be stationed strategically near the bustling gates of the city. Josephus claimed there were millions who would make the journey. Many historians claim the number would have been around 200,000. Accommodations for sleeping and feasting were sought out in every available space. To help defuse the Jewish resentment of the Romans, the Roman authorities would release a prisoner at Passover time.

The animal (preferably a lamb) was selected on the 10th day of Nisan. Families or groups of at least 10 people were required to eat the entire lamb in one sitting at the Passover meal. No part of the animal was to remain until the next day.

Before the common meal on Passover eve, the day was filled with preparing for the event. A full contingent of priests – twenty-four divisions instead of the usual one – came early to the Temple. Their first task was to burn the chametz (leaven) which had been searched for by candlelight in each home the night before and then removed for burning the next morning.

The afternoon was spent performing the ritual slaughtering of the lambs. The offering of the Pesach (Passover) sacrifice at the Temple began about 3:00 pm and was conducted in massive shifts. When the Temple court was filled with the first group of offerors, the gates of the court were closed. The shofar (ram's horn) was sounded and the sacrifice began. Each Jew slaughtered his own lamb. The priests stood in two rows, one holding gold basins and the other silver. After the blood was brought to the basin, it was tossed against the base of the altar. While the offerings were going on, the Levites sang the Hallel (Psalms 113-118). Each lamb was then skinned and its fat with its kidneys were removed for burning on the altar. Before leaving the Temple, each offeror slung his lamb – wrapped in its own hide – over his shoulder. He then left the Temple courts with his group to prepare the Passover meal. Immediately, the next group of offerors filed into the Temple court and the ritual was repeated (Wilson, 1989, pp. 243-244).

Thousands of Jewish men and women could gather in The Court of the Women (pictured). The Levitical choir would sing as they stood on the fifteen semi-circular steps that were in front of the Gate of Nicanor. The Gate of Nicanor led to the Court of the Israelites and the Court of the Priests. The large altar of the Temple could be seen through the open gates (Ritmeyer, 2015). Illustration: Court of the Women by Debbie Willey

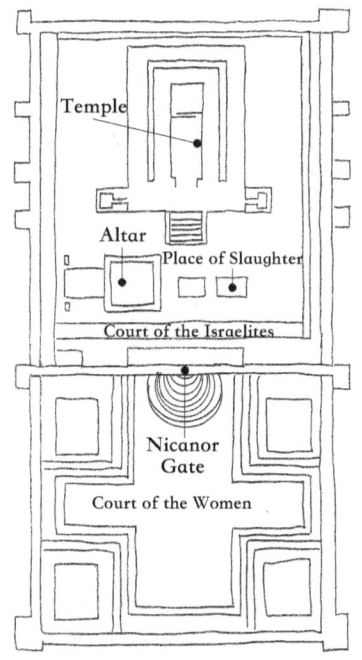

The first group would enter the Court of the Israelites with their Passover lambs. The Nicanor Gate would be shut. Each individual would slaughter their own lamb. The priests threw the sacrificial blood against the base of the altar (Ritmeyer, 2006, pg. 352).

(Temple Diagram: Debbie Willey)

"The Bible means a lot to me, but there's so much I still need to learn. The Bible is the truth. It gives us knowledge of the past. It allows us to learn some of the most important events that happened in Jesus' time. It allows me to reflect on personal things. The Bible has so many different life lessons. The Bible leads us straight to the Lord."
Grady James – Class of 2021

Passover Seder

Seder means "order of service." The Passover evening meal was held at home or in a room within the city reserved for the occasion. The lamb would be roasted in the courtyard of the home. The room would be prepared with floor cushions for reclining and small tables for serving. The festival celebrated freedom, the celebrants reclined while they ate; and each person participated in the event as if he or she had personally come out of Egypt. Ritual hand washings, prayers, and symbolic foods were part of the event. The ceremony would conclude late, as the participants sang the *Hallel*. Many would spend the rest of the evening in prayer and worship (Wilson, 1989, pp. 244-245).

22:14) When the evening time arrived, He reclined for the meal with the authoritative emissaries along with Him. 22:15) He said to them, "I have earnestly desired to eat this Pesach lamb with you before I die. 22:16) I tell you, I will not eat from it again until a new one is eaten, fulfilled in the kingdom of God." 22:17) Having taken a cup, after giving thanks, He said, "Take this and share among yourselves. 22:18) I tell you, I will not drink of the fruit of the vine from now until the kingdom of God comes." 22:19) Having taken some Matzah bread, after giving thanks, He broke it and gave it to them saying "This is My body. *22:21) Yet look! The hand of the one betraying Me is with Me on the table. 22:22) Surely the Son of Man is going as it has been determined, but severe retribution threatens that man through whom he is betrayed!" 22:23) They began questioning among themselves which one of them it might be who was going to do this.

GOSPEL OF LUKE

- In verses 19-20, after the words, *"This is my body," there is a longer manuscript reading and a shorter text. Based upon the manuscript evidence, here the shorter text has been accepted which stresses the intense feeling of betrayal by showing a direct connection between Jesus' broken body and the hand of the one who betrayed Him. The longer text reconstructs 1 Cor 11:23-25. So other manuscripts add the longer text after the words, "This is my body" in Luke 22:19: "...which is given for you. 20) In the same way, the cup after supper, 'This cup which is poured out for you is the renewed covenant in my blood.'" See David Flusser, Jesus, 142 (Young, 2019).

Yeshua's Last Supper

Yeshua instituted the Lord's Supper by associating it with the third cup of wine, which came after the Pesach (Passover) meal was eaten. The third cup is known as the "cup of redemption," which in rabbinic tradition linked to the third of the fourfold promise of redemption in Exodus 6:6-7. Yeshua associated this cup of wine with his atoning death in saying in verse 20 (Wilson, 1989, p. 246), "The cup which is poured out for you is the renewed covenant in my blood."

The blessing over the bread is *Baruch ata Adonai Eloheinu Melech ha'olam hamotzi lechem min ha'aretz.* (Blessed are you, Lord our God, king of the universe, who brings forth bread from the earth.)

The blessing over wine or grape juice is *Baruch ata Adonai Eloheinu Melech ha'olam borei p'ri hagafen.* (Blessed are you, Lord our God, king of the universe, who creates the fruit of the vine.)

- The necessity of slaughtering a Passover lamb on the Day of Unleavened Bread and Yeshua sending Kefa (Peter) and Yochanan (John) portrays Yeshua as a Torah-abiding Jew rather than as a renegade.
- The emissaries (apostles) reclining with Yeshua emphasizes the table fellowship between friends.
- Yeshua has eagerly desired to eat this meal because it will be His last opportunity until the messianic banquet in God's Kingdom.
- Yeshua reminds His emissaries (apostles) that the greatest person is to become like the youngest and the leader to become like one who is the server at the table. The theme of table fellowship is maintained as service is taught without a denial of greatness (Gundry, 2003).

> "Studying the Bible and listening to what God has to say have greatly impacted me. Whenever I am going through hard times, I know to look toward God and His word because He always has the answer. When my grandpa died a few years ago, I became severely depressed. However, when I began to read my Bible, all of that went away. I began to put my trust back in God. I began studying His word more. I would not be who I am today if it weren't for God's word." Jenna Pearcy – Class of 2021

22:24) So there arose also a quarrel among them as to which one of them was to be regarded as leader. 22:25) But He said to them, "The kings of the pagans lord it over their subjects. Those who exercise authority over them are called 'Benefactors.' 22:26) But not so with you; but let the one who is the greatest among you become like the youngest, and let the leader be like one who serves. 22:27) For who is more important, the one who reclines for the meal or the one who serves? Is it not the one who reclines at the table for dinner? Yet I am among you as the one who serves. 22:28) You are those who have persevered with Me through the trials that have tested Me. 22:29) I also covenant with you just as My Father covenanted with Me His kingly power 22:30) that you may eat and drink around My table in My kingdom. You will sit upon thrones judging the twelve tribes of Yisrael. 22:31) Shimon, Shimon, look out! Satan has demanded permission to sift through all of you like wheat. 22:32) But I have prayed for you that you will not lose your [chutzpah style] faith, so that when you make your comeback, you will strengthen your brothers and sisters." 22:33) He said to him, "Lord, I am ready to go with You both to prison and even to death!" 22:34) He answered, "I tell you, Kefa, the rooster will not crow this day before you will deny three times that you know Me."

- In verse 29, some later manuscripts use the word "covenant" instead of "kingdom." The internal evidence from the Greek text supports this reading. The alternate reading reflected in most translations would be, "and I appoint for you—just as My Father appointed for Me a kingdom" (Young, 2019).
- Sifting like wheat stands for an attempt to shake loyalty (Gundry, 2003).
- "'Shimon, Shimon' Saying Shimon (Simon) twice in Hebrew usage is an expression either of affection or urgency. In the school of R. Hiyya it was taught: This is an expression of love and an expression of encouragement" (Lachs, 1987, p. 410).
- "Satan has demanded..." is reminiscent of Job 1-2, Zech. 3:1, "Fear the Lord and love your neighbor, even though the spirits of Beliar [i.e. Satan] claim to afflict you with every evil, they shall not have dominion over you" (Lachs, 1987, p. 410).
- Ancient literature associate roosters crowing with dawn (Cultural Backgrounds Study Bible, 2016).

22:35) He said to them, "When I sent you out with no money bag or traveler's pack, were you in need of anything?" They replied, "Nothing." 22:36) He said to them, "But now let the one who has a money bag take it along and in the same way, also a traveler's pack. Let the one who has no money sell his robe and buy a sword. 22:37) Because I tell you that this Scripture must be fulfilled in Me, 'Moreover, he was numbered with the transgressors' (Isa 53:12), for all that refers to Me is finding its fulfillment. 22:38) They responded, "Look, Lord, here we have two swords." He said to them, "It is enough."

- In verse 35, many textual witnesses add sandals to the list after, "money bag or traveler's pack." But this is missing in numerous authorities (Young, 2019).

22:39) He went out and walked over to the Mount of Olives which was where He was accustomed to stay. The disciples followed Him. 22:40) When He arrived at the place, He warned them, "Pray that you will not be overcome with temptation." 22:41) He withdrew from them about a stone's throw away; bending down to his knees, He began to pray, 22:42) "Father, if You are willing, spare Me from this cup. Nonetheless do not do what I want, but let Your will be done." 22:43) [[An angel from heaven appeared to Him, giving Him more strength. 22:44) Being in deep anguish, He prayed more fervently; and it happened that His sweat became like drops of blood falling down upon the ground.]] 22:45)

- In verse 43, this is likely an interpolation based upon tradition (Young, 2019).

When He rose up from prayer, He went over to His disciples and found them asleep, weary from sorrow. 22:46) He said to them, "Why are you sleeping? Rise and pray that you will not be overcome with temptation." 22:47) While He was still speaking, behold, a crowd came up, and the one called Yehudah, one of the twelve, was leading them. He came near Yeshua to kiss Him. 22:48) But Yeshua said to him, "Yehudah! Are you going to betray the Son of Man with a kiss?" 22:49) When those who were standing around Him saw what was going to happen, they asked, "Lord, shall we fight back with the sword?" 22:50) One of them slashed at the slave of the high priest and cut off his right ear. 22:51) But Yeshua called them down and said, "Stop! No more of this." Then He touched his ear and healed him. 22:52) Yeshua spoke to the chief priests, the Temple police, and the elders who had wanted to find Him, "Have you come out with swords and clubs like you would arrest a rebel? 22:53) While I was with you every day in the Temple courts, you did not lay hands on Me. But now in this time, the power of darkness is yours."

- The Gospel of Matthew names Gethsemane as the specific location on the Mount of Olives where these events occurred.

- The cup is the symbol of pain and suffering – Ezekiel 23:32-34; also, destiny and fate – Isaiah 51:17, 22 (p. 414).
- This arrest describes an official arrest by some of the Jewish leaders and the Roman garrison (Lachs, 1987).
- The kiss here is a form of greeting and hence it is the worst type of hypocrisy. The disciple is not permitted to greet the teacher first, since this would imply equality and therefore be an insult to the master.
- Could the one who slashed the slave with the sword have been a *sicarii*? (Lachs, 1987).
- The *sicarii* (dagger men) was a Jewish rebel group who carried daggers beneath their clothes. Mixing with pilgrims on the Temple hill, they murdered their political opponents (Roth, 1962, p. 1717).
- Some later Jewish traditions complained that the servants of the high priest in this period used clubs when abusing people (*Cultural Backgrounds Study Bible*, 2016).

Photo: The ancient olive trees in the Garden of Gethsemane. This location is the traditional site of Yeshua's prayer and arrest before His crucifixion.

Lower Photo: The view across the Kidron Valley from the Garden of Gethsemane looks toward the Eastern Gate of the Temple Mount.

Photo credits: David Anderson, 2018

> "At some point in everyone's life they will feel alone – alone and lost – looking for comfort from anywhere that is easy. Reading the Bible is reading God's word, and God is the ultimate comforter. Through reading and studying His word, we find His path for us. We will never be alone with God by our side. There is an unbelievable amount of comfort in God's word. Even when we doubt, He is always there in His word to lead us in the way we need to go." Brady Thomas – Class of 2021

22:54) Having arrested Him, they marched Him off and brought Him to the house of the high priest. All the while, Kefa followed at a distance away. 22:55) After they had kindled a fire in the middle of the courtyard, they sat down together. Kefa was sitting among them. 22:56) A servant girl spotted him as he sat in the firelight. Looking straight at him, she declared, "This man was also with Him." 22:57) But he denied it saying, "Woman, I do not know Him." 22:58) A little while later, someone else recognized him and said, "You are one of them too!" But Kefa denied it, "No way, sir, I am not!" 22:59) After about an hour had passed, another man emphatically was asserting, "Unquestionably this man was with Him also; the proof is that he is a Galilean." 22:60) But Kefa disputed the remark, "Man, I do not know what you are talking about." At that moment, while he was still speaking, a rooster crowed. 22:61) Then the Lord turned and looked at Kefa. At once Kefa remembered the word of the Lord, how He said to him, "Before a rooster crows today, you will deny Me three times." 22:62) He went outside and burst into tears of bitter anguish.

- The high priest was Caiaphas, and the gathering may have taken place at his house to ensure secrecy (*Archaeological Study Bible*, 2005).
- Mansions of the Jewish aristocracy during the time of Yeshua were large and spacious. They had rooms built around an open-air courtyard. Kefa (Peter) would have had the cover of being in a public place and could have heard or possibly seen what was happening to Yeshua in His appearance before the high priest.
- Kefa would have had a Galilean accent (*ESV Archaeology Study Bible*, 2017).

22:63) The men who were holding Yeshua as a prisoner made cruel sport and tortured Him. 22:64) They blindfolded Him and taunted Him, "Now play the prophet: who is the one who hit You?" 22:65) They were saying many other abusive words against Him, even blaspheming God.

22:66) At daybreak, some elders of the people, the chief priests, and [their] scribes convened together and brought Him to their committee meeting, asking Him, 22:67) "If You are the Anointed One, then tell us." But he answered them, "If I tell you, you will not believe. 22:68) Moreover, if I ask you a question, you will not answer. 22:69) But from now on the Son of Man will be seated at the right hand of the power of God" (Dan 7:13; Ps 110:1). 22:70) At that, they all declared, "Then You are the Son of

God!" He said to them, "You say that I am." 22:71) They concluded, "What further need do we have of testimony? We have heard it ourselves from His own mouth."

Caiaphas was the high priest from AD 18-36. He had been appointed by Rome and was the son-in-law of Annas who had served from AD 6-15. The reputation of the high priest had been ruined. The Essenes were especially critical of this "Roman puppet," whom they called the "Wicked Priest" (*Archaeological Study Bible*, 2005).

The Caiaphas family burial cave was discovered in southeastern Jerusalem. His full name appears twice on this elaborately decorated ossuary – which indeed has been determined to belong to the Caiaphas from the New Testament. Soft limestone. (Photo: Israel Museum, Jerusalem, 2019).

- Jewish law demanded a day's wait between the arrest and trial in capital cases, and no one could be tried on a festival day (such as Passover) or the eve of such an event. However, this event at Caiaphas' house was probably an informal hearing before Annas and Caiaphas. Once He was considered to be a blasphemer, Yeshua could be beaten before His official trial at daybreak (Young, 2019).

- The trial occurred early enough that Yeshua could still appear before Pilate and Herod Antipas before His crucifixion at noon. 22:66) The pronoun [their] refers to scribes employed for the chief priests who were Sadducees. It is added for clarity. The word scribe identifies a profession rather than a political or religious group. A scribe often was employed to serve a governmental entity. But the profession was needed by other groups like the Pharisees and the Sadducees. The well-educated scribe was able to prepare records, copy scrolls, or provide information. It is highly probable that the scribes mentioned in the NT should be connected to the group, sect, or governmental entity cited in the immediate context. Here Luke specifies clearly that this was "their," namely the chief priests' or Sadducees' council meeting. Their leader, the High Priest Caiaphas, conducted the meeting. Their scribes participated (Young, 2019).

Questions for review and discussion

What is the most important thing you learned from your study of Exodus chapters 1-13:10?

Summarize what you learned in "Preparing for Pesach"

What does *seder* mean?

What is a Passover Seder?

Summarize "Yeshua's Last Supper"

What is the "third cup"?

How is this related to communion?

What does *sicarii* mean?

Who was Caiaphas?

What was discovered in Jerusalem in Caiaphas' family tomb?

Summarize the study notes from this chapter and discuss:

___

Summarize in one or two sentences the most important or the most interesting thing you learned in this chapter from your study:

___

What makes it important or interesting to you?

___

Re-read Luke Chapter 22 from the *Hebrew Heritage Bible* translation used in this book. Discuss. Summarize Luke Chapter 22 in one paragraph and discuss:

_____
_____
_____
_____
_____
_____
_____
_____
_____
_____
_____

Choose one verse from Luke Chapter 22 that you think is the most important and write it here. Discuss why you think it is the most important verse:

_____
_____

How did your understanding of Luke Chapter 22 change after you studied it and read it again? Discuss.

_____
_____
_____
_____

How can you apply what you learned from Luke Chapter 22 to your life? Discuss.

_____
_____
_____
_____

What question or questions do you still have about Luke Chapter 22 that you don't understand or want to know more about? Discuss.

_____
_____
_____
_____

If you have the opportunity, participate in a Passover Seder in your local community or host a Seder in your classroom or at home. Discuss what you learned.

THE GOSPEL OF LUKE CHAPTER TWENTY-THREE

Lesson 25

Before you begin your study, read Luke Chapter 23 out loud (as a group) from your Bible.

In your own words, summarize Luke Chapter 23 in one paragraph and write at least two questions that you had about the chapter as you read the biblical text: (Discuss)

_____
_____
_____
_____
_____
_____
_____
_____
_____
_____
_____
_____
_____
_____

The events documented in Luke Chapter 23 are foundational to the Christian faith. After the Passover meal with His emissaries on Thursday evening, Yeshua is arrested and led away to the house of Caiaphas for a hearing. On Friday morning He appears before a council and is brought before Pilate and Herod Antipas. He is crucified, dies, and is buried. This is the Passion of Yeshua for humanity.

Ruling from AD 26-36, Pontius Pilate was the fifth Roman governor of Judea. After Herod the Great's son Archelaus was banished in AD 6, Rome began to rule Judea directly (*ESV Archaeology Study Bible*, 2017). Research more about Pilate. Where was he from? What were his duties in Judea? Where did he live when he was governor? Why would he be in Judea for Passover? Why did Rome recall him in AD 36? Write and discuss:

Chapter 23

23:1) Then the whole group of them arose and marched Him off to Pilate. 23:2) They began to make charges against Him saying, "We found this man misleading our nation, forbidding to pay taxes to Caesar, and claiming that He is anointed to reign as King." 23:3) Pilate questioned Him saying, "Are You then the King of the Jewish people?" He answered him and said, "This is what you say." 23:4) Pilate said to the chief priests and the crowds, "I do not find this man guilty." 23:5) But they kept on pressing the charges saying, "He stirs up the people, teaching all over Yehudah, beginning in the Galil and even spreading the message here." 23:6) But when Pilate heard this, he asked whether the man was a Galilean. 23:7) After learning that He belonged to Herod's jurisdiction, he sent him to Herod, who himself also was in Yerushalayim at that time.

- "In reality, it is highly doubtful if Yeshua ever appeared before the Sanhedrin. Leaders like Gamaliel would never have allowed such unfair proceedings in a trial [see Acts 5:34-41]. The Greek word *sunedrion* is the term used for council. Sometimes it has wrongly been understood to mean the prestigious high court of the Sanhedrin. During the trial of Yeshua, it becomes clear that this was their council, that is, the committee of the Sadducean priests (Luke 22:66)" (Young, 1995, p. 231).
- The council wanted to charge Yeshua with refusing to pay taxes to Caesar. This would help them in their judicial process (Young, 1995).
- Pilate probably tried Yeshua at the palace compound built by Herod the Great in the western part of Yerushalayim. Both Herod's palace and the Antonia Fortress (located on the northwestern corner of the Temple Mount) had a praetorium.
- Pilate was the governor of Judea, and he did not have jurisdiction in Galil. Herod Antipas did have jurisdiction over Galil (ESV Archaeology Study Bible, 2017).
- The trial of Yeshua is very much an affair of the Roman officials in charge of Yerushalayim.
- The Pharisees (spiritual leaders) and the majority of the Jewish people opposed such actions against Yeshua. The Sadducees, who received their power from Rome, felt it was in their best interest to cooperate with the empire (Young, 1995).

23:8) Now when Herod saw Yeshua, he was delighted. For a long time, he had wanted to see Him because he had been hearing about Him and was hoping to see some miraculous sign performed by Him. 23:9) He questioned Him in depth, but He would not answer him a word. 23:10) The chief priests and the scribes were standing there, pressing charges against Him vigorously. 23:11) Herod and his soldiers treated Him with contempt and ridiculed Him. Then they dressed Him up in a gorgeous robe and sent Him back to Pilate. 23:12) That very day Herod and Pilate became friends with one another. Before that, they had been feuding with each other.

23:13) Pilate called a meeting for the chief priests, the rulers, and the people. 23:14) He said to them, "You brought this man to me charged as one who incites the people to rebellion. Listen, having examined the case against Him before you, I have found this man not guilty of the charges of which you accuse Him. 23:15) Neither has Herod because he sent Him back to us. Nothing deserving the death sentence has been done by Him. 23:16) So I will give Him a flogging and release Him." 23:17) Now he was forced to release one prisoner to them during the feast. 23:18) But they called out together saying, "Take this man away and release Bar Abba for us!" 23:19) He was one who had been thrown into prison for an insurrection which he instigated in the city and for murder. 23:20) So Pilate wanted to release Yeshua to them. He asked them again, 23:21) but they kept on calling out, saying, "Crucify, crucify Him!" 23:22) He said to them for the third time, "Why, what crime has this man done? I have not found Him guilty of charges deserving the death penalty. I will give Him a flogging and release Him." 23:23) But they were insistent, with loud voices asking that

He be crucified. Their voices and the demands of the chief priests were compelling. 23:24) Pilate pronounced the death sentence, and hence, their request was granted. 23:25) So he released the man they were asking for who had been thrown into prison for insurrection and murder, but he turned Yeshua over as they had wanted.

- "Transferring Yeshua over to Herod Antipas was like sending a notorious criminal to the kangaroo court of the hanging judge…Pilate was interested in improving his relationship with Herod and winning some further political favor for imperial Rome, which he represented" (Young, 1995, p. 232).
- The actions between Pilate and Herod demonstrate the "political nature of Yeshua's arrest and the miscarriage of justice which He endured in His final hours before crucifixion" (Young, 1995, p. 232).
- Both politicians benefited from the prisoner transfer (Young, 1995).
- Two important facts need to be remembered about Pilate:
  - The Roman governor [Pilate] was required to grant amnesty to someone. During the festival he had to release one prisoner.
  - Pilate was a cruel, self-serving tyrant. Philo, the first century Jewish philosopher said this about Pilate, "…the briberies, the insults, the robberies, the outrages and wanton injuries, the executions without trial constantly repeated, the ceaseless and supremely grievous cruelty…" (Young, 1995, pp. 232-233).
- Pilate was a Roman official who showed little compassion and cared only about his position and the policies of the empire (Young, 1995).
- Verse 17 is missing in some authorities, but it is well attested in other manuscripts. It is paralleled in Matt. 27:15, Mark 15:6, and John 18:39. It is well grounded in the rock-solid sources of the Gospels. The internal evidence supports the inclusion of verse 17 because the scene of Pilate asking the chief priests whom they want released for the Passover amnesty is incomprehensible without it. Pilate wanted the least dangerous figure for Rome to be released. Barabbas, the murderer and insurrectionist, was more troublesome for him than Jesus. On the other hand, the Sadducees viewed the popularity of Jesus and the momentum of His messianic movement with greater concern for political stability than Barabbas and his activities. Pilate and the Sadducees both wanted to keep the "peace" of the Roman Empire (Young, 2019).
- The group of Sadducees and priests who had gathered together urged Pilate to stop Yeshua. Unlike the Pharisee Gamaliel who would later argue in favor of Kefa (Peter) and the other apostles, the Sadducees felt that Yeshua's movement threatened the nation.
- Pilate gave the death sentence. Roman soldiers carried it out (Young, 1995).

23:26) When [the Roman soldiers] led Him away, they compelled Shimon from Cyrene, who was coming in from the country, and loaded the cross beam on him to carry behind Yeshua. 23:27) There were following Him a great throng of people and of women who were pounding their chests in lament and mourning for Him. 23:28) But Yeshua turned toward them and said, "Daughters of Yerushalayim, stop weeping for Me, but weep for yourselves and for your children. 23:29) Look, the days are coming when they will say, 'Blessed are the barren and wombs that never gave birth and the breasts that never nursed.' 23:30) Then they will begin to say to the mountains, 'Fall on us' and to the hills, 'Hide us' (Hos 10:8). 23:31) For if they do these things to the green tree (Ezek. 20:47), what will happen when [they do it] to the dry tree?" 23:32) Two others who were criminals also were being led away to be put to death with Him. 23:33) When they came to the place called the Skull, there they crucified Him and the criminals, one on the right and the other on the left. 23:34) But Yeshua was saying, "Father, forgive them for they do not know what they are doing." They threw dice to divide up His clothes among themselves (Ps 22:18). 23:35) The people stood by watching. Some of the rulers sneered at him saying, "He saved others; let Him save Himself, if this is the Anointed of God, his Chosen One." 23:36) The soldiers also mocked Him, coming up to Him, offering Him sour wine, 23:37) and saying, "If You are the King of the Jewish people, then save Yourself!" 23:38) Now there was also an inscription above him [[written in Greek, Latin, and Hebrew]], "This is the King of the Jewish people."

- In verse 26, the way to execution was directed by the Roman soldiers. Only Roman soldiers could conscript and force (Shimon) Simeon to carry the cross beam. The fear of Rome prevented the Gospel writers from mentioning the Roman soldiers directly. Only John's Gospel portrays this fear, "...the Romans will take action and destroy both our place and our nation" (11:48). Jewish messianic movements were brutally suppressed by the empire's superior military might. The King of the Jewish people will be crucified by the Roman Empire and the movement will be destroyed (Young, 2019).

- Usually the condemned person carried their own cross beam to the place of execution, but Yeshua was probably too weak from the severe beatings he had received.

- Shimon was a Jew from Cyrene in North Africa and was in Yerushalayim to celebrate Passover (Cultural Backgrounds Study Bible, 2016).

- In verse 27, literally, all the crowds of people who had gathered around to witness the scene were, "beating themselves and wailing," in mourning for the dead. See Josephus on the mourning for the death of King Saul, in the same words his folk were "beating the breast and wailing in lament for the king" (Ant. 6.14,8; 377). Clearly while the Gospel shows that some sneered consenting to what happened, the great multitudes of Jewish people assembled there were deeply saddened and were opposed to the crucifixion of a Jew from their family of Abraham's children—loyal to their Torah, to the one true God, and to their country (Young, 2019).

- Verse 31 was prophetic. Dry wood burns faster than green wood; Yeshua was unjustly executed, but wider bloodshed was eminent (Cultural Backgrounds Study Bible, 2016).

- Yeshua had endured humiliation and inhumane beatings.
- In verse 36, the soldiers were mocking Him as they offered Yeshua sour wine. It was a narcotic and was regularly given to Jewish criminals...so that his mind would become confused (Lachs, 1987).
- Pilate wanted the inscription of the charge against Yeshua to read "This is the King of the Jewish people" in three languages (Matthew 27:37, Mark 15:26, Luke 23:38, John 19:19). The Sadducees were offended. "But Pilate wanted to make a political statement in the form of a severe warning. The sign was a threat. It mocked the Jewish faith and practice. Pilate's words ridiculed the people. In Pilate's mind Rome had crucified the King of the Jews. His action demonstrated the might of the Roman empire and the weakness of Jewish faith in God's future deliverance" (Young, 1995, pp. 236-237).

23:39) Of the criminals who were being hanged there, one was hurling abuse at Him saying, "Are you not the Anointed One? Save Yourself and us!" 23:40) But the other answered and rebuked him, "Do you not even fear God? After all, you have received the same sentence of death. 23:41) We justly received condemnation because we are receiving what we deserve for our actions; but this man has done nothing wrong." 23:42) Then he implored, "Yeshua, remember me when You come into Your kingdom!" 23:43) He said to him, "In truth I tell you, today, you shall be with Me in Paradise." 23:44) It was now about midday, and darkness fell over the whole land until late afternoon. 23:45) While the sun was hidden, [[the veil of the Temple was torn down the middle.]] 23:46) Yeshua cried out with a loud voice and said, "Father, into Your hands I commit My spirit" (Ps 31:5). After He said this, He breathed His last. 23:47) Now when the centurion saw what had taken place, he sanctified God saying, "Beyond all doubt, this man was righteous." 23:48) All the crowds who had gathered together to watch this terrible scene felt heartbroken after they saw what had happened. They began to return, beating their chests in mourning. 23:49) Also His close friends and the women who had accompanied Him from the Galil were standing at a distance, watching what was going on.

- Yeshua was crucified with two other men. These men were political offenders (Lachs, 1987). Executing the condemned during festivals sent a wider warning against those who would dare defy Rome.
- Darkness often appears as judgement in the TANAK (Exodus 10:31-23), including darkness at noon (Am. 8:9) (Cultural Backgrounds Study Bible, 2016).
- The darkness was from noon until 3:00 pm. "'The earth quakes before them, the heavens tremble, the sun and the moon are darkened, and the stars withdraw their shining' (Joel 2:10). Rabbinic sources also recount strange occurrences at the death of notable rabbis" (Lachs, 1987, p. 434).

- The curtain's tearing may imply new access to the Most Holy Place (*Cultural Backgrounds Study Bible*, 2016).

- "There were two curtains, an inner curtain and an outer, but here what is meant is the outer, so that it was visible to the people. There is an interesting story that forty years before the destruction of the Temple the western light dimmed. Among other strange happenings, the doors of the sanctuary opened on their own accord" (Lachs, 1987, pp. 434-435).

- In verse 34, Yeshua had prayed for the forgiveness of His persecutors. In verse 46, Yeshua echoes Psalm 31:5; a Jewish tradition says that this prayer was recited during the evening offering at the Temple about the same time Yeshua died (*Cultural Backgrounds Study Bible*, 2016).

The curtain of the Temple separated the Holy Place from the Most Holy Place. The curtain (Veil) was made of "blue and purple and scarlet, and fine twined linen of cunning work." It was one hand-breadth thick. Its length was forty cubits (69 feet) and its width was twenty cubits (34.4 feet) (Ritmeyer, 2015, p. 25). Illustration: The Holy Place by Debbie Willey

GOSPEL OF LUKE 343

23:50) Then came forward a man named Yosef, who was a member of the council. He was a good and righteous man. 23:51) This man had objected to the plan and actions taken against Yeshua. He was from Harmatayim, a city of the Jewish people. He himself was living in expectation for the kingdom of God. 23:52) This man approached Pilate and asked for the body of Yeshua. 23:53) He took the body down from the cross and wrapped it in linen cloths and laid the body in a tomb cut into the rock where no person had ever been buried. 23:54) It was the preparation day, as the Shabbat observance was about to begin. 23:55) Now following after all this, the women who had accompanied Him from the Galil watched the tomb and saw how His body was laid to rest. 23:56) They returned and prepared some sweet-smelling spices and perfumes for His burial. On the day of Shabbat they rested in observance of the commandment.

- Yosef of Arimathea. Arimathea is Harmatayim. It was 10 miles east of Lydda (roughly 20 miles northwest of Yerushalayim) (Lachs, 1989).

- Yosef's wealth and position allowed him to construct a new tomb [outside the walls] in Yerushalayim, the center of his religious and political life (ESV Archaeology Study Bible, 2017).

- "It is recorded that the Patriarch Gamaliel II decreed that all Jews regardless of their station in life were to be buried in linen shrouds. It is difficult to determine if the use of linen shrouds was current before the decree of Rabban Gamaliel or because of it" (Lachs, 1987, p. 436).

- The corpse would normally be washed and anointed with oil, and its chin bound (in order for the mouth not to fall open) (ESV Archaeology Study Bible, 2017).

- Yards of linen and large quantities of spices were used in preparing the body for burial. Seventy-five pounds of myrrh and aloes were already used on this first day (John 19:39-40). More was purchased by the women after Shabbat before they returned to the tomb (Archaeological Study Bible, 2005).

- This was Friday, the day before Shabbat. Shabbat begins at sundown on Friday. Because Yeshua was buried just before sundown, the women rested until Shabbat was over on Saturday evening (ESV Archaeology Study Bible, 2017).

Gethsemane on the Mount of Olives and the place of Yeshua's crucifixion, burial, and resurrection (the Church of the Holy Sepulchre). Photo: Modern Yerushalayim from the Tower of David (near Herod's ancient palace where Yeshua may have stood trial before Pilate).

Yeshua was charged with blasphemy, but the power to execute lay in the hands of Rome. Yeshua was sent to Pilate. Pilate had come to Yerushalayim because of the Passover holiday. This holiday always had the potential for anti-Roman riots. Pilate would not have cared about blasphemy. So, Yeshua was charged with misleading the Jews, forbidding them to pay taxes to Rome, and insurrection. Pilate sent Yeshua to Herod (who was also in Yerushalayim because of Passover), and Herod sent Him back to Pilate. Pilate had Yeshua crucified (*ESV Archaeological Study Bible*, 2017).

The act of crucifixion included these events: the condemned was scourged; he was forced to carry his crossbar to the site of execution; and he was fastened to the crossbar by nails; the crossbar was affixed to an upright beam that was already set in the ground (*ESV Archaeological Study Bible*, 2017).

Photo: Heel bone and iron nail from Jerusalem (1st Century AD) Israel Museum, Jerusalem, 2019

The Church of the Holy Sepulchre in Jerusalem

Photo Credit: David Anderson, 2018

GOSPEL OF LUKE   345

The Church of the Holy Sepulchre stands over the spot where the earliest Christian tradition places Golgotha and the tomb of Jesus. In the fourth century Queen Helena, Emperor Constantine's mother, visited Jerusalem and was shown "the very spot of the Savior's sufferings" (Eusebius). This spot had been previously covered over by a shrine to Roman deities by Emperor Hadrian around AD 135 in his attempt to stamp out Judaism in Jerusalem (Hoffmeier, 2008).

Take a trip online to the Church of the Holy Sepulchre in Jerusalem. Locate the traditional site of Yeshua's crucifixion and His tomb. What does the inside of the church look like? What have scholars recently discovered about His tomb? Why did some scholars reject this church as the location of Yeshua's tomb? This church has a long and fascinating history. Write and discuss:

_____
_____
_____
_____
_____
_____
_____
_____

Questions for review and discussion

Which group of Jewish leaders made the charges against Yeshua?
_____

What motivated them to press these charges against Yeshua?
_____

How did the Pharisees (spiritual leaders) and most Jewish people feel about the hostile treatment of Yeshua?
_____
_____

Why did Pilate want the inscription to read "The King of the Jews?"
_____
_____

What did the darkness represent?

What happened to the curtain (veil) in the Temple?

What did this represent?

What were the dimensions of the veil?

What were the other strange events that may have coincided with Yeshua's death?

Where was Yeshua buried?

How was His body prepared for burial?

What happened on Shabbat?

Summarize the study notes from this chapter and discuss:

Summarize in one or two sentences the most important or the most interesting thing you learned in this chapter from your study:

What makes it important or interesting to you?

_____
_____

Re-read Luke Chapter 23 from the *Hebrew Heritage Bible* translation used in this book. Discuss. Summarize Luke Chapter 23 in one paragraph and discuss:

_____
_____
_____
_____
_____
_____
_____
_____
_____
_____
_____
_____

Choose one verse from Luke Chapter 23 that you think is the most important and write it here. Discuss why you think it is the most important verse:

_____
_____

How did your understanding of Luke Chapter 23 change after you studied it and read it again? Discuss.

_____
_____
_____
_____

How can you apply what you learned from Luke Chapter 23 to your life? Discuss.

_____
_____
_____

What question or questions do you still have about Luke Chapter 23 that you don't understand or want to know more about? Discuss.

_____
_____
_____
_____

THE GOSPEL OF LUKE CHAPTER TWENTY-FOUR

Lesson 26

Before you begin your study, read Luke Chapter 24 out loud (as a group) from your Bible.

In your own words, summarize Luke Chapter 24 in one paragraph and write at least two questions that you had about the chapter as you read the biblical text: (Discuss)

_____
_____
_____
_____
_____
_____
_____
_____
_____
_____
_____
_____
_____
_____

In 1883, General Charles Gordon found what is known as the "Garden Tomb" near a stone escarpment north of the Damascus Gate in Yerushalayim. Every year thousands of Christians from around the world visit this site that Gordon believed was Yeshua's tomb (Hoffmeier, 2008).

Photo: Garden Tomb, Jerusalem

Take a trip online to Jerusalem and visit the Garden Tomb. Why did Gordon think this was the site of Yeshua's burial? Who owns the Garden Tomb? The tombs that have been uncovered at this site date to which time period? What did you learn? Write and discuss:

Hebrew Names and their English Equivalents

Hebrew	English
Miryam	Mary
Yochana	Joanna
Yaakov	Jacob (James)
Moshe	Moses
Yisrael	Israel
Natzeret	Nazareth
Shimeon	Simon
Beit Anyah	Bethany

Chapter 24

24:1) Early in the first day of the week, they went to the tomb, bringing the sweet-smelling spices which they had prepared. 24:2) Then they discovered that the stone had been rolled away from the tomb entrance. 24:3) When they went in, they did not find the body of the Lord Yeshua. 24:4) While they were bewildered about what they had discovered, suddenly it happened that two figures stood before them whose clothes flashed like lightning. 24:5) The women were terrified and bowed their faces to the ground. The men said to them, "Why do you look for the living One among the dead? 24:6) He is not here, but He has risen. Remember how He explained to you while He was still in the Galil 24:7) saying, 'The Son of Man must be betrayed into the hands of sinful men, and be crucified, and yet on the third day rise again.'" 24:8) At that, they remembered His words. 24:9) Upon returning from the tomb, they reported news of all this to the eleven and to all the rest. 24:10) Now it was Miryam from Migdal, Yochana, Miryam the mother of Yaakov, and also the other women with them who were telling these things to the authoritative emissaries. 24:11) Even so, these reports seemed like nonsense to them, and they chose not to believe them. 24:12) [[But Kefa arose and ran to the tomb. Stooping down and looking in, he saw only the grave cloth wrappings, and he went away to his home wondering what had actually happened.]]

- They rested on Shabbat according to the commandment.
- By Jewish time, the first day of the week (Sunday) began at sundown on Saturday. The women probably bought spices after sunset on Saturday and were ready to travel to the tomb early on Sunday morning. When they began their journey it was still dark, and when they arrived at the tomb it was early in the morning (*Archaeological Study Bible*, 2005).

- The stone had been rolled away – not for Yeshua to get out of the tomb – it was removed so they could see it was empty and witness the awesome delivering power of God.
- A tomb's entrance was usually kept closed to prevent vandals and animals from disturbing the bodies. Typically, a disk-shaped stone was rolled over the opening of the tomb. These stones usually weighed between one and three tons.
- Yeshua's tomb had been sealed by the Romans. The seal was a security device with a cord attaching the stone to the tomb and a Roman seal anchoring both ends (Archaeological Study Bible, 2005).
- The two angels parallel the two angels at the ascension (Acts 1:10) and provide two witnesses to the important fact of the resurrection (Marshall, 1978).
- The angels "clothes flashed like lightning." Different biblical accounts demonstrate that people could mistake angels for humans, but they could also appear dressed in white (Daniel 10:5) or as if made of fire (2 Kings 6:17) (Cultural Backgrounds Study Bible, 2016).
- The tomb was empty! Yeshua has risen and He is Lord!
- The women were reminded of what Yeshua had said earlier.
- The women received the news of the fulfillment of God's promise. They are portrayed as "loyal, pious Jews" (p. 883) and were messengers of the news of the resurrection to the emissaries (Marshall, 1978).
- Both Jewish and Roman law normally regarded a woman's testimony as of limited value, treating women as unstable. It is to the women, however, that God's angels first entrust the testimony of Yeshua's resurrection (Cultural Backgrounds Study Bible, 2016).

"The Bible is where I can find peace and guidance. I can always count on it. I can rely on its truth. It helps us talk to and know God." Lauren Force – Class of 2021

24:13) Then that very day two men were walking toward a village named Motza, which was located about seven miles distance from Yerushalayim. 24:14) They were discussing with one another about all these things which had taken place. 24:15) It happened that while they were absorbed in deep discussion and debate, Yeshua himself came near and began walking along beside them. 24:16) But something obstructed the vision of their eyes so that they could not recognize him. 24:17) He said to them, "What are these events which you are discussing with one another as you are walking?" They stood still feeling sad. 24:18) One of them, named Cleopas, answered and said to Him, "Are You the only stranger visiting Yerushalayim who has not heard about all the events which have happened there within these last few days?" 24:19) But He said to them, "What events?" So they explained to Him, "The events surrounding Yeshua from Natzeret who proved Himself a prophet, powerful in working miracles and in teaching, both in the sight of God and all the people. 24:20) Then the chief priests and our rulers delivered Him up to the sentence of death. The [Roman soldiers] crucified Him.

24:21) But we were hoping that it was He who was going to redeem Yisrael. In fact, besides all this, it is now the third day since these things happened. 24:22) Moreover, some women from among our group amazed us. When they went to the tomb early 24:23) and did not find His body, they returned telling that they had actually seen a vision of heavenly messengers, who said that He was alive. 24:24) Some of those who were with us went to the tomb and found it just exactly as the women had described, but they did not see Him." 24:25) Then He said to them, "O simple minded fools and slow of heart to believe all that the prophets have spoken! 24:26) Was it not necessary for the Anointed One to die and to enter into His glory?" 24:27) Beginning with Moshe and with all the prophets, He explained to them the teachings concerning Himself in all the writings of Scripture. 24:28) They came near the village where they were going. He acted as though He would go on farther. 24:29) But they urged Him saying, "Stay with us, for it is getting late toward evening, and the day is nearly over." So he went in to stay with them. 24:30) Then it happened as He reclined at the table with them, He took the bread and recited a blessing over it, broke it, and began to give it to them. 24:31) At this, their eyes were opened and they recognized Him. He vanished from their sight. 24:32) They said one to the other, "Did not our hearts burn within us while He was teaching us on the road, while He was explaining the Scriptures to us?" 24:33) At that very hour, they arose and returned to Yerushalayim. They found the eleven gathered together along with others who were with them. 24:34) They exclaimed, "The Lord has really risen and has appeared to Shimeon. 24:35) They began to relate their experiences on the road and how they recognized Him in the breaking of the bread.

- In verse 13, literally 60 *stadia* which is 7 miles rounded off from 6.8 miles (10.95 kms). The *stadion* is thought to be 202.3 yards (186.7 meters). The location could be Motza if the distance is reckoned as a day journey to and from Jerusalem (Young, 2019).

"The most detailed account in the Gospel of Luke of an appearance of Yeshua after His resurrection is that of His encounter with two disciples on the road." Usually translated as "Emmaus" the village is probably Motza. It is only 3.5 miles from Yerushalayim. Luke probably indicated the distance of the round trip since the men traveled both ways (ESV *Archaeology Study Bible*, 2017, p. 1533).

Take a trip online to Motza, Israel. It is considered a neighborhood in Jerusalem. Exciting excavations have been occurring at this location. Where is it located in Jerusalem? What has been discovered at this site? What does it look like? What Bible verses refer to this site? Write and discuss:

_____
_____
_____
_____
_____

> "Studying the Bible helps you come closer to God. You begin to understand how magnificent He is. He is loving and caring. Bringing others to Christ and giving God glory is our goal as Christians. We need to be closer to God so we can bring others to Him."
> Harrison Hunnicutt – Class of 2021

- The two men are walking to Motza on the same day as the discovery of the empty tomb. They were probably returning home after their celebration of Passover in Yerushalayim (Marshall, 1978).
- It is possible they were so focused on their disappointments and problems that they missed recognizing Yeshua when He was walking along beside them.
- The news about Yeshua's crucifixion had spread throughout Yerushalayim because it occurred during Passover week. Jews from all over the Roman empire knew about His death (Life Application Study Bible, 2000).
- It is also quite possible that these two men do not recognize Yeshua due to "Spiritual blindness" (p. 893). "Something obstructed the vision of their eyes" (v. 16). "Its purpose is to enable the disciples to be prepared for the revelation of the risen Yeshua by a fresh understanding of the prophecies of His resurrection; it may also be meant to show that one can know the presence of the risen Yeshua without being able to see Him" (p. 893). To these two men, Yeshua is just another festival pilgrim returning home (Marshall, 1978, p. 894).
- Luke identifies one of the men as Cleopas. Because he is identified, it is assumed he was well-known to Luke's audience. Perhaps he was the father of Simeon (who later became bishop of Yerushalayim). The other person is not named. It is possible the other person was Cleopas' son or his wife (Marshall, 1978, p. 894).
- Before they knew about the resurrection, the highest description they could have applied to Yeshua was that of a prophet (Marshall, 1978).
- Yeshua's activities such as proclaiming the word of God, raising the dead, cleansing the lepers, and feeding the crowds were the same actions as biblical prophets like Elijah and Elisha (Cultural Backgrounds Study Bible, 2016).
- Their hope was that Yeshua would crown His prophetic work by setting the Jewish people free from their Roman enemies (Marshall, 1978, p. 895).
- Many Jews believed that the "'Old Testament' prophecies had pointed to a military and political Messiah. They didn't realize that Yeshua's death offered the greatest hope possible" (Life Application Study Bible, 2000).

- The reference to the third day appears to reflect the Jewish belief that by the fourth day the soul has left the body, or possibly a faint memory that Yeshua had spoken of something that would happen on the third day (Marshall, 1978).
- The reference to Moshe (Moses) and all the prophets in verse 27, means the whole TANAK ("Old Testament") (Archaeological Study Bible, 2005).
- Yeshua gives them the opportunity to offer Him an invitation to join them. He will not force His presence on them.
- Because this event occurred during the Festival of Unleavened Bread, the bread at the meal would have been unleavened.
- Verse 30 was reminiscent of the last supper of Yeshua (and perhaps the feeding of the multitudes). These actions helped identify the stranger as Yeshua to the disciples. Their eyes were opened when He recited the blessing, broke the bread, and gave it to them.
- The risen Yeshua is portrayed as a supernatural visitor (p. 898).
- They could not keep the news to themselves; others in Yerushalayim had not heard that Yeshua had risen from the dead. Therefore, they went quickly to Yerushalayim (Marshall, 1978).

24:36) Then while they were telling these things, He Himself stood in the middle of the gathering, [[and said to them, "Shalom to you all."]] 24:37) But they were startled and frightened. They thought that they were seeing a spirit. 24:38) But He said to them, "Why are you troubled and why do doubts take hold of your hearts? 24:39) See My hands and My feet that it is I Myself; touch and examine Me because a spirit does not have flesh and bones as You see that I have." 24:40) When He had said this He showed them His hands and His feet. 24:41) But they still could not believe it for sheer joy and were marveling, when He asked them, "Do you have something here to eat?" 24:42) They gave him a piece of grilled fish. 24:43) He took it and ate it in their sight. 24:44) Now he said to them, "These are My teachings which I taught you while I was still with you because all the things which are written about Me in the Torah of Moshe and the Prophets and the Writings must be fulfilled." 24:45) Then he opened their minds to understand the Scriptures. 24:46) He taught them, "Thus it is written, that the Anointed One should die and rise again from the dead on the third day. 24:47) Repentance for forgiveness of sins should be proclaimed in His name beginning from Yerushalayim. 24:48) You are witnesses of these events. 24:49) Take notice of this! I am sending the promise of My Father upon you, but you must stay in the city until you are clothed with power from above." 24:50) He led them out as far as Beit Anyah, and He lifted up His hands and blessed them. 24:51) It happened that while He was blessing them, He departed from them [[and ascended into heaven]]. 24:52) They [[worshiped Him]] and returned to Yerushalayim with great joy. They were continually in the Temple praising God.

- The traditional Jewish greeting is shalom (Peace be with you). This greeting constituted an implicit prayer to God for well-being of the person addressed (*Cultural Backgrounds Study Bible*, 2016, p. 1800).

- The promise of peace (shalom) associated with the coming of Yeshua now reaches its fulfillment, and the conventional greeting is transformed (Marshall, 1978).

- It may seem strange that the disciples should be frightened at Yeshua appearing to them if they knew He had risen, but it is understandable that a supernatural appearance would cause alarm even when it is half-expected (Marshall, 1978).

- They might think they are seeing a ghost, but the risen Yeshua removes their doubts by
  - Proving that it is He who is present.
  - Showing that He is not a spirit. He has flesh and bones (Marshall, 1978).

- Some Jewish people believed in ghosts or spirits associated with the dead. Some ancients believed in a "shadowy afterlife"; such shadows could not be grasped with hands. Many Jewish sources doubted that angels did not eat human food (*Cultural Backgrounds Study Bible*, 2016, p. 1800).

- In verse 44, the Torah of Moshe and the Prophets refers to the TANAK.

- "'For the forgiveness of sins…beginning in Yerushalayim' is a common theme that the beginnings of the messianic age shall first be noticeable in Yerushalayim. R. Levi said: 'All goodness and blessings and consolation which the Holy One, blessed be He, will give to Israel comes only from Zion'" (Lachs, 1987, p. 444).

- In verse 49, "spirit from on high… 'Spirit from His Shekhinah in the height of the Heaven'" (Lachs, 1987, p. 444).

- In verse 50, Yeshua led them to Beit Anyah (Bethany) and He lifted His hands to bless them…the priestly blessing. In Jewish tradition, priests lifted their hands when they blessed the people (*Cultural Backgrounds Study Bible*, 2016).

- In verse 46, the third day, by Jewish reckoning part of a day counted as a day (*Cultural Backgrounds Study Bible*, 2016).

- In verse 51, some important manuscripts delete, "and ascended into heaven." However, the reading appears in the early witness Papyrus 75, fits the context, and connects with Acts 1:2, "until the day when He was taken up…." (Young, 2019).

- In verse 52, the words, "they worshiped Him" are omitted in important manuscript witnesses. Although it may be a later addition, it is possible that a scribe may have omitted the phrase by skipping from the word autoi to the word autos in the Greek text. The alternate reading would be, "They returned to Yerushalayim with great joy" (Young, 2019).

- The Gospel of Luke closes like it had opened (1:8-10) with the Jews in the Temple in Yerushalayim praying and worshiping God (*Cultural Backgrounds Study Bible*, 2016).

Faith, History, and Theology

"Yeshua proclaims His ultimate victory over the cruel Roman cross through His resurrection. He overcame death in victory....The misunderstanding of the historical issues pertaining to His trial and crucifixion has caused untold pain to the Jewish people.... The pages of church history have been dyed red with the blood of the Jewish faithful.... Christians should never blame modern Jews for the errors of the Sadducean priests. Neither should they place guilt upon Italians...for Pilate's activities and the policies of the Roman empire...The study of history should prevent a new generation from repeating the mistakes of the past. The uncompromising message of Yeshua's love should challenge His followers to demonstrate the truth of his message in action. Love is stronger than hatred. Divine love expressed in human action will overcome racial hatred and prejudice...In Christian theology the real reason for Yeshua's death is not related to the historical circumstances of the trial. It was both the human need for forgiveness and divine grace that mandated the cross. The theology of the Christian faith attaches deep significance to the cross. Without death there is no resurrection... When Christians read Isaiah 53, they see Yeshua...Though modern Jews and Christians view the cross from different vantage points, perhaps both faith communities share something in common when they consider the pain of Yeshua. He loved His people and suffered as one of his own... He made the supreme sacrifice...However, His sufferings on the cross invoke a challenge...He called upon His disciples to deny themselves and walk in His footsteps. The foundation of His ministry was healing love for others. The sacrificial love of Yeshua was deeply rooted in the Jewish understanding of divine compassion for people created in the image of God" (Young, 1995, pp. 237-238).

"Studying the Bible has impacted me by solidifying my faith through proven historical accounts. I grew up knowing the stories and thinking there was no meaning behind them except what was on the surface. However, when I began studying the Bible and really digging into the history of it, God revealed Himself and showed me why I should believe. Not only did the outside sources I found prove biblical accounts, I discovered there was so much of the Jewish faith that matched what the outside accounts had said."
Molly Nickell – Class of 2020.

Questions for review and discussion

What do you think when you hear that the women were the first ones to testify about Yeshua's resurrection?

What happened on the road to Motza?

_____
_____

Why didn't the two on the road know they were talking to Yeshua?

_____

Summarize "Faith, History, and Theology."

_____
_____

What does it mean to you?

_____
_____

Summarize the study notes from this chapter and discuss:

_____
_____
_____
_____
_____
_____
_____
_____
_____
_____
_____
_____
_____
_____

Summarize in one or two sentences the most important or the most interesting thing you learned in this chapter from your study:

_____
_____

What makes it important or interesting to you?

_____
_____

Re-read Luke Chapter 24 from the *Hebrew Heritage Bible* translation used in this book. Discuss. Summarize Luke Chapter 24 in one paragraph and discuss:

_____
_____
_____
_____
_____
_____
_____
_____
_____
_____
_____
_____
_____

Choose one verse from Luke Chapter 24 that you think is the most important and write it here. Discuss why you think it is the most important verse:

_____
_____

How did your understanding of Luke Chapter 24 change after you studied it and read it again? Discuss.

_____
_____

How can you apply what you learned from Luke Chapter 24 to your life? Discuss.

_____
_____

What question or questions do you still have about Luke Chapter 24 that you don't understand or want to know more about? Discuss.

_____
_____
_____

> "Studying the Bible helps us learn about who God is. It helps us better understand who we are as humans and the plan and purpose of our life. Being able to understand ourselves and acknowledge God as our Lord and Savior will help us navigate life and our relationships." Gillian Tredway – Class of 2020

Reflect on Luke Chapters 1-24. What were the most important things that you learned in each chapter? List and discuss them here: *(See pages 363-365 "Additional Notes" if you need more space for your answers.)*

_____

What have been your three favorite verses from Luke?

_____

What is the most important thing you learned from studying Luke?

_____

Why is it so important to you?

How has your understanding of the Gospel of Luke changed?

How has this study impacted your life?

Why do you think it is important to study the Bible?

Has your testimony changed as a result of your study of Luke? How?

What questions do you still have?

Other comments:

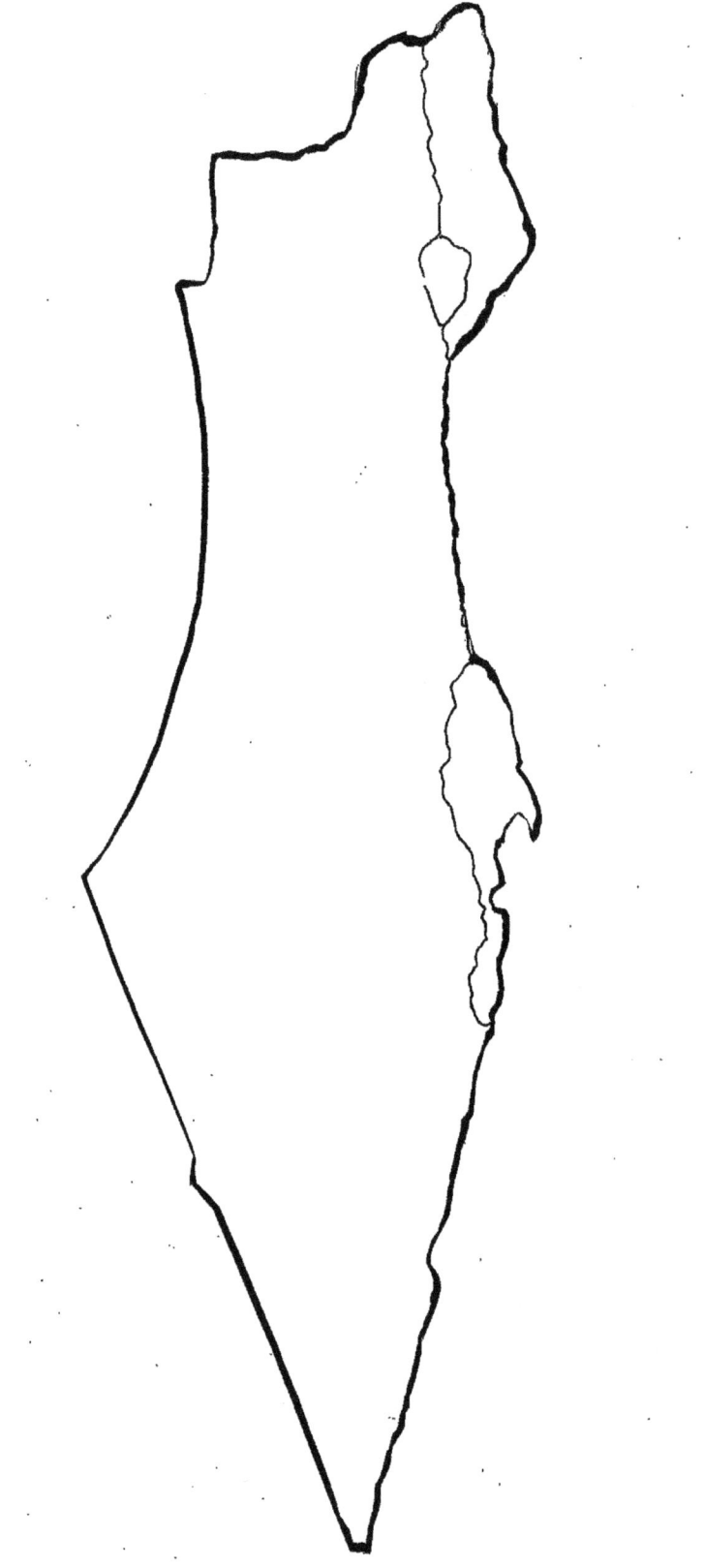

Teachers may use and copy this map as a resource for this workbook.

Additional Notes

Additional Notes

Additional Notes

References

Aharoni, Y., Avi-Yonah, M., Rainey, A., & Safrai, Z. (2002). *The Carta Bible Atlas: Fourth Edition*. Jerusalem, Israel: Carta, The Israel Map and Publishing Co.

Amit, D. (2016). *The Model of Jerusalem in the Second Temple Period*. Jerusalem, Israel: The Israel Museum, Jerusalem and Holyland Tourism (1992). Ltd.

Anderson, R. S. (2001). *The Shape of Practical Theology: Empowering Ministry with Theological Praxis*. Downers Grove, IL: InterVarsity Press.

Archaeological Study Bible. (2005). Grand Rapids, MI: Zondervan.

Bailey, K. E. (2008). *Jesus through Middle Eastern Eyes: Cultural Studies in the Gospels*. Downers Grove, IL: InterVarsity Press.

Beers, R. A. (Gen. Ed.). (2000). *Life Application Study Bible: New American Standard Bible*. Grand Rapids, MI: Zondervan.

Belkin, S. (1960). *In His image: The Jewish Philosophy of Man Expressed in Rabbinic Tradition*. New York, NY: Abelard-Schuman Limited.

Bivin, D. & Blizzard, R., Jr. (2001). *Understanding the Difficult Words of Jesus: New Insights from a Hebraic Perspective*. Shippensburg, PA: Destiny Image Publishers.

Blomberg, C. L. (2006). On Building and Breaking Barriers: Forgiveness, Salvation, and Christian Counseling with Special Reference to Matthew 18:15-35. *Journal of Psychology and Christianity*, 25(2), 137-154.

Bruce, F. F. (1988). *The Book of Acts: Revised Edition*. Grand Rapids, MI: William B. Eerdmans Publishing Company.

Buxbaum, Y. (2004). *The Life and Teachings of Hillel*. Lanham, MD: Rowman and Littlefield Publishers.

Cultural Backgrounds Study Bible. (2016). Grand Rapids, MI: Zondervan.

Darom, D. *Animals of the Bible*. Herzlia, Israel: Palphot.

Eckstein, Y. (1997). *How Firm a Foundation: A Gift of Jewish Wisdom for Christians and Jews*. Brewster, MA: Paraclete Press.

Edersheim, A. (1993). *The Life and Times of Jesus the Messiah*. Peabody, MA: Hendrickson Publishers.

Edersheim, A. (1994). *Sketches of Jewish Social Life: Updated Edition*. Peabody, MA: Hendrickson Publishers.

ESV Archaeology Study Bible. (2017). Wheaton, IL: Crossway.

Fee, G. D. (2002). *New Testament Exegesis Third Edition: A Handbook for Students and Pastors*. Louisville, KY: Westminster John Knox Press.

Flusser, D. (2001). *Jesus*. Jerusalem, Israel: The Hebrew University Magnes Press.

Flusser, D. (2009). *Judaism of the Second Temple Period Volume 2: The Jewish Sages and Their Literature*. Grand Rapids, MI: William B. Eerdmans Publishing.

Grayzel, S. (1947). *A History of the Jews*. Philadelphia, PA: The Jewish Publication Society of America.

Grudem, W. (2000). *Systematic Theology*. Grand Rapids, MI: Zondervan.

Gundry, R. H. (2003). *A Survey of the New Testament: Fourth Edition*. Grand Rapids, MI: Zondervan.

Hart, L. D. (2005). *Truth Aflame: Theology for the Church in Renewal*. Grand Rapids, MI: Zondervan.

Henrich, S. S. (2007). *Great Themes of the Bible: Volume 2*. Louisville, KY: Westminster John Knox Press.

Hoffmeier, J. K. (2008) *The Archaeology of the Bible*. Oxford, England: Lion Hudson.

Israel Pocket Library: Jewish Values. (1974). Jerusalem, Israel: Keter Publishing House.

Jeremias, J. (1972). *The Parables of Jesus*. Upper Saddle River, NJ: Prentice-Hall.

Jeremias, J. (1975). *Jerusalem in the Time of Jesus*. Fortress Press.

Kaiser, W. C. Jr., (2015). *Tough Questions about God and His Actions in the Old Testament*. Grand Rapids, MI: Kregel Publications.

Lachs, S. T. (1987). *A Rabbinic Commentary on the New Testament: The Gospels of Matthew, Mark, and Luke*. Hoboken, NY: KTAV Publishing House, Inc.

Lindsey, R. (2017). *Jesus Rabbi and Lord: The Hebrew Story of Jesus Behind our Gospels*. GSM Media.

Marshall, I. H. (1978). *Commentary on Luke: New International Greek Testament Commentary*. Grand Rapids, MI: William B. Eerdmans Publishing Company.

McCullough, M. E. (2001). Forgiveness: Who Does It and How Do They Do It? *Current Directions in Psychological Science*, 10(6), 194-197.

Mounce, W. D. (Gen. Ed.). (2006). *Mounce's Complete Expository Dictionary of Old & New Testament Words*. Grand Rapids, MI: Zondervan.

Nelson, J. B. (2004). *Thirst: God and the Alcoholic Experience*. Louisville, KY: Westminster John Knox Press.

Ritmeyer, L. (2006). *The Quest: Revealing the Temple Mount in Jerusalem*. Jerusalem, Israel: Carta.

Ritmeyer, L. & Ritmeyer, K. (2015). *The Ritual of the Temple in the Time of Christ*. Jerusalem, Israel: Carta.

Ritmeyer, L. & Ritmeyer, K. (2017). *Understanding the Holy Temple Jesus Knew*. Jerusalem, Israel: Carta.

Roitman, A. (2009). *The Bible in the Shrine of the Book: From the Dead Sea Scrolls to the Aleppo Codex*. Jerusalem, Israel: The Israel Museum.

Roth, C. B. (Ed.). (1962). *The Standard Jewish Encyclopedia*. Jerusalem, Israel: Massadah Publishing Company.

Rozenberg, S. & Mevorah, D. (Ed.). (2014). *Herod the Great: The King's Final Journey*. Jerusalem, Israel: The Israel Museum, Jerusalem.

Schama, S. (2013). *The Story of the Jews: Finding the Words 1000 BC – 1492 AD*. New York, NY: HarperCollins Publishers.

Stern, D. H. (1992). *Jewish New Testament Commentary*. Clarksville, MD: Jewish New Testament Publications.

Stern, D. H. (2016). *The Complete Jewish Study Bible*. Peabody, MA: Hendrickson.

Walvoord, J. F., & Zuck, R. B. (Ed.). (1983). *The Bible Knowledge Commentary: An Exposition of the Scriptures by Dallas Seminary Faculty New Testament Edition*. Wheaton, IL: Victor Books.

Whiston, W. (2016). *Josephus Carta's Illustrated the Jewish War*. Jerusalem, Israel: Carta.

Wilson, M. R. (1989). *Our Father Abraham: Jewish Roots of the Christian Faith*. Grand Rapids, MI: William B. Eerdmans Publishing.

Wilson, M. R. (2014). *Exploring Our Hebraic Heritage: A Christian Theology of Roots and Renewal*. Grand Rapids, MI: William B. Eerdmans Publishing Company.

Worthington, E. L., Jr. (2006). *Forgiveness and Reconciliation: Theory and Application*. New York, NY: Routledge Taylor & Francis Group.

Young, B. (1995). *Jesus the Jewish Theologian*. Peabody, MA: Hendrickson Publishers.

Young, B. (1998). *The Parables: Jewish Tradition and Christian Interpretation*. Peabody, MA: Hendrickson Publishers.

Young, B. (2001). *The Jewish Background of the Lord's Prayer*. Tulsa, OK: Gospel Research Foundation, Inc.

Young, B. (2007). *Meet the Rabbis: Rabbinic Thought and the Teachings of Jesus*. Grand Rapids, MI: Baker Academic.

Young, B. (2019). *Hebrew Heritage Bible Translation*. Tulsa, OK: The Hebrew Heritage Bible Society.

www.ingramcontent.com/pod-product-compliance
Lightning Source LLC
Chambersburg PA
CBHW081415230426
43668CB00016B/2245